T0224018

Communications in Computer and Information Science 882

Commenced Publication in 2007
Founding and Former Series Editors:
Phoebe Chen, Alfredo Cuzzocrea, Xiaoyong Du, Orhun Kara, Ting Liu,
Dominik Ślęzak, and Xiaokang Yang

Lian Li · Pinyan Lu
Kun He (Eds.)

Theoretical Computer Science

36th National Conference, NCTCS 2018
Shanghai, China, October 13–14, 2018
Proceedings

 Springer

Editors
Lian Li
Hefei University of Technology
Hefei
China

Pinyan Lu
Shanghai University of Finance
  and Economics
Shanghai
China

Kun He
Huazhong University of Science
  and Technology
Wuhan
China

ISSN 1865-0929   ISSN 1865-0937 (electronic)
Communications in Computer and Information Science
ISBN 978-981-13-2711-7   ISBN 978-981-13-2712-4   (eBook)
https://doi.org/10.1007/978-981-13-2712-4

Library of Congress Control Number: 2018955641

This Springer imprint is published by the registered company Springer Nature Singapore Pte Ltd.
The registered company address is: 152 Beach Road, #21-01/04 Gateway East, Singapore 189721, Singapore

Preface

The National Conference of Theoretical Computer Science (NCTCS) is the main academic activity in the area of theoretical computer science in China. To date, NCTCS has been successfully held 35 times in over 20 cities. It provides a platform for researchers in theoretical computer science or related areas to exchange ideas and start cooperations.

This volume contains the papers presented at NCTCS 2018: the 36th National Conference of Theoretical Computer Science held during October 13–14, 2018, in Shanghai, China. Sponsored by the China Computer Forum (CCF), NCTCS 2018 was hosted by the CCF Theoretical Computer Science Committee and Institute for Theoretical Computer Science at Shanghai University of Finance and Economics (SUFE).

NCTCS 2018 received 49 English submissions (including 18 published papers accepted only for communication at the conference) in the area of algorithms and complexity, software theory and methods, data science and machine learning theory, web science base theory, parallel and distributed computing and computational models, etc. Each of the 31 submissions was reviewed by at least three Program Committee members. The committee decided to accept 11 papers that are included in these proceedings published Springer's *Communications in Computer and Information Science* (CCIS) series.

NCTCS 2018 invited well-reputed researchers in the field of theoretical computer science to give keynote speeches, carry out a wide range of academic activities, and introduce recent advanced research results. We had eight invited plenary speakers at NCTCS 2018: Yijia Chen (Fudan University), Yi Deng (Institute of Information Engineering, Chinese Academy of Sciences), Nick Gravin (Shanghai University of Finance and Economics), Angsheng Li (Institute of Software Chinese Academy of Sciences), Jianzhong Li (Harbin Institute of Technology), Xiangyang Li (University of Science and Technology of China), Shengyu Zhang (The Chinese University of Hong Kong), and Zhihua Zhang (Peking University). We express our sincere thanks to them for their contributions to the conference and the proceedings.

We would like to thank the Program Committee members and external reviewers for their hard work in reviewing and selecting papers. We are also very grateful to all the editors at Springer and the local organization chairs for their hard work in the preparation of the conference.

September 2018

Lian Li
Pinyan Lu
Kun He

Organization

General Chairs

Lian Li	Hefei University of Technology, China
Pinyan Lu	Shanghai University of Finance and Economics, China

General Co-chairs

Kerong Ben	Naval University of Engineering, China
Zhigang Chen	Central South University, China
Yuxi Fu	Shanghai Jiao Tong University, China
Xiaoming Sun	Institute of Computing Technology, CAS, China
Jinyun Xue	Jiangxi Normal University, China

Program Chair

Pinyan Lu	Shanghai University of Finance and Economics, China

Program Co-chair

Kun He	Huazhong University of Science and Technology, China

Program Committee

Xiaohui Bei	Nanyang Technological University, Singapore
Kerong Ben	Naval University of Engineering, China
Jinyi Cai	University of Wisconsin-Madison, USA
Zhiping Cai	National University of Defense Technology, China
Yongzhi Cao	Peking University, China
Juan Chen	National University of Defense Technology, China
Wei Chen	Microsoft Research Asia, China
Zhigang Chen	Central South University, China
Kaimin Chung	Academia Sinica, Taiwan, China
Dingzhu Du	The University of Texas at Dallas, USA
Yuxi Fu	Shanghai Jiao Tong University, China
Heng Guo	The University of Edinburgh, UK
Yiliang Han	Engineering University of CAPF, China
Jinkao Hao	University of Angers, France
Zhenyan Ji	Beijing Jiaotong University, China
Min Jiang	Xiamen University, China
Dongkui Li	Baotou Teachers' College, China
Yongming Li	Shaanxi Normal University, China

Yujian Li	Beijing University of Technology, China
Chumin Li	University of Picardie Jules Verne, France
Zhanshan Li	Jilin University, China
Jian Li	Tsinghua University, China
Shizhong Liao	Tianjin University, China
Guohua Liu	Donghua University, China
Huawen Liu	Zhejiang Normal University, China
Tian Liu	Peking University, China
Xiaoguang Liu	Nankai University, China
Jun Long	National University of Defense Technology, China
Shuai Lv	Jilin University, China
Xinjun Mao	National University of Defense Technology, China
Xiangwu Meng	Beijing University of Posts and Telecommunications, China
Jun Niu	Ningbo University, China
Dantong Ouyang	Jilin University, China
Richard Peng	Georgia Institute of Technology, USA
Zhiyong Peng	Wuhan University, China
Zhengwei Qi	Shanghai Jiao Tong University, China
Jiaohua Qin	Central South University of Forestry and Technology, China
Kaile Su	Griffith University, Australia
Haoxuan Tang	Harbin Institute of Technology, China
Jianxin Wang	Central South University, China
Zihe Wang	Shanghai University of Finance and Economics, China
Jigang Wu	Guangdong University of Technology, China
Mingji Xia	Chinese Academy of Sciences, China
Meihua Xiao	East China Jiaotong University, China
Mingyu Xiao	University of Electronic Science and Technology of China
Jinyun Xue	Jiangxi Normal University, China
Yan Yang	Southwest Jiaotong University, China
Jianping Yin	National University of Defense Technology, China
Mengting Yuan	Wuhan University, China
Defu Zhang	Xiamen University, China
Jianming Zhang	Changsha University of Science and Technology
Peng Zhang	Shandong University, China
Jialin Zhang	Institute of Computing Technology, CAS, China
Yuan Zhou	Indiana University Bloomington, USA
Daming Zhu	Shandong University, China
En Zhu	National University of Defense Technology, China

Organizing Committee

Huili Liang	Shanghai University of Finance and Economics, China
Yuan Lin	Shanghai University of Finance and Economics, China
Zihe Wang	Shanghai University of Finance and Economics, China

Contents

Semi-online Machine Covering on Two Hierarchical Machines with Discrete Processing Times

Gangxiong Wu[1(✉)] and Weidong Li[1,2(✉)]

[1] School of Mathematics and Statistics, Yunnan University, Kunming 650504, China
`1317630396@qq.com, weidongmath@126.com`
[2] Dianchi College of Yunnan University, Kunming 650504, China

Abstract. In this paper, we study the semi-online machine covering problem on two hierarchical machines, whose objective is to maximize the minimum machine load. When the processing times are discrete by $\{1, 2, 2^2, \ldots, 2^k\}$ with $k \geq 2$, we prove that no algorithm can have a competitive ratio less than 2^k and present an optimal semi-online algorithm with competitive ratio 2^k.

Keywords: Machine covering · Semi-online · Competitive ratio
Hierarchy · Discrete processing times

1 Introduction

Given m hierarchical machines and n jobs, each job can only be processed on a subset of the machines and each job can only be processed on a machines. The hierarchical scheduling problem, denoted by $P|GoS|C_{max}$, is to minimize the maximum load of all machines (makespan). Hwang et al. [2] studied the offline problem $P|GoS|C_{max}$ and designed an approximation algorithm with the mankspan no more than $\frac{5}{4}$-times the optimum for $m = 2$, and no more than $2 - \frac{1}{m-1}$-times the optimum for $m \geq 3$. Ou et al. [7] designed a 4/3-approximation algorithm and a polynomial time approximation scheme (PTAS, for short) for $P|GoS|C_{max}$. Li et al. [6] designed an efficient PTAS with running time $O(nlogn)$ for a special case of the problem $P|GoS|C_{max}$ and present a simple fully polynomial time approximation scheme (FPTAS, for short) with running time $O(n)$ for the problem $P_m|GoS|C_{max}$, where m is a constant. For the online version, Park et al. [8] and Jiang et al. [3] designed an optimal online algorithm with a competitive ratio of $\frac{5}{3}$ for the case of two machines, respectively. Wu et al. [10] designed several optimal semi-online scheduling algorithm on two hierarchical machines. Zhang et al. [11] designed some optimal online algorithms on two hierarchical machines with tightly-grouped processing times.

Machine covering on hierarchical machines with the objective of maximizing the minimum machine load, denoted by $P|GoS|C_{min}$, is not a well-studied scheduling problem. Li et al. [4] presented a PTAS for $P|GoS|C_{min}$. Wu et al.

© Springer Nature Singapore Pte Ltd. 2018
L. Li et al. (Eds.): NCTCS 2018, CCIS 882, pp. 1–7, 2018.
https://doi.org/10.1007/978-981-13-2712-4_1

[9] designed two semi-online optimal algorithms for $P|GoS|C_{min}$ on two hierarchical machines, when both the processing time and the class of the largest job are known. Luo et al. [5] presented an optimal online algorithm with a competitive ratio of $(1 + \alpha)$ for $P|GoS|C_{min}$ on two hierarchical machines, when the processing time of each job is bounded by an interval $[1, \alpha]$. Chassid and Epstein [1] considered the machine covering problem on two hierarchical machines of possibly different speeds.

In this paper, we consider the online machine covering problem on two hierarchical machines with discrete processing times. The processing time of all jobs are discrete by $\{1, 2, 2^2, \ldots, 2^k\}$, where $k \geq 2$. We prove that no algorithm can have a competitive ratio less than 2^k and give an optimal algorithm with the competitive ratio of 2^k. The paper is organized as follows. Section 2 gives some basic definitions. Section 3 presents an optimal semi-online algorithm. Section 4 presents concluding remarks.

2   Preliminaries

We are given two machines and a series of jobs arriving online which are to be scheduled irrevocably at the time of their arrivals. The first machine can process all the jobs while the second one can process only part of the jobs. The arrival of a new job occurs only after the current job is scheduled. Let $J = \{J_1, J_2, \ldots, J_n\}$ be the set of all jobs arranged in the order of arrival. We denote each job as J_i with p_i and g_i, where $p_i > 0$ is the processing time (also called job size) of the job J_i and $g_i \in \{1, 2\}$ is the hierarchy of the job J_i. If $g_i = 1$, the job J_i must be processed by the first machine, and if $g_i = 2$, the job J_i can be processed by either of the two machines. p_i and g_i are not known until the arrival of the job J_i.

The schedule can be seen as the partition of J into two subsets, we denote as $<S_1, S_2>$, where S_1 and S_2 contain job indices assigned to the first and the second machine, respectively. Let $p(S_1) = \sum_{J_i \in S_1} p_i$ and $p(S_2) = \sum_{J_i \in S_2} p_i$ denote the load of the first machine and the second machine, respectively.

For the first i jobs, we define that T^i denote total processing time, TG_1^i is total processing time the jobs with hierarchy 1; p_{max}^i is the largest job time; $p(S_1^i)$ denote total processing time of the jobs scheduled on M_1 after the job J_i is scheduled; $p(S_2^i)$ is total processing time of the jobs scheduled on M_2 after the job J_i is scheduled; $V_i(opt)$ denote the optimal minimum machine load after scheduling the job J_i; V_{opt} is the optimal function value of the problem in an offline version; V_{out} denote the output objective function value by a algorithm.

So, according to the define of above, we have $S_1 = S_1^n$ and $S_2 = S_2^n$. The minimum value of $p(S_1)$ and $p(S_2)$, i.e., $min\{p(S_1), p(S_2)\}$, is defined as the minimum machine load of the schedule $<S_1, S_2>$. The objective is to find a schedule $<S_1, S_2>$ that maximizes the minimum machine load.

For the first i jobs, let $L^i = min\{T^i - TG_1^i, \frac{T^i}{2}, T^i - p_{max}^i\}$ and L^i is a standard upper bound of the optimal minimum machine load. Then we can get following lemma.

Lemma 1. *The optimal minimum machine load is at most L^i after scheduling the job J_i.*

Definition 1. *For a job sequence J and an algorithm, then the competitive ratio of algorithm is defined as the smallest η such that for any J, $V_{opt} \leq \eta V_{out}$.*

At first, we give a lower bounded for the problem.

Theorem 1. *There exists no algorithm with a competitive ratio less than 2^k.*

Proof: Consider an algorithm B and the following job sequence. The first job J_1 with $p_1 = 1$ and $g_1 = 2$. If algorithm B schedules J_1 on M_1, we further generate the last job J_2 with $p_2 = 2^k$ and $g_2 = 1$ must be scheduled on M_1. Therefore, we have $V_{opt} = 1$ and $V_{out} = 0$, which lead to the competitive ratio is unbounded.

Otherwise, if algorithm B schedules J_1 with $p_1 = 1$ and $g_1 = 2$ on M_2. The job J_2 with $p_2 = 2^k$ and $g_2 = 2$, the algorithm B must schedule J_2 with $p_2 = 2^k$ and $g_2 = 2$ on M_1. If the algorithm B schedule J_2 with $p_2 = 2^k$ and $g_2 = 2$ on M_2, we have $V_{opt} = 1$ and $V_{out} = 0$, which lead to the competitive ratio is unbounded. The job J_3 with $p_3 = 2^k$ and $g_3 = 1$ must be scheduled on M_1. We have $V_{opt} = 2^k$ and $V_{out} = 1$. Hence, there exists no algorithm with a competitive ratio less than 2^k.

3 An Optimal Semi-online Algorithm

In the section, we consider that the hierarchical load balancing problem on two machines with discrete processing times. All processing times belong to $\{1, 2, 2^2, \ldots, 2^k\}$, where $k \geq 2$ in this problem. We present an optimal algorithm.

Algorithm A
Input : $J_i = (p_i, g_i)$
Output : $< S_1, S_2 >$;
Step 0: $S_1^0 = \emptyset$, $S_2^0 = \emptyset$, $i = 1$;
Step 1: On receiving $J_i = (p_i, g_i)$, update T^i, TG_1^i, p_{max}^i and L^i;
Step 2: If $g_i = 1$, schedule J_i on M_1. Go to **Step 4**;
Step 3: If $g_i = 2$ and when $p(S_1^{i-1}) < \frac{1}{2^k} L^i$, schedule J_i on M_1. Else schedule it on M_2. Go to **Step 4**;
Step 4: If there is a new job, let $i = i + 1$ and go to **Step 1**. Else, output S_1 and S_2.

For the problem and the algorithm, we define that $V_{out} = min\{p(S_1^n), p(S_2^n)\}$ is the output of the Algorithm A and V_{opt} is the output of the optimal offline algorithm.

Lemma 2. *If Algorithm A schedule the job J_i with $g_i = 2$ on M_1, then $L^i \neq T^i - TG_1^i$.*

Proof: According to Algorithm A, if the job J_i with $g_i = 2$ is scheduled on M_1, we have $p(S_1^{i-1}) < \frac{1}{2^k}L^i$.

If $L^i = min\{T^i - TG_1^i, \frac{T^i}{2}, T^i - p_{max}^i\} = T^i - TG_1^i$, then we get $T^i - TG_1^i \leq \frac{T^i}{2}$, which implies $TG_1^i \geq \frac{T^i}{2}$. Since $p(S_1^{i-1}) \geq TG_1^{i-1} = TG_1^i$, then we have

$$p(S_1^{i-1}) \geq \frac{T^i}{2} \geq L^i > \frac{L^i}{2^k}$$

and it is contradictory with $p(S_1^{i-1}) < \frac{L^i}{2^k}$. Thus, the proof is complete.

Lemma 3. *If Algorithm A schedule the job J_i with $g_i = 2$ on M_1 and $L^i = T^i - p_{max}^i$, then $p(S_2^i) \geq \frac{1}{2^k}(T^i - TG_1^i)$.*

Proof: Since $L^i = T^i - p_{max}^i$, according to the definition of L^i, we get $T^i - p_{max}^i \leq \frac{T^i}{2}$, which means

$$p_{max}^i \geq \frac{T^i}{2}.$$

In the first i jobs, we denote job J_j where $j \in \{1, 2, 3 \cdots i\}$ has largest processing time, i.e., $p_j = p_{max}^i$. Now, we will discuss two cases:

Case 1. $p_{max}^i \neq p_i$.

If J_j belongs to S_1^{i-1}, we have

$$p(S_1^{i-1}) \geq p_{max}^i \geq \frac{T^i}{2} > \frac{1}{2^k}L^i$$

and this is contradictory with that Algorithm A schedule the job J_i on M_1.

If J_j belongs to S_2^i, we have

$$p(S_2^i) \geq p_{max}^i \geq \frac{T^i}{2} \geq \frac{1}{2^k}T^i \geq \frac{1}{2^k}(T^i - TG_1^i). \tag{1}$$

Case 2. $p_{max}^i = p_i$.

We have

$$T^i - p_{max}^i = p(S_2^i) + p(S_1^{i-1}). \tag{2}$$

Since Algorithm A schedule the job J_i on M_1, we have

$$p(S_1^{i-1}) < \frac{1}{2^k}L^i = \frac{1}{2^k}(T^i - p_{max}^i). \tag{3}$$

Hence, according to the inequalities of (2), (3), we have

$$p(S_2^i) = T^i - p_{max}^i - p(S_1^{i-1}) > T^i - p_{max}^i - \frac{1}{2^k}(T^i - p_{max}^i) = \frac{2^k - 1}{2^k}(T^i - p_{max}^i).$$

Since $k \geq 2$ and according to the inequalities of (3), we have

$$p(S_2^i) > \frac{2^k - 1}{2^k}(T^i - p_{max}^i) > (2^k - 1)p(S_1^{i-1}) \geq 3p(S_1^{i-1}). \tag{4}$$

Since $p(S_1^{i-1}) \geq 1$, we have $p(S_2^i) > 3$. Since $p_i = p_{max}^i \geq \frac{T^i}{2} > p(S_1^{i-1})$ and $p_i \leq 2^k$, we have

$$\frac{T^i - TG_1^i}{p(S_2^i)} \leq \frac{T^i}{p(S_2^i)} = 1 + \frac{p(S_1^{i-1}) + p_i}{p(S_2^i)} < 1 + \frac{2^{k+1}}{3} < 2^k. \qquad (5)$$

The proof is complete.

Lemma 4. *If Algorithm A schedule the job J_i with $g_i = 2$ on M_1 and $L^i = \frac{T^i}{2}$, then $p(S_2^i) \geq \frac{T^i - TG_1^i}{2^k}$.*

Proof: Since the job J_i with $g_i = 2$ is scheduled on M_1, we have $p(S_1^{i-1}) < \frac{L^i}{2^k} = \frac{T^i}{2 \times 2^k}$. Since

$$L^i = min\{T^i - TG_1^i, \frac{T^i}{2}, T^i - p_{max}^i\} = \frac{T^i}{2}.$$

So, we have $T^i - p_{max}^i \geq \frac{T^i}{2}$ holds, which implies $p_{max}^i \leq \frac{T^i}{2}$. Then, we have $p_i \leq p_{max}^i \leq \frac{T^i}{2}$ and

$$p(S_2^i) = T^i - p(S_1^{i-1}) - p_i > T^i - \frac{T^i}{2 \times 2^k} - \frac{T^i}{2} = \frac{2^k - 1}{2 \times 2^k} T^i.$$

Since $k \geq 2$ and $T^i \geq T^i - TG_1^i$, we have

$$p(S_2^i) > \frac{2^k - 1}{2 \times 2^k} T^i > \frac{T^i}{2^k} \geq \frac{T^i - TG_1^i}{2^k}.$$

We complete the proof.

Theorem 2. *If $V_{out} = min\{p(S_1^n), p(S_2^n)\} = p(S_1^n)$, then $\frac{V_{opt}}{V_{out}} \leq 2^k$.*

Proof: According to the question, we know that $S_2^n \neq \emptyset$.

We assume that the job J_i is the last job that scheduled on M_2. According to Algorithm A, we have $p(S_1^{i-1}) \geq \frac{1}{2^k} L^i$. Since

$$L^n - L^i \leq T^n - T^i \qquad (6)$$

and all the jobs arrived after the job J_i will be scheduled on M_1.

According to the definition of L^n and $L^n \geq V_{opt}$, we have

$$\frac{1}{2^k} L^i + (L^n - L^i) \geq \frac{1}{2^k}(L^i - L^n) + \frac{L^n}{2^k} + (L^n - L^i)$$

$$\geq (1 - \frac{1}{2^k})(L^n - L^i) + \frac{L^n}{2^k} \qquad (7)$$

$$\geq 0.$$

Then, according to inequality (7), we have

$$\frac{1}{2^k} L^i + (L^n - L^i) \geq \frac{1}{2^k} L^n. \qquad (8)$$

So, according to the inequalities of (6), (8), we have

$$p(S_1^n) = p(S_1^{i-1}) + (T^n - T^i) \geq \frac{1}{2^k}L^i + (L^n - L^i) \geq \frac{1}{2^k}L^n \geq \frac{1}{2^k}V_{opt}. \qquad (9)$$

Thus, according to inequality (9), when $V_{out} = min\{p(S_1^n), p(S_2^n)\} = p(S_1^n)$, we have

$$\frac{V_{opt}}{V_{out}} \leq 2^k.$$

We complete the proof.

Theorem 3. *The competitive ratio of Algorithm A is 2^k.*

Proof: According to Theorem 2, if $V_{out} = min\{p(S_1^n), p(S_2^n)\} = p(S_1^n)$, then

$$\frac{V_{opt}}{V_{out}} \leq 2^k. \qquad (10)$$

Therefore, we only need to prove when $V_{out} = min\{p(S_1^n), p(S_2^n)\} = p(S_2^n)$, the inequality (10) holds.

We discuss the following two cases:

Case 1. Algorithm A doesn't schedule jobs with hierarchy 2 on M_1.

In this case, according to the definition of L^n. We have

$$p(S_2^n) = T^n - TG_1^n \geq L^n \geq V_{opt} > \frac{1}{2^k}V_{opt}. \qquad (11)$$

Case 2. At least one job with hierarchy 2 is scheduled on M_1.

Let J_a denote the last job with $g_a = 2$ that scheduled on M_1. According to Lemmas 2, 3 and 4, we have

$$p(S_2^a) \geq \frac{1}{2^k}(T^a - TG_1^a).$$

Since remaining the jobs with hierarchy 2 are scheduled on M_2 after job J_a and we have $k \geq 2$ and

$$T^n - TG_1^n \geq T^a - TG_1^a,$$

then we get

$$\begin{aligned}
p(S_2^n) &= p(S_2^a) + ((T^n - TG_1^n) - (T^a - TG_1^a)) \\
&\geq \frac{1}{2^k}(T^a - TG_1^a) + ((T^n - TG_1^n) - (T^a - TG_1^a)) \\
&= \frac{1 - 2^k}{2^k}(T^a - TG_1^a) + (T^n - TG_1^n) \\
&\geq \frac{1 - 2^k}{2^k}(T^n - TG_1^n) + (T^n - TG_1^n) \qquad (12) \\
&= \frac{1}{2^k}(T^n - TG_1^n) \\
&\geq \frac{1}{2^k}L^n \\
&\geq \frac{1}{2^k}V_{opt}.
\end{aligned}$$

According to the definition of V_{out} and the inequalities of (11), (12). We have the inequality (10) holds.

According to Theorem 1, the optimal competitive ratio of Algorithm A is 2^k. We complete the proof of competitive ratio.

4 Conclusion

In the paper, we study the semi-online version of hierarchical scheduling problem on two parallel machines with the objective of maximizing the minimum machine load. If the processing times are discrete by $\{1, 2, 2^2, \ldots, 2^k\}$, where $k \geq 2$. We prove the lower bound of the competitive ratio of any online algorithm is 2^k and present an algorithm which is shown to be optimal.

Acknowledgement. The work is supported in part by the National Natural Science Foundation of China [Nos. 11761078, 61662088], the Natural Science Foundation of Education Department of Yunnan Province [No. 2017ZZX235], IRTSTYN and Program for Excellent Young Talents, Yunnan University.

References

1. Chassid, O., Epstein, L.: The hierarchical model for load balancing on two machines. J. Comb. Optim. **15**(4), 305–314 (2008)
2. Hwang, H.C., Chang, S.Y., Lee, K.: Parallel machine scheduling under a grade of service provision. Comput. Oper. Res. **31**(12), 2055–2061 (2004)
3. Jiang, Y., He, Y., Tang, C.: Optimal online algorithms for scheduling two identical machines under a grade of service. J. Zhejiang Univ. Sci. A. **7**(3), 309–314 (2006)
4. Li, J., Li, W., Li, J.: Polynomial approximation schemes for the max-min allocation problem under a grade of service provision. Discret. Math. Algorithms Appl. **1**(3), 355–368 (2009)
5. Luo, T., Xu, Y.: Semi-online hierarchical load balancing problem with bounded processing times. Theor. Comput. Sci. **607**, 75–82 (2015)
6. Li, W., Li, J., Zhang, T.: Two approximation schemes for scheduling on parallel machines under a grade of service provision. Asia-Pac. J. Oper. Res. **29**(5), Article No. 1250029 (2012)
7. Ou, J., Leung, J.Y.T., Li, C.L.: Scheduling parallel machines with inclusive processing set restrictions. Nav. Res. Logist. **55**(4), 328–338 (2008)
8. Park, J., Chang, S.Y., Lee, K.: Online and semi-online scheduling of two machines under a grade of service provision. Oper. Res. Lett. **34**(6), 692–696 (2006)
9. Wu, Y., Cheng, T.C.E., Ji, M.: Optimal algorithm for semi-online machine covering on two hierarchical machines. Theor. Comput. Sci. **531**, 37–46 (2014)
10. Wu, Y., Ji, M., Yang, Q.: Optimal semi-online scheduling algorithm on two parallel identical machines under a grade of service provision. Int. J. Prod. Econ. **135**(1), 367–371 (2012)
11. Zhang, A., Jiang, Y., Fan, L., Hu, J.: Optimal online algorithms on two hierarchical machines with tightly-grouped processing times. J. Comb. Optim. **29**(4), 781–795 (2015)

Improved Algorithms for Properly Learning Mixture of Gaussians

Xuan Wu$^{(\boxtimes)}$ and Changzhi Xie$^{(\boxtimes)}$

Institute for Interdisciplinary Information Sciences,
Tsinghua University, Beijing 100084, China
`wu3412790@gmail.com`, `xcz15@mails.tsinghua.edu.cn`

Abstract. We study the problem of learning Gaussian Mixture Model (GMM) in one dimension. Given samples access to a mixture f of k Gaussians and an accurate parameter $\epsilon > 0$, our algorithm takes $\tilde{O}(\frac{k}{\epsilon^5})$ samples, runs in polynomial time and outputs a mixture g of at most $\tilde{O}(\min\{\frac{k^2}{\epsilon^2}, \frac{k}{\epsilon^3}\})$ Gaussians such that the total variation distance between f and g is at most ϵ. This improves the previous result by [4], which uses $O(\frac{k^2}{\epsilon^6})$ samples and outputs a mixture of $O(\frac{k}{\epsilon^3})$ Gaussians. Our algorithm uses LP rounding technique to find the sparse solution of a linear programming. The main technical contribution of us is a non-trivial inequality for Gaussians, which may be interesting in its own right.

We also consider the problem of properly learning mixture of two Gaussians. We show how to reduce the learning task to the closest pair problem in L_∞-norm. Our algorithm takes $\tilde{O}(\frac{1}{\epsilon^2})$ samples and runs in time $\tilde{O}(\frac{1}{\epsilon^{4.001}})$. Our result improves the previous result by [7], which uses $\tilde{O}(\frac{1}{\epsilon^2})$ samples and runs in time $\tilde{O}(\frac{1}{\epsilon^5})$.

Keywords: Gaussian mixture model · LP rounding
Proper learning · L_∞-closest pair

1 Introduction

We study the problem of learning Gaussian Mixture Model (GMM) in one dimension. A one-dimensional GMM is simply a convex combination of Gaussian distributions. A GMM with k components has density function:

$$f(x) = \sum_{i=1}^{k} \omega_i N(\mu_i, \sigma_i^2)(x),$$

where ω_is are nonnegative and $\sum_i \omega_i = 1$. Here, $N(\mu, \sigma^2)(x) = \frac{1}{\sqrt{2\pi\sigma^2}} e^{-\frac{(x-\mu)^2}{2\sigma^2}}$ denotes the density function of a Gaussian distribution whose mean is μ and variance is σ^2.

© Springer Nature Singapore Pte Ltd. 2018
L. Li et al. (Eds.): NCTCS 2018, CCIS 882, pp. 8–26, 2018.
https://doi.org/10.1007/978-981-13-2712-4_2

Gaussian Mixture Model is one of the most important and well-studied statistical mixture models. Given sample access of a Gaussian mixture, our goal is to recover the underlying mixture. There are three popular objectives, parameter learning, proper learning and improper learning. In parameter learning, the task is to recover each constitute component and its weight, up to a given error parameter ϵ. Starting from Dasgupta's seminal paper [5], there is a long line of work in parameter learning GMM (e.g. [12,14,15]). A relaxed problem is the density estimation problem, in which we only need to output a density function g such that $|f - g|_1 \leq \epsilon$. We call the density estimation problem a *proper learning* problem if we require the output is also a GMM with the same number of components as the underlying GMM. Otherwise, we call it *improper learning*.

Recently, [1] provided an algorithm for estimating the density of GMM with nearly optimal sample complexity and in nearly linear time but their algorithm outputs a piecewise polynomial density function rather than a Gaussian mixture. So their result is an improper learning result. Proper learning is more difficult. [16] provided an algorithm for properly learning GMM in exponential time. Given a candidate set of Gaussians, they basically enumerated all possible k-mixtures of Gaussians and applied a modified Scheffe hypothesis learning algorithm (see e.g. [8]). Recently, [13] provided an algebraic algorithm for properly learning mixtures of Gaussians with nearly optimal sample complexity and nearly linear time for any constant k. But their algorithm still runs in time exponential on k.

Obtaining a polynomial time algorithm that properly learns GMM without any separation assumption is a long-standing open problem. In this paper, we consider a relaxation of the problem. Given sample access to a mixture f of k-Gaussians, we still require the output g is a mixture of Gaussians. However, we allow the number of components of g to be somewhat larger than k. In a recent paper, [4] obtain such a result by finding a sparse solution of an LP via the multiplicative weights updating (MWU) method. Their algorithm takes $O(\frac{k^2}{\epsilon^6})$ samples and output a mixture of at most $O(\frac{k}{\epsilon^3})$ Gaussians. In this paper, we improve the above result, as in the following theorem.

Theorem 1. *Given an integer k, a positive real number $\epsilon > 0$ and sample access to a mixture f of k Gaussians, there is a polynomial time algorithm which takes $\tilde{O}(\frac{k}{\epsilon^5})$ samples from f and outputs a mixture g of at most $\tilde{O}(\min\{\frac{k^2}{\epsilon^2}, \frac{k}{\epsilon^3}\})$ Gaussians, such that with probability at least 0.99, we have $|f - g|_1 \leq \epsilon$.*

In this paper, we also consider a special but important case, properly learning a mixture of two Gaussians. Given sample access to a mixture f of two Gaussians and a constant $\epsilon > 0$, one needs to output a mixture of two Gaussians g such that $|f - g|_1 \leq \epsilon$. Previously, the best result is due to [7]. Their algorithm uses $\tilde{O}(\frac{1}{\epsilon^2})$ samples and runs in $\tilde{O}(\frac{1}{\epsilon^5})$ time. Their algorithm is also based on a modified version of Scheffe's algorithm. We provide two algorithms which improve both sample and time complexity, as follows.

Theorem 2. *Given $\epsilon > 0$, the sample access to an unknown mixture f of two Gaussians, there is an algorithm which takes $O(\epsilon^{-2})$ samples from f, runs in $\tilde{O}(\epsilon^{-5})$ and outputs a mixture g of two Gaussians such that with probability at least 0.99, $|f - g|_1 \leq \epsilon$.*

For any $p > 0$, there is a different algorithm which takes $O((\log\log\frac{1}{\epsilon})^2 p^{-2}\epsilon^{-2})$ samples from f, runs in $\tilde{O}(\epsilon^{-4-2p})$ time and outputs a mixture of two Gaussians g such that with probability at least 0.99, $|f - g|_1 \leq \epsilon$. If we take $p = 0.0005$, the sample and time complexity become $O((\log\log\frac{1}{\epsilon})^2\epsilon^{-2})$ and $\tilde{O}(\epsilon^{-4.001})$ respectively.

1.1   Related Work

Gaussian Mixture Model (GMM) is introduced over 100 years ago by Pearson. In an 1895 paper, Pearson used GMM to estimate the distribution of local crabs' leg length. He guessed that the distribution is a mixture of two Gaussians and used a moment-based method to find parameters which fit the first six empirical moments the best.

The problem of learning Gaussian mixture model has been studied extensively by computer scientists from last century. In a seminal paper, [5] provided a clustering algorithm for recovering the mixture components and their weights, under some separation assumption. This result was improved by some subsequent work (see e.g., [6,17]). Two breakthrough papers [12] and [14] gave the first algorithm to efficiently recover the components of the Gaussian mixture without any separation assumption, their algorithm's sample complexity is super-exponential on k, where k is the number of mixture components. It is also shown in their paper [14] that exponential dependence on k is unavoidable. A similar upper bound is also obtained by [3] in which they used an algebraic algorithm to show the existence of a super-exponential bound. Recently, [10] showed that for learning the parameters of a mixture of two Gaussians, the tight bound is $\Theta(\epsilon^{-12})$.

Recently, [9] shows that under the smoothed analysis setting, learning GMM is significantly easier in high dimensional space. Another paper [2] used tensor methods to show there is a polynomial time algorithm to recover GMM under a certain non-degenerate condition in general high-dimensional space.

1.2   Preliminaries

In this section, we list notations and classical results used in this paper.

A_k distance: a proxy of L_1-distance

Definition 1 (A_k-norm and A_k distance). *Denote by S_k the set containing all possible ways to partition the real axis into at most k intervals, i.e. $S_k = \{(s_1, s_2, \ldots, s_{k-1}) : s_1 \leq s_2 \leq \ldots \leq s_{k-1}\}$ where the partition defined by $(s_1, s_2, \ldots, s_{k-1})$ is naturally*

$$(-\infty, s_1], (s_1, s_2], \ldots, (s_{k-1}, \infty)$$

Let $f : \mathbb{R} \to \mathbb{R}$. We define the A_k-norm of f to be

$$|f|_{A_k} = \sup_{(s_1,\ldots,s_{k-1}) \in S_k} \sum_{i=1}^{k} |\int_{s_{i-1}}^{s_i} f(x) dx|$$

where s_0 is defined to be $-\infty$ and s_k is ∞. We also define the A_k-distance between f and g to be

$$d_{A_k}(f,g) = |f - g|_{A_k}$$

In probability theory, $d_K(f,g) = \frac{1}{2} d_{A_2}(f,g) = \sup_x |\int_{-\infty}^x (f(y)-g(y)) dy|$ is called Kolmogorov's distance.

The following theorem proved in [14] explains why A_k-distance can be used as a proxy for L_1-distance.

Theorem 3 ([14]). *If f is a mixture of n Gaussians and g is a mixture of m Gaussians, then f and g have at most $2(n+m) - 2$ crossing points.*

Consequently, we have the following theorem.

Theorem 4. *If f and g are two mixture of k-Gaussians, then $d_{A_{4k-2}}(f,g) = |f - g|_1$.*

The following simple lemma will be used in Sect. 4:

Lemma 1. *Let f, g be both mixtures of two Gaussians. We have that*

$$|f - g|_1 = d_{A_6}(f,g) = \Theta(d_K(f,g)).$$

Proof. By Theorem 4 we have $|f - g|_1 = d_{A_6}(f,g)$. By definition $d_K(f,g) \leq d_{A_6}(f,g)$. For a partition determined by $S = (Y_1, \ldots, Y_5)$ (as usual, $Y_0 = -\infty, Y_6 = \infty$), by triangle inequality we have,

$$\sum_{i=0}^{5} |\int_{Y_i}^{Y_{i+1}} (f(x) - g(x)) dx| \leq \sum_{i=0}^{5} |\int_{-\infty}^{Y_{i+1}} (f(x) - g(x)) dx| + \sum_{i=0}^{5} |\int_{-\infty}^{Y_i} (f(x) - g(x)) dx|$$
$$\leq 12 d_K(f,g)$$

This holds for each partition of $\mathbb{R}$ containing 6 intervals. So we conclude that,

$$d_K(f,g) \leq d_{A_6}(f,g) \leq 12 d_K(f,g)$$

The Empirical Distribution. The empirical distribution is also used in this paper, we require the following definition and classical result.

Definition 2 (Empirical distribution). *Let p denote a probability density over $\mathbb{R}$, the empirical distribution $\hat{p}_n$ of p is defined by n i.i.d samples $X_1, X_2, \ldots, X_n$ from p as follows:*

$$\hat{p}_n(x) = \frac{1}{n} \sum_{i=1}^{n} \delta_{X_i}(x),$$

where $\delta_{X_i}(x)$ is the delta function.

Theorem 5 (VC-inequality). *Let p denote a probability density over $\mathbf{R}$, $\hat{p}_n$ is its empirical distribution defined by $n = \Omega(k\epsilon^{-2})$ samples, then with probability at least 0.9999 the A_k distance between p and $\hat{p}_n$ is bounded by ϵ i.e.,*

$$d_{A_k}(p, \hat{p}_n) \leq \epsilon.$$

When $k = 2$ the inequality is also called DKW-inequality.

The Candidate Set. Our analysis of the algorithm highly depends on the structural construction of a candidate set of Gaussians given in [16],

Definition 3 ([16]). *Let f be a mixture of k-Gaussians. Let $n = O(\frac{k \log k}{\epsilon})$ and $X_1, X_2, \ldots, X_n$ are n samples from f. Define the candidate set of Gaussians*

$$\mathcal{H}_f = \{N_{ij}(x) = N(X_i, (X_i - X_j)^2)(x) : i, j \in [n], j \neq i\}$$

Theorem 6 ([16]). *Let f be a mixture of k-Gaussians and $\mathcal{H}_f$ denote the candidate set in Definition 3. Then with probability at least 0.99, there exists a mixture of k Gaussians from $\mathcal{H}_f$ denoted by g such that $|f - g|_1 \leq \epsilon$.*

1.3   High Level Description

Our algorithm is based on LP rounding. Firstly we follow [16] to construct a candidate set of $\tilde{O}(k^2/\epsilon^2)$ many Gaussians such that there is a convex combination of these Gaussians which is close to f in L_1-distance. We use an LP to compute this convex combination, it is a mixture of $\tilde{O}(k^2/\epsilon^2)$ many Gaussians, we then round its coefficients to multiple of $\frac{1}{q}$ for $q = \tilde{O}(\frac{k}{\epsilon^3})$. Next, we analyze the $A_{O(q)}$ distance between the rounded mixture and original mixture, we prove a non-trivial concentration bound and conclude that the distance is less than ϵ. Since each non-zero coefficient is a multiple of $1/q$ and there is at most $\tilde{O}(\frac{k^2}{\epsilon^2})$ candidate components, the resulting mixture will have at most $\tilde{O}(\min\{\frac{k^2}{\epsilon^2}, \frac{k}{\epsilon^3}\})$ components.

The concentration bound depends on the structural construction of the candidate set, the problem here seems to be of independent interest. We prove an interesting fact that given arbitrary n different real numbers $x_1, \ldots, x_n$, we have

$$\int_{-\infty}^{\infty} \max_{i,j \in [n], i \neq j} N(x_i, (x_i - x_j)^2)(x)dx = \Theta(n).$$

2   The Linear Programming

In this section, we define the LP in our learning algorithm. It's used for learning a mixture of Gaussians from $\mathcal{H}_f$ as in Definition 3. Precisely, we prove following theorem in this section:

Theorem 7. *Let f denote a mixture of k-Gaussians, let $\mathcal{H}_f$ be the candidate set in Definition 3. Given $\tilde{O}(\frac{k}{\epsilon^5})$ samples from f, one can learn a density function g which is a convex combination of Gaussians in $\mathcal{H}_f$ such that $d_{A_{4q}}(f, g) \leq \epsilon$ for $q = \tilde{O}(k/\epsilon^3)$, with probability at least 0.99.*

The algorithm is simply to solve an LP defined as follows:

Definition 4 (The Linear Programming). *Let f denote a mixture of k-Gaussians, H_f is the candidate set in Definition 3, $n = O(\frac{k \log \frac{k}{\epsilon}}{\epsilon})$ is the parameter in Definition 3, $q = \tilde{O}(\frac{k}{\epsilon^3}), m = O(\frac{q}{\epsilon^2})$, $\hat{f}_m$ is the empirical distribution of f as defined in 2. In the following LP, a_{ij} represents for the weight of each candidate Gaussians N_{ij} in $\mathcal{H}_f$:*

$$\min \delta$$
$$s.t. (1) \sum_{i,j \in [n], j \neq i} a_{ij} = 1$$
$$(2) \; a_{ij} \geq 0, i, j \in [n], i \neq j$$
$$(3) \; d_{A_{4q}}\left(\sum_{i,j \in [n], j \neq i} a_{ij} N_{ij}, \hat{f}_m\right) \leq \delta$$

Firstly, we need to show the program in Definition 4 is indeed an LP and can be solved in polynomial time.

Lemma 2. *The programming in Definition 4 is an LP and can be solved in polynomial time. The solution of this program satisfies $\delta \leq \epsilon$, with probability at least 0.99.*

Proof. Firstly, note that constraints (1), (2) are linear constraints, constraint (3) can be written as exponentially many linear constraints since we only need to enumerate all possible partitions. By Theorems 6 and 5, with probability 0.99, this LP has a solution which is less than ϵ.

To solve this LP in polynomial time, we use the ellipsoid method. We only need to show a polynomial separation oracle exists for constraints of this LP.

Assume the empirical distribution $\hat{f}_m$ is determined by $Y_1 < Y_2 < \ldots < Y_m$. Given a set of value of variables $\{b_{ij} : i, j \in [n]i \neq j\}$, we use a dynamic programming to compute $d_{A_{4q}}(\sum_{i,j \in [n], j \neq i} b_{ij} N_{ij}, \hat{f}_m)$. Note the end points of the optimal partition should be at Y_i by monotonicity. Let $F[i, j]$ denote the A_j-distance between $\sum_{i,j \in [n], j \neq i} b_{ij} N_{ij} i$ and $\hat{f}_m$ restricted on $(-\infty, Y_i)$. We have:

$$F[i, j] = \max_{l < i} \left\{ F[l, j-1] + \left| \sum_{i,j \in [n], j \neq i} b_{ij} N_{ij}((Y_l, Y_i)) - \frac{i-l}{m} \right| \right\}, j > 1.$$

and

$$F[i, 1] = \left| \sum_{i,j \in [n], j \neq i} b_{ij} N_{ij}((-\infty, Y_i)) - \frac{i}{m} \right|.$$

Given such separation oracle, the ellipsoid method can return the optimal solution.

Proof (Proof of Theorem 7). The algorithm is simply to solve the LP in Definition 4, where we need $O(\frac{k \log \frac{k}{\epsilon}}{\epsilon})$ many samples to construct the candidate set and $m = O(\frac{q}{\epsilon^2}) = \tilde{O}(\frac{k}{\epsilon^5})$ many samples to construct the empirical distribution by Theorem 5. By lemma 2, the A_{4q} distance between the mixture returned by solving LP and the underlying GMM is at most ϵ. The algorithm obviously runs in polynomial time since LP has polynomial algorithm.

3   Main Theorem

In this section, we give our algorithm for Theorem 1 and prove its correctness. In what follows, we use $[x]$ and $\{x\}$ to denote the integral and fractional part of a real number x.

Algorithm 1. Learning GMM

Require: $k, \epsilon > 0$ and sample access to f which is an unknown k-mixture of Gaussians.
Ensure: A mixture g of at most $\tilde{O}(\min\{\frac{k^2}{\epsilon^2}, \frac{k}{\epsilon^3}\})$ Gaussians.
1: Define $q = \tilde{\Theta}(\frac{k}{\epsilon^3}), n = \tilde{O}(\frac{k}{\epsilon}), m = O(\frac{q}{\epsilon^2})$. Take $n + m$ independent samples from f to construct the empirical distribution and the candidate set. Let $\mathcal{H}_f$ denote the candidate set of Gaussians in Definition 3, let $\hat{f}_m$ denote the empirical distribution in Definition 2.
2: Solve the LP in Definition 4, obtain a solution $\{a_{ij} : i, j \in [n], i \neq j\}$.
3: Independently round a_{ij} to a multiple of $1/q$ as follows: define r_{ij} to be independent random variables where $\mathbf{P}\big(r_{ij} = [qa_{ij}]\big) = 1 - \{qa_{ij}\}$ and $\mathbf{P}\big(r_{ij} = [qa_{ij} + 1]\big) = \{qa_{ij}\}$. Round a_{ij} to $\omega_{ij} = \frac{r_{ij}}{q}$.
4: Arbitrarily add multiple of $1/q$ (may be negative if sum of ω_{ij} is larger than 1) into some ω_{ij} such that they remain non-negative and sum to 1.
5: **return** $g(x) = \sum_{i,j \in [n], j \neq i} \omega_{ij} N_{ij}(x)$.

Theorem 8. *The algorithm Learning GMM outputs a mixture of at most $\tilde{O}(\min\{\frac{k^2}{\epsilon^2}, \frac{k}{\epsilon^3}\})$-Gaussians g such that the L_1-distance between f and g is at most $O(\epsilon)$, with probability at least 0.99.*

Proof. Note the output is a mixture of Gaussians where each component's coefficient is a multiple of $1/q$, so the total number of positive coefficients is at most q. That means g is a mixture of at most q Gaussians. Next we prove that with probability at least 0.99, $|f - g|_1 = O(\epsilon)$.

By multiplicative Chernoff bound we have that:

$$\mathbb{P}\bigg(\big| \sum_{i,j \in [n], j \neq i} \frac{r_{ij}}{q} - 1\big| > \epsilon \bigg) < e^{-4q\epsilon^2} < e^{-\Omega(k)} < 0.00001.$$

Let $g'(x) = \sum_{i,j\in[n],j\neq i} \frac{r_{ij}}{q} N_{ij}(x)$. Since f is a mixture of k Gaussians and g is a mixture of q Gaussians, we have, with probability at least 0.9999,

$$
\begin{aligned}
|f - g|_1 &= d_{A_{O(q)}}(f, g) \\
&\leq d_{A_{O(q)}}(f, g') + d_{A_{O(q)}}(g, g') \\
&\leq d_{A_{O(q)}}(f, g') + \left| \sum_{i,j\in[n],j\neq i} \frac{r_{ij}}{q} - 1 \right| \\
&= d_{A_{O(q)}}(f, g') + O(\epsilon)
\end{aligned}
$$

Next we prove that with probability at least 0.9999 (on the randomness of constructing $\mathcal{H}_f$ and $\hat{f}_m$), $\mathbb{E}[d_{A_{O(q)}}(f, g')] = O(\epsilon)$ (on the randomness of variables r_{ij}). Then the theorem follows by using Markov's inequality.

Recall the empirical distribution $\hat{f}_m(x) = \frac{1}{m}\sum_{i=1}^{m} I(Y_i = x)$, where $\{Y_1, Y_2, \ldots, Y_m\}$ are m samples from f. Without loss of generality, assume that

$$
-\infty = Y_0 < Y_1 < Y_2 < \ldots < Y_m < Y_{m+1} = \infty.
$$

Note that by 5 and $m = O(q/\epsilon^2)$, with probability at least 0.9999 we have:

$$
\begin{aligned}
d_{A_{O(q)}}(f, g') &\leq d_{A_{O(q)}}(f, \hat{f}_m) + d_{A_{O(q)}}(\hat{f}_m, g') \\
&\leq \epsilon + d_{A_{O(q)}}(\hat{f}_m, g')
\end{aligned}
$$

Now look at $d_{A_{O(q)}}(\hat{f}_m, g')$, note that by monotonicity the $A_{O(q)}$-distance between g' and $\hat{f}_m$ is determined by all ways to partition the real axis into at most $O(q)$ intervals where each interval's endpoints are at some Y_i. Let $\mathcal{S}$ be the set of all such partitions then we know that:

$$
d_{A_{O(q)}}(\hat{f}_m, g') = \sup_{S\in\mathcal{S}} \sum_{s\in S} |g'(s) - \hat{f}_m(s)|
$$

where $g'(s) = \int_s g(x)dx$ i.e., the probability mass of g on interval s.

Let $f'(x) = \sum_{i,j\in[n],j\neq i} a_{ij} N_{ij}(x)$ denote the corresponding Gaussian mixture determined by the LP solution. For any $S \in \mathcal{S}$, by triangular inequality,

$$
\sum_{s\in S} |g'(s) - \hat{f}_m(s)| \leq \sum_{s\in S} |g'(s) - f'(s)| + \sum_{s\in S} |f'(s) - \hat{f}_m(s)|
$$

By union bound, the probability of all previous inequality holds and the algorithm ends successfully is at least 0.999. Conditioned on this we have that:

$$
\begin{aligned}
\sum_{s\in S} |f'(s) - \hat{f}_m(s)| &\leq \sum_{s\in S} |f'(s) - f(s)| + \sum_{s\in S} |f(s) - \hat{f}_m(s)| \\
&\leq d_{A_{O(q)}}(f', f) + d_{A_{O(q)}}(f, \hat{f}_m) \\
&\leq 2\epsilon.
\end{aligned}
$$

Here $d_{A_{O(q)}}(f', f) \leq \epsilon$ is by the fact that f' is the solution returned by the linear programming (Lemma 2).

So

$$\sum_{s \in S} |g'(s) - \hat{f}_m(s)| \leq \sum_{s \in S} |g'(s) - f'(s)| + 2\epsilon$$

$$\leq \sum_{i=0}^{m} |g'([Y_i, Y_{i+1}]) - f'([Y_i, Y_{i+1}])| + 2\epsilon$$

It means that

$$\mathbb{E}[d_{A_{O(q)}}(\hat{f}_m, g')] = \mathbb{E}[\sup_{S \in S} \sum_{s \in S} |g'(s) - \hat{f}_m(s)|] \leq \mathbb{E}[\sum_{i=0}^{m} |g'([Y_i, Y_{i+1}]) - f'([Y_i, Y_{i+1}])|] + 2\epsilon$$

$$= \sum_{i=0}^{m} \mathbb{E}[|g'([Y_i, Y_{i+1}]) - f'([Y_i, Y_{i+1}])|] + 2\epsilon$$

Note that by definition we have:

$$\mathbb{E}[g'([Y_i, Y_{i+1}])] = \mathbb{E}[\sum_{l,j \in [n], j \neq l} \frac{r_{lj}}{q} N_{lj}([Y_i, Y_{i+1}])] = \sum_{l,j \in [n], j \neq l} a_{lj} N_{lj}([Y_i, Y_{i+1}])$$

$$= f'([Y_i, Y_{i+1}]).$$

To upper bound $\mathbb{E}[|g'([Y_i, Y_{i+1}]) - f'([Y_i, Y_{i+1}])|]$ we use the following simple lemma:

Lemma 3. *Let $b_1, b_2, \ldots, b_n$ be n independent 0–1 variables such that $\mathbb{P}(b_i = 1) = p_i$ and $\mathbb{P}(b_i = 0) = 1 - p_i$. $r_1, r_2, \ldots, r_n$ are positive numbers and $\mu = \mathbb{E}[\sum_{i=1}^{n} b_i r_i] = \sum_{i=1}^{n} p_i r_i$, then*

$$\mathbb{E}[|\sum_{i=1}^{n} r_i b_i - \mu|] = O\left(\sqrt{\mu \max_{i \in [n]} r_i}\right)$$

Proof. By independence,

$$\mathbb{E}^2[|\sum_{i=1}^{n} r_i b_i - \mu|] \leq Var[\sum_{i=1}^{n} r_i b_i] = \sum_{i=1}^{n} Var[r_i b_i] = \sum_{i=1}^{n} b_i^2 p_i (1 - p_i)$$

$$\leq \max_{i \in [n]} b_i \cdot \sum_{i=1}^{n} b_i p_i = \mu \max_{i \in [n]} b_i$$

So we have a corresponding upper bound for the deviation,

$$\mathbb{E}[|g'([Y_i, Y_{i+1}]) - f'([Y_i, Y_{i+1}])|] = O\left(\sqrt{q^{-1} f'([Y_i, Y_{i+1}]) \max_{l,j \in [n], l \neq j} N_{lj}([Y_i, Y_{i+1}])}\right)$$

So by Cauchy-Schwarz's inequality,

$$\mathbb{E}[d_{A_{O(q)}}(\hat{f}_m, g')] \leq \sum_{i=0}^{m} \mathbb{E}[|g'([Y_i, Y_{i+1}]) - f'([Y_i, Y_{i+1}])|] + 2\epsilon$$

$$\leq O\left(\sum_{i=0}^{m} \sqrt{q^{-1} f'([Y_i, Y_{i+1}]) \max_{l,j \in [n], l \neq j} N_{lj}([Y_i, Y_{i+1}])} \right) + 2\epsilon$$

$$\leq O\left(\sqrt{q^{-1} \left(\sum_{i=0}^{m} f'([Y_i, Y_{i+1}])\right)\left(\sum_{i=0}^{m} \max_{l,j \in [n], l \neq j} N_{lj}([Y_i, Y_{i+1}])\right)} \right) + 2\epsilon$$

$$= O\left(\sqrt{q^{-1} \left(\sum_{i=0}^{m} \max_{l,j \in [n], l \neq j} N_{lj}([Y_i, Y_{i+1}])\right)} \right) + 2\epsilon.$$

Since $q = \tilde{\Theta}(\frac{k}{\epsilon^3})$, we only need to prove

$$\sum_{i=0}^{m} \max_{l,j \in [n], l \neq j} N_{lj}([Y_i, Y_{i+1}]) = \tilde{O}(k/\epsilon)$$

Indeed we have the following stronger lemma, and we put the proof in Appendix A.

Lemma 4.

$$\int_{-\infty}^{\infty} \max_{i,j \in [n], i \neq j} N_{ij}(x)dx = O(n).$$

So we have that

$$\sum_{i=0}^{m} \max_{l,j \in [n], l \neq j} N_{lj}([Y_i, Y_{i+1}]) \leq \int_{-\infty}^{\infty} \max_{i,j \in [n], i \neq j} N_{ij}(x)dx = O(n) = \tilde{O}(k/\epsilon).$$

Proof (Proof of Theorem 1). We use the algorithm in Theorem 8, and the output mixture of Gaussians g is what we need. By union bound, the success probability is at least 0.99, the sample complexity is

$$O(m + n) = O\left(\frac{q}{\epsilon^2} + \frac{k \log \frac{k}{\epsilon}}{\epsilon} \right) = \tilde{O}(\frac{k}{\epsilon^5})$$

Obviously, the running time is polynomial on the sample complexity.

4   Properly Learning Mixture of Two Gaussians

In this section, we provide two algorithms for properly learning mixture of two Gaussians. The algorithms search for a mixture of two Gaussians which is close to the empirical distribution in A_6 distance.

Let $\hat{f}_n$ be the empirical distribution of f defined by $n = O(\frac{1}{\epsilon^2})$ many samples. By DKW-inequality (Theorem 5), we have $d_K(f, \hat{f}_n) \leq O(\epsilon)$. Lemma 1 motivates us to look for a mixture of two Gaussians g such that $d_K(g, \hat{f}_n) \leq O(\epsilon)$. The same as in the general case, g can be a mixture from the candidate set $\mathcal{H}_f$ in Definition 3. We show that this problem can be reduced to a well-studied geometric problem, the closest pair problem in L_∞-norm. We then give two algorithms. One uses a good property of Gaussian distribution to speed up the search and the other is a consequence of Indyk's result [11].

4.1   Reduce to L_∞-Closest Pair

Assume $\hat{f}_n$ is the empirical distribution defined by samples $Y_1, Y_2, \ldots, Y_n$, for $n = O(\frac{1}{\epsilon^2})$, i.e., $\hat{f}_n(x) = \frac{1}{n}\sum_{i=1}^{n}\delta_{Y_i}(x)$. W.l.o.g assume that

$$-\infty = Y_0 < Y_1 < Y_2 < \ldots < Y_n < Y_{n+1} = \infty,$$

Recall the construction of $\mathcal{H}_f$. We draw $m = \tilde{O}(\frac{1}{\epsilon})$ samples $x_1, \ldots, x_m$ from f and define

$$\mathcal{H}_f = \{N_{ij}(x) = N(x_i, (x_i - x_j)^2)(x) : i, j \in [m], i \neq j\}.$$

By Theorem 6, we know there is a mixture of two Gaussians in $\mathcal{H}_f$ which is close to $\hat{f}_n$ in Kolmogorov distance. We need to look for it. Being more precise, we look for a real number $\omega \in [0, 1]$ and index $i, j, k, l \in [m]$ where $i \neq j, k \neq l$ such that

$$d_K\big(\omega N_{ij}(x) + (1 - \omega)N_{kl}(x), \hat{f}_n(x)\big) \leq O(\epsilon)$$

This also reads as

$$\forall t \in [n], \; \left|\omega N_{ij}((-\infty, Y_t]) + (1 - \omega)N_{kl}((-\infty, Y_t]) - \frac{t}{n}\right| \leq \epsilon.$$

Now we enumerate ω over all multiples of $\frac{\epsilon}{3}$ in $[0, 1]$ which takes $O(\frac{1}{\epsilon})$ time. For all $i, j \in [m], i \neq j$, we define n-dimensional vectors u_{ij} and v_{ij} as follows:

$$v_{ij} = (v_{ij}^{(t)})_{t=1}^{n}, v_{ij}^{(t)} = \omega \cdot \left(N_{ij}((-\infty, Y_t)) - \frac{t}{n}\right)$$

$$u_{ij} = (u_{ij}^{(t)})_{t=1}^{n}, u_{ij}^{(t)} = -(1 - \omega) \cdot \left(N_{ij}((-\infty, Y_t)) - \frac{t}{n}\right)$$

By definition, we have that:

Lemma 5.

$$d_K\left(\omega N_{ij}(x) + (1 - \omega)N_{kl}(x), \hat{f}_n(x)\right) \leq O(\epsilon)$$

if and only if

$$|v_{ij} - u_{kl}|_\infty = O(\epsilon).$$

The problem now is to look for an approximation of the closest pair between $\{v_{ij}\}$ and $\{v_{ij}\}$. We give two algorithms in next subsection which are faster than the naive searching algorithm.

There is one remaining trouble before we state and prove the correctness of our algorithm. The trouble is the number of coordinates are large (it's $n = O(\frac{1}{\epsilon^2})$). However, we can reduce it to $O(\frac{1}{\epsilon})$ through the following simple lemma.

Lemma 6. *Let the empirical distribution* $\hat{f}_n(x) = \frac{1}{n} \sum_{i=1}^{n} \delta_{Y_i}(x)$. *Let* $d = [\epsilon n]$, $k_i = [\frac{i}{\epsilon}]$, *for* $i = 1, \ldots, d$. *Define a distribution* $\hat{g}(x) = \frac{1}{d} \sum_{i=1}^{d} \delta_{Y_{k_i}}(x)$. *Let* g *be a probability density function. We have that,*

- *If* $d_K(\hat{f}_n, g) \le \epsilon$, *then* $d_K(\hat{g}, g) \le \epsilon$.
- *If* $d_K(\hat{g}, g) \le \epsilon$, *then* $d_K(\hat{f}_n, g) \le O(\epsilon)$.

So in order to find some g which is close to $\hat{f}_n$ in Kolmogorov's distance, we can indeed only consider the values of v_{ij} and u_{ij} on $k_1, k_2, \ldots, k_d$-th coordinates.

Definition 5. *For each* $\omega \in [0,1]$, *define* $U_\omega = \{u_{ij}\}$ *and* $V_\omega = \{v_{ij}\}$ *to be vectors sets in d-dimensions such that,*

$$v_{ij}^{(t)} = \omega \left(N_{ij}\big((-\infty, Y_{k_t})\big) - \frac{k_t}{n} \right)$$

and

$$u_{ij}^{(t)} = -(1 - \omega) \left(N_{ij}\big((-\infty, Y_{k_t})\big) - \frac{k_t}{n} \right)$$

4.2   Proof of Theorem 2

We use the following simple fact to speed up the brute force searching algorithm through a binary search.

Lemma 7. *Let* $F(\mu, \sigma^2)(x)$ *denote the CDF of* $N(\mu, \sigma^2)$, *that is* $F(\mu, \sigma^2)(x) = \int_{-\infty}^{x} N(\mu, \sigma^2)(y)dy$. *If* $y < \mu$ *then* $F(\mu, \sigma^2)(y)$ *is monotone decreasing on* σ. *If* $y > \mu$ *then* $F(\mu, \sigma^2)(y)$ *is monotone increasing on* σ.

Back to our problem, we want to find a real number $\omega \in [0, 1]$ and four indexes i, j, k, l such that $|u_{ij} - v_{kl}|_\infty \le \epsilon$. If we naively enumerate ω over all multiples of $\frac{\omega}{3}$ and all possible i, j, k, l then compute the L_∞ norm in $O(d) = O(\frac{1}{\epsilon})$ time, the overall time is $\tilde{O}(\frac{1}{\epsilon^6})$. Thanks to the previous observation, we can improve the running time by using a binary search. We first enumerate ω and construct U_ω and V_ω then we enumerate $i, j, k \in [m]$. By the previous observation $u_{ij}^{(t)} - v_{kl}^{(t)} = \omega N_{ij}\big((-\infty, Y_{k_t})\big) + (1 - \omega)N_{kl}\big((-\infty, Y_{k_t})\big) - \frac{k_t}{n}$ is monotone decreasing on the variance when $Y_{k_t} < x_k$ and monotone increasing on the variance when $Y_{k_t} > x_k$. So for each t, we can use a binary search to find all l which satisfies that $|u_{ij}^{(t)} - v_{kl}^{(t)}| < \epsilon$ (which is a continuous interval). Finally we check if there is a l which satisfies all constraints. The overall running time is $\tilde{O}(\epsilon^{-5})$.

The second algorithm for Theorem 2 uses a classical result of the Nearest Neighbor Search (NNS) problem in L_∞ norm by [11] as a subroutine. The Nearest Neighbor Search (NNS) problem in L_∞^d is defined as follows: given a set of points in a d dimensional space, build a data structure to answer efficiently the queries which ask for the closest point to some point q in L_∞ norm. The C-NNS problem requires returning a point which is at most C times the minimum distance close to the query point in L_∞ norm. Obviously, the closest pair problem can be solved by simply asking the queries on each input point for a built NNS data structure. In this section, we use a classical algorithm for L_∞-nearest neighbor by [11].

Theorem 9 ([11]). *Assume there are n points in d dimensional space. For any $p > 0$ there is a data structure, uses $\tilde{O}(dn^{1+p})$ storage and $\tilde{O}(d)$ query time for $4\log_{1+p}\log d + 1$-NNS algorithm in L_∞^d. Moreover, the data structure can be constructed in nearly linear time.*

So we can simply enumerate ω and construct the previous data structure for U_ω. Then we obtain an $O(\log_{1+p}\log d) = O(\frac{\log\log\frac{1}{\epsilon}}{p})$ -approximation of the closest pair through the data structure by querying each point in V_ω. Note we only obtain a mixture of two Gaussians which is $O(p^{-1}\epsilon\log\log\frac{1}{\epsilon})$ close to f in L_1-distance. So we need to work on a smaller ϵ at the beginning. We lose a $(p^{-1}\log\log\frac{1}{\epsilon})^2$ factor on the sample complexity. Note that in our problem the number of points is $\tilde{O}(\frac{1}{\epsilon^2})$ and we need another $O(\frac{1}{\epsilon})$ factor to enumerate ω. So the total time complexity is $\tilde{O}(\frac{1}{\epsilon}\cdot dn^{1+p} + \frac{1}{\epsilon}\cdot nd) = \tilde{O}(\frac{1}{\epsilon^{4+2p}})$. Theorem 2 then follows.

Acknowledgement. Thanks Jian Li for very useful discussion.

A   Proof of Technique Lemma

In this section, we prove that:

$$\int_{-\infty}^{\infty} \max_{p,q\in[n],p\neq q} N(x_p,(x_p-x_q)^2)(x)\,dx = O(n).$$

Define $\max(\emptyset) = 0$. Set $x_0 = -\infty$, $x_{n+1} = \infty$, and, w.l.o.g., assume $x_0 < x_1 < x_2 < \cdots < x_n < x_{n+1}$. For convenience, let $S = \{(p,q)|p,q \in [n], p \neq q\}$ and $N_{p,q} = N(x_p,(x_p-x_q)^2)$ for any $(p,q) \in S$.

To estimate LHS, a nature idea is to consider for what kind of p,q and x, $N(p,q)(x)$ will be maximized. More specifically, we want to find a subset S_i of S such that

$$\max_{(p,q)\in S} N_{p,q}(x) = \max_{(p,q)\in S_i} N_{p,q}(x)$$

for any $x \in [x_i, x_{i+1}]$. Unfortunately, there does not exist such good S_i. But if we relax the restriction, then we can get a pretty good result: for any $x \in [x_i, x_{i+1}]$,

$$\max_{(p,q)\in S, p\leq i} N_{p,q}(x) \leq 2\max\left(g_i(x), N_{i,i+1}(x)\right), \tag{1}$$

where

$$g_i(x) = \max_{k\in[n], k_i\leq k\leq i-1} N_{i,k}(x)$$

and k_i denotes the smallest k such that $x_i - x_k < x_{i+1} - x_i$ for any $i \in [n]$.

The proof of (1) is in Appendix A.1.

Note that

$$\int_{-\infty}^{\infty} \max_{(p,q)\in S} N_{p,q}(x)\, dx = \sum_{i=1}^{n} \int_{x_i}^{x_{i+1}} \max\left(\max_{(p,q)\in S, p\leq i} N_{p,q}(x); \max_{(p,q)\in S, p\geq i+1} N_{p,q}(x)\right) dx$$

$$\leq \sum_{i=1}^{n} \int_{x_i}^{x_{i+1}} \max_{(p,q)\in S, p\leq i} N_{p,q}(x)\, dx + \sum_{i=1}^{n} \int_{x_i}^{x_{i+1}} \max_{(p,q)\in S, p\geq i+1} N_{p,q}(x)\, dx.$$

By symmetricity, we only need to prove that

$$\sum_{i=1}^{n} \int_{x_i}^{x_{i+1}} \max_{(p,q)\in S, p\leq i} N_{p,q}(x)\, dx = O(n).$$

By inequality (1),

$$\sum_{i=1}^{n} \int_{x_i}^{x_{i+1}} \max_{(p,q)\in S, p\leq i} N_{p,q}(x)\, dx \leq \sum_{i=1}^{n} \int_{x_i}^{x_{i+1}} 2\max\left(g_i(x), N_{i,i+1}(x)\right) dx$$

$$\leq \sum_{i=1}^{n} \int_{x_i}^{x_{i+1}} 2g_i(x)\, dx + \sum_{i=1}^{n} \int_{x_i}^{x_{i+1}} 2N_{i,i+1}(x)\, dx$$

$$\leq \sum_{i=1}^{n} \int_{-\infty}^{\infty} 2g_i(x)\, dx + 2n.$$

So we only need to prove that:

$$\sum_{i=1}^{n} \int_{-\infty}^{\infty} g_i(x)dx = O(n). \tag{2}$$

We put proof of (2) in Appendix A.2.

A.1

In this section, we show that for any $x \in [x_i, x_{i+1}]$

$$\max_{(p,q)\in S, p\leq i} N_{p,q}(x) \leq 2\max\left(g_i(x), N_{i,i+1}(x)\right),$$

where k_i denotes the smallest k such that $x_i - x_k < x_{i+1} - x_i$ and

$$g_i(x) = \max_{k \in [n], k_i \le k \le i-1} N_{i,k}(x)$$

for any $i \in [n]$.

By definition, we have $k_i \le i$. It is easy to find that some $N_{p,q}(x)$ are always bigger than any other. To illustrate it, we need a lemma:

Lemma 8. *For any real number* $a < b \le x \le c$ *such that* $b - a \ge c - b$,

$$N(b, (b-c)^2)(x) \ge N(b, (b-a)^2)(x).$$

Proof. When $t \ge x - b$,

$$\frac{d}{dt} N(b, t^2)(x) = \frac{1}{\sqrt{2\pi}} \frac{(x-b)^2 - t^2}{t^4} e^{-\frac{(x-b)^2}{2t^2}} \le 0.$$

Since $b - a \ge c - b \ge x - b$, we have

$$N(b, (b-c)^2)(x) \ge N(b, (b-a)^2)(x).$$

So it is easy to find two deductions (3) and (4) of Lemma 8:

For any $k, i \in [n]$ such that $k < k_i$, any $x \in [x_i, x_{i+1}]$, let $a = x_k$, $b = x_i$, $c = x_{i+1}$. Since $k < k_i \le i$, we have $a < b < c$. By definition of k_i and $k < k_i$, we have $x_i - x_k \ge x_{i+1} - x_i$, which means $b - a \ge c - b$. Obviously, $b \le x \le c$. So we can use Lemma 8 to conclude:

$$N_{i,k}(x) \le N_{i,i+1}(x). \tag{3}$$

For any p, q, i such that $p \le i, q \ge i + 1$ and any $x \in [x_i, x_{i+1}]$,

$$N_{p,q}(x) = \frac{1}{\sqrt{2\pi(x_p - x_q)^2}} e^{-\frac{(x-x_p)^2}{2(x_p-x_q)^2}}$$

$$\le \frac{1}{\sqrt{2\pi(x_p - x_q)^2}} e^{-\frac{(x-x_i)^2}{2(x_p-x_q)^2}}$$

$$= N(x_i, (x_p - x_q)^2)(x).$$

Let $a = x_i - (x_q - x_p)$, $b = x_i$, $c = x_{i+1}$. Obviously, $a < b \le x \le c, b - a \ge c - b$. So we can use Lemma 8 to conclude:

$$N(x_i, (x_p - x_q)^2)(x) \le N_{i,i+1}(x).$$

Combining two inequalities, we have

$$N_{p,q}(x) \le N_{i,i+1}(x). \tag{4}$$

To compare $N_{q,p}(x)$ and $N_{i,p}(x)$ for $p < q \le i$, we need a lemma:

Lemma 9. *For any real numbers* a, b, c, x *such that* $a < b \leq c \leq x$,

$$2N(c, (c-a)^2)(x) \geq N(b, (b-a)^2)(x).$$

Proof. Note that for any real number t,

$$(1+t)^2 \leq 2(1+t^2) \leq 2e^{t^2}.$$

So

$$1 + t \leq \sqrt{2e^{t^2}} \leq 2e^{\frac{1}{2}t^2}.$$

Let $t = \frac{c-b}{b-a}$. Then we have

$$\frac{c-a}{b-a} \leq 2exp\left(\frac{(c-b)^2}{2(b-a)^2}\right).$$

Since

$$\begin{aligned}
\frac{(x-b)^2}{2(b-a)^2} - \frac{(x-c)^2}{2(c-a)^2} &\geq \frac{(x-b)^2}{2(b-a)^2} - \frac{(x-c)^2}{2(b-a)^2} \\
&= \frac{2(c-b)x + b^2 - c^2}{2(b-a)^2} \\
&\geq \frac{2(c-b)c + b^2 - c^2}{2(b-a)^2} \\
&= \frac{(c-b)^2}{2(b-a)^2},
\end{aligned}$$

we have

$$\begin{aligned}
2exp\left(\frac{(x-b)^2}{2(b-a)^2} - \frac{(x-c)^2}{2(c-a)^2}\right) &\geq 2exp\left(\frac{(c-b)^2}{2(b-a)^2}\right) \\
&\geq \frac{c-a}{b-a}.
\end{aligned}$$

That is

$$2\frac{1}{c-a}exp\left(-\frac{(x-c)^2}{2(c-a)^2}\right) \geq \frac{1}{b-a}exp\left(-\frac{(x-b)^2}{2(b-a)^2}\right),$$

which means

$$2N(c, (c-a)^2)(x) \geq N(b, (b-a)^2)(x).$$

For any $p, q, i \in [n]$ such that $p < q \leq i$ and any $x \in [x_i, x_{i+1}]$, note that

$$\begin{aligned}
N_{p,q}(x) &= \frac{1}{\sqrt{2\pi(x_p - x_q)^2}} e^{-\frac{(x-x_p)^2}{2(x_p - x_q)^2}} \\
&\leq \frac{1}{\sqrt{2\pi(x_p - x_q)^2}} e^{-\frac{(x-x_q)^2}{2(x_p - x_q)^2}} \\
&= N_{q,p}(x).
\end{aligned}$$

Let $a = x_p$, $b = x_q$, $c = x_i$. Obviously, $a < b \le c \le x$. So we can use Lemma 9 to conclude that:

$$N_{q,p}(x) \le 2N_{i,p}(x).$$

Combining two inequalities, we have that:

$$N_{p,q}(x) \le N_{q,p}(x) \le 2N_{i,p}(x). \tag{5}$$

By inequality (3) and definition of $g_i(x)$, for any $k < i$ and any $x \in [x_i, x_{i+1}]$ we have:

$$N_{i,k}(x) \le \max\left(g_i(x) + N_{i,i+1}(x) \right). \tag{6}$$

Combining inequalities (4), (5) and (6), for any $p \le i$ and any $x \in [x_i, x_{i+1}]$,

$$N_{p,q}(x) \le 2\max\left(g_i(x), N_{i,i+1}(x) \right).$$

A.2

In this section, we show that:

$$\sum_{i=1}^{n} \int_{-\infty}^{\infty} g_i(x)\, dx = O(n).$$

To estimate the LHS, we need a lemma:

Lemma 10. *For any real number $a < b < c$,*

$$\int_{-\infty}^{\infty} \max\left(N(c, (c-b)^2)(x) - N(c, (c-a)^2)(x), 0 \right) dx \le \frac{b-a}{c-a}.$$

Proof.

$$N(c, (c-a)^2)(x) = \frac{1}{\sqrt{2\pi(c-a)^2}} e^{-\frac{(x-c)^2}{2(c-a)^2}}$$

$$\ge \frac{1}{\sqrt{2\pi(c-a)^2}} e^{-\frac{(x-c)^2}{2(c-b)^2}}$$

$$= \frac{c-b}{c-a} N(c, (c-b)^2)(x).$$

That is

$$\frac{b-a}{c-a} N(c, (c-b)^2)(x) \ge N(c, (c-b)^2)(x) - N(c, (c-a)^2)(x).$$

Also since $\frac{b-a}{c-a} N(c, (c-b)^2)(x) \ge 0$, we have

$$\max\left(N(c, (c-b)^2)(x) - N(c, (c-a)^2)(x), 0 \right) \le \frac{b-a}{c-a} N(c, (c-b)^2)(x).$$

So

$$\int_{-\infty}^{\infty} \max\left(N(c, (c-b)^2)(x) - N(c, (c-a)^2)(x), 0 \right) dx \leq \int_{-\infty}^{\infty} \frac{b-a}{c-a} N(c, (c-b)^2)(x)\, dx$$

$$= \frac{b-a}{c-a}.$$

Note that for any $i, j \in [n]$ such that $k_i \leq j \leq i-1$,

$$N_{i,j} = N_{i,k_i} + \sum_{k=k_i}^{j-1} N_{i,k+1} - N_{i,k}$$

$$\leq N_{i,k_i} + \sum_{k=k_i}^{i-2} \max\left(N_{i,k+1} - N_{i,k}, 0 \right).$$

So

$$\max_{k_i \leq k \leq i-1} N_{i,j} \leq N_{i,k_i} + \sum_{k=k_i}^{i-2} \max\left(N_{i,k+1} - N_{i,k}, 0 \right).$$

By Lemma 10, we have:

$$\sum_{i=1}^{n} \int_{-\infty}^{\infty} g_i(x)\, dx \leq \sum_{i=1}^{n} \left(\int_{-\infty}^{\infty} N_{i,k_i}(x)\, dx + \sum_{k=k_i+1}^{i-1} \int_{-\infty}^{\infty} \max\left(N_{i,k+1} - N_{i,k}, 0 \right)(x)\, dx \right)$$

$$\leq n + \sum_{i=1}^{n} \sum_{k=k_i}^{i-2} \frac{x_{k+1} - x_k}{x_i - x_k}$$

$$= n + \sum_{k=1}^{n} (x_{k+1} - x_k) \sum_{i \in T_k} \frac{1}{x_i - x_k},$$

where $T_k = \{i | k_i \leq k \leq i-2\}$.

Fix a subscript k. Assume all elements in T_k are $i_1 < i_2 < \cdots < i_m$. For any i_t, by the definition of k_i and $k_{i_t} \leq k \leq i_t - 2$, we have $x_{i_t+1} - x_{i_t} > x_{i_t} - x_k$. So

$$x_{i_{t+1}} - x_k \geq x_{i_t+1} - x_{i_t} + x_{i_t} - x_k$$

$$\geq 2(x_{i_t} - x_k).$$

So

$$(x_{k+1} - x_k) \sum_{i \in T_k} \frac{1}{x_i - x_k} \leq \frac{x_{k+1} - x_k}{x_{i_1} - x_k}\left(1 + \frac{1}{2} + \frac{1}{4} + \cdots + \frac{1}{2^{m-1}}\right)$$

$$\leq \frac{x_{k+1} - x_k}{x_{i_1} - x_k} \cdot 2$$

$$\leq 2.$$

Since k is arbitrary, we have

$$\sum_{i=1}^{n} \int_{-\infty}^{\infty} g_i(x)\, dx \leq n + 2n = 3n = O(n).$$

References

1. Acharya, J., Diakonikolas, I., Li, J., Schmidt, L.: Sample-optimal density estimation in nearly-linear time. In: Proceedings of the Twenty-Eighth Annual ACM-SIAM Symposium on Discrete Algorithms, SIAM, pp. 1278–1289 (2017)
2. Anandkumar, A., Ge, R., Hsu, D.J., Kakade, S.M., Telgarsky, M.: Tensor decompositions for learning latent variable models. J. Mach. Learn. Res. **15**(1), 2773–2832 (2014)
3. Belkin, M., Sinha, K.: Polynomial learning of distribution families. In: 2010 51st Annual IEEE Symposium on Foundations of Computer Science (FOCS), pp. 103–112. IEEE (2010)
4. Bhaskara, A., Suresh, A.T., Zadimoghaddam, M.: Sparse solutions to nonnegative linear systems and applications. In: AISTATS (2015)
5. Dasgupta, S.: Learning mixtures of Gaussians. In: 1999 40th Annual Symposium on Foundations of Computer Science, pp. 634–644. IEEE (1999)
6. Dasgupta, S., Schulman, L.: A probabilistic analysis of EM for mixtures of separated, spherical Gaussians. J. Mach. Learn. Res. **8**(Feb), 203–226 (2007)
7. Daskalakis, C., Kamath, G.: Faster and sample near-optimal algorithms for proper learning mixtures of Gaussians. In: COLT, pp. 1183–1213 (2014)
8. Devroye, L., Lugosi, G.: Combinatorial Methods in Density Estimation. Springer Science & Business Media, New York (2012)
9. Ge, R., Huang, Q., Kakade, S.M.: Learning mixtures of Gaussians in high dimensions. In: Proceedings of the Forty-Seventh Annual ACM on Symposium on Theory of Computing, pp. 761–770. ACM (2015)
10. Hardt, M., Price, E.: Tight bounds for learning a mixture of two Gaussians. In: Proceedings of the Forty-Seventh Annual ACM on Symposium on Theory of Computing, pp. 753–760. ACM (2015)
11. Indyk, P.: On approximate nearest neighbors under l infinity norm. J. Comput. Syst. Sci. **63**(4), 627–638 (2001)
12. Kalai, A.T., Moitra, A., Valiant, G.: Efficiently learning mixtures of two Gaussians. In: Proceedings of the Forty-Second ACM Symposium on Theory of Computing, pp. 553–562. ACM (2010)
13. Li, J., Schmidt, L.: A nearly optimal and agnostic algorithm for properly learning a mixture of k Gaussians, for any constant k. arXiv preprint arXiv:1506.01367 (2015)
14. Moitra, A., Valiant, G.: Settling the polynomial learnability of mixtures of Gaussians. In: 2010 51st Annual IEEE Symposium on Foundations of Computer Science (FOCS), pp. 93–102. IEEE (2010)
15. Sanjeev, A., Kannan, R.: Learning mixtures of arbitrary Gaussians. In: Proceedings of the Thirty-Third Annual ACM Symposium on Theory of Computing, pp. 247–257. ACM (2001)
16. Suresh, A.T., Orlitsky, A., Acharya, J., Jafarpour, A.: Near-optimal-sample estimators for spherical Gaussian mixtures. In: Advances in Neural Information Processing Systems, pp. 1395–1403 (2014)
17. Vempala, S., Wang, G.: A spectral algorithm for learning mixture models. J. Comput. Syst. Sci. **68**(4), 841–860 (2004)

A New Method for Retinal Image Semantic Segmentation Based on Fully Convolution Network

Yuning Cao[1,2], Xiaojuan Ban[1,2(✉)], Zhishuai Han[1], and Bingyang Shen[1]

[1] University of Science and Technology Beijing, Beijing, China
mail@caoyuning.com, banxj@ustb.edu.cn, zsani.han@gmail.com,
shenbingyang1995@163.com
[2] Beijing Key Laboratory of Knowledge Engineering for Materials Science,
Beijing, China

Abstract. Retina images contain a lot of useful information for medical judgment, blood vessel extrusion, the ratio of the arteriovenous width and whether there is lesion area are vital to disease judgment, it is difficult to draft a unified standard for artificial judgment due to subjectivity. Traditional approaches to obtain the three indicators mentioned above include image processing and machine learning, these approaches have relatively poor accuracy or too many restrictions. In order to solve these problems, we propose a customized fully convolutional network, RI-FCN, based on image semantic segmentation for retina image detection. In our proposed method, there are five convolution layers, three down-pooling layers and two up-pooling layers. This structure can classify every pixel into predefined categories and show in different colors and small features can also be presented which is vital in the detection of blood vessel extrusion. Using the RI-FCN model, identification accuracy rate of arteriovenous width ratio, extrusion and lesion area can be increased to 92.23%, 90.99% and 98.13% respectively.

Keywords: RI-FCN · Semantic segmentation · Deep learning
Retina images

1 Introduction

Retina adjuvant therapy is an important part of intelligent medical system. Retinal blood vessels are the only blood vessels that can be observed of the body [1,2]. Doctors can infer the health situation of the patients according to whether there is lesion and blood vessel extrusion area or whether the ratio of the arteriovenous width is in normal range [1,3]. However, in this process, the evaluation criteria are greatly influenced by the subjective judgment of doctors.

Y. Cao—Graduate student majoring in computer science at University of Science and Technology Beijing.

© Springer Nature Singapore Pte Ltd. 2018
L. Li et al. (Eds.): NCTCS 2018, CCIS 882, pp. 27–45, 2018.
https://doi.org/10.1007/978-981-13-2712-4_3

For the same retinal image, different doctors may give different conclusions, resulting this kind of traditional medical treatment is not accurate [1,3,4]. A quick and accurate extraction of the required information from an existing retinal image is an urgent problem to be solved.

The main difficulty in the identification of retinal lesions lies in lesion and extrusion area extraction and corresponding spatial position localization [5,6]. The artery, vein, blood vessel extrusion area and lesion area have their own unique characteristics, these characteristics are necessary for feature extraction [7,8]. However, these characteristics are very difficult to address. Firstly, the width of the arteries and veins are particularly fine, it is very difficult to determine which pixel is or is not on the blood vessel [9]. Secondly, at the intersection of the arterial and venous vessels, the area of the cross obstruction will be much smaller due to the small width of the arteriovenous blood vessels [10]. In retinal images, the RGB values of the vascular area and non-vascular regions are not immutable in different locations, which is difficult to set the threshold for the traditional method of image processing [11]. Given retinal image resolution, calculation error caused by pure image processing is inevitable.

The difficulty in the lesion region extraction is the uncertainty of the location of the lesion region [12]. The lesion may occur in the fundus region, or it may occur in the vascular region. When the lesion occurs in the eye, it presents bright red, distinct from the color of other areas of the retina ground. However, there is a partial overlap with the color of the vascular region, it is difficult to ensure that a part of the normal vascular area is extracted when the lesion is extracted, and this error may cause the misjudgment of doctor [13]. When the lesion region is on the vessel, the problem at this point is the difficulty of extracting the lesion. As mentioned above, the width of the vessel is very fine, therefore, the corresponding lesion region is also very fine. Usually, there is only one or two pixels in the retinal image dataset. After setting the static threshold, the lesion region in some raw images may not be extracted at all. In those dynamic threshold setting literatures, it is difficult to set the dynamic threshold for each of these regions, considering the chromaticity changes in the vascular region [11]. Although there is some difference in color between the lesion area and the surrounding vascular region, the RGB value in the vascular region has a certain range, and the RGB value of the lesion region may have the same RGB value as the distant vessel [14]. Similarly, some blood vessel regions may be extracted when the region of interest is extracted, or the region of interest cannot be extracted at all when the vascular region is removed.

At present, the method of pure image processing is to find the feature of the region for a certain area, perform some transformations in frequency domain and time domain. Antal et al. [15] propose a combination of internal components of micro aneurysm detectors, but the performance of this method depends on more preprocessing methods and candidate extractors. Agurto et al. [12] adopt multiscale amplitude-modulation-frequency-modulation methods for discriminating between normal and pathological retinal images, however, this method emphasizes lesion area detection, it does not work well in classification. Ramlugun et al.

[16] introduce a systematic approach for segmentation of retinal blood vessels. The key components of this method include 2D-Match (Gabor) filters, a double sided thresholding scheme and hysteresis thresholding, but the threshold has to be manually set to for the best result, hence it is not universal.

Traditional image processing has inevitable drawbacks as introduced above. With the developing of machine learning, more and more machine learning approaches have been applied in medical image processing. Shanmugam et al. [17] uses a 7-D feature vector based on pixel classification, and this approach can categorize each pixel into two classes, vessel and non-vessel area respectively, but this method cannot extract lesion region because of its small size. Narasimhan et al. [18] also presents a method to classify normal and abnormal images, but uses Support Vector Machine (SVM) and Bayesian Network to train their model. This model is very effective on linear separable problems, as for complex pixel localization problems, SVM cannot work nicely. Lachure et al. [19] compares SVM and KNN classifier, giving method to detect both exudates and micro-aneurysms. Though this method has a great improvement on specificity and accuracy, the structure is relatively simple and can only be used for classification, but not to locate lesion region accurately. Besides, there are many machine learning based methods in the literature [20–23], although machine learning based classification is more accurate than pure image processing, some deep-seated features cannot be extracted.

Compared to pure image processing and machine learning combined, deep learning can reach more accurate classification and segmentation results. Li et al. [24] offers a new supervised method for retinal vessel segmentation. This method transforms the segmentation task to a problem of cross-modality data transformation from retinal image to vessel map based on a wide and deep neural network. Holbura et al. [25] presents a deep neural network for optic disc segmentation, this method can learn different features between parapapillary atrophy and optic disc. Based on extracted features, the method can reach a least mean overlapping error 9.7%. However, machine learning based methods yield relatively few features, therefore, they have limited accuracy in segmentation.

In order to solve the problems mentioned above and obtain three key indicators, in this paper, we propose a method of semantic segmentation for retinal images based on fully convolution network. This method uses the idea of deep learning to classify every pixel in the retinal image, and solves the problem of image segmentation at semantic level [26]. The traditional method is to do some transformation in the time and frequency domain, or to do some trick in the dynamic threshold setting, and then multiple morphological transformations are performed to extract interest regions. This method has great limitations, especially in the attribution of fuzzy pixel points, often results in great errors and misjudgment. In contrast, our method marks each pixel and the object or area around the pixel, and determines the pixel attribute according to the comprehensive information, hence it is more universal in applicability. Moreover, compared to the deep convolutional networks based on semantic segmentation, RI-FCN can accept any size of the input image. The last convolution layer feature map is sampled by a convolution kernel to restore it to the same size as the input image. This method can predict the category of each pixel, and preserve the spatial pixels information of the original input image. After the up-sampling is completed, RI-FCN classifies each pixel on their feature map and calculates the error of each pixel classification. In our method, the five-layer convolution structure can preserve the edge information of the blood vessel when extracting the blood vessel characteristics, and reduce the misclassification rate. The latter two convolution operations make a further classification of the third convolution layer, guarantying the integrity of the minimum granularity of the interest region (Fig. 1).

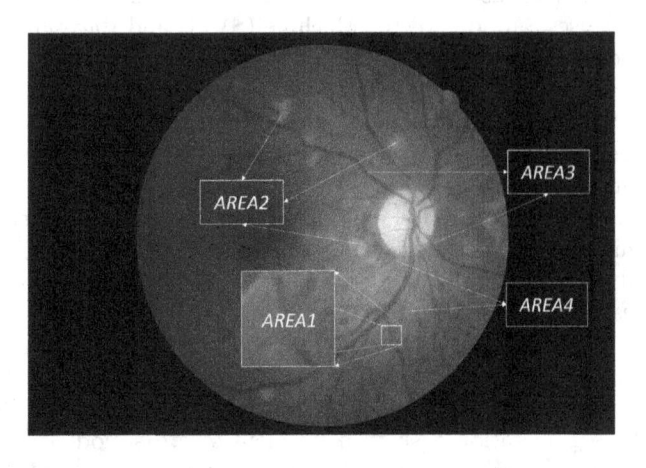

Fig. 1. Schematic diagram of vein, artery, extrusion and lesion region. AREA1, AREA2, AREA3 and AREA4 denote extrusion region, lesion region, vein and artery respectively.

2   Related Works

2.1   Semantic Image Segmentation

Semantic image segmentation is the key technology of image processing. Now deep learning is getting more and more popular in the field of image segmentation, many excellent methods have emerged, one of the most representative is fully convolutional network. FCN was presented by Jonathan Long on the CVPR2015 and has gotten the best paper [26]. It is a pioneering work in the task of image semantic segmentation based on deep learning. The principle of semantic image segmentation is to carry out the end-to-end semantic segmentation of pixel level in order to achieve the state-of-the-art results. The core processing of FCN consists of three parts: convolution, pooling and hopping, which will be described in detail in next sections. FCN is a semantic segmentation method based on convolution neural network training, on the basis of pre-training supervision, accuracy has been greatly improved. In the past two years, FCN is increasingly being applied to image segmentation, a number of papers based on FCN and its optimization algorithms appear in top conferences and journals, such as CVPR. For example, in order to solve the large representation domain and many pooling layers in FCN, Bertasius [27] proposes BNF based on the existing FCN to enhance the consistency of semantic segmentation and improve the localization of objects.

2.2 Edge Detection

Edge detection is a kind of supervised learning problem. Ganin et al. [28] proposes a new architecture for complex image processing operations, adopting natural edge detection and thin object segmentation. The architecture uses nearest neighbor search to improve the results considerably and account for the underfitting effect. Wang [29] presents a supervised method combining two superior classifiers: Convolutional Neural Network (CNN) and Random Forest (RF), the proposed method is able to learn features from the raw images automatically based on trained edge detection patterns. Therefore, using deep learning technique in edge detection can improve image segmentation performance greatly.

3 Methodology

On the basis of general FCN framework, we add image preprocessing and improved convolution kernel, propose a deep learning algorithm for retinal images. FCN uses a locally aware convolution layer, for retinal images with relatively fixed range, adding a certain process to the convolution layer will yield better effect than pure FCN. The most important training process in FCN is the second convolution layer, the feature extraction is obvious. The processing of our optimization model is mainly focused on the input level and the second convolution stage to process the edge feature data of the object to be extracted. FCN differs from CNN in that there is no fully connected layer, the two connections between the last volume of the CNN or the sub sampling layer to the output layer are fully connected. In FCN, the two connections are replaced by two volumes, and output a labeled retinal images.

3.1 Customized Pretreatment

The training accuracy of retinal images depends largely on the quality of the training set, in this paper, we propose a customized pretreatment for retinal image processing. The preprocessing layer is used to filter out the noise and redundant information in the original image and intercept the interesting region. The images of the original training set and the test set are substantially more than 1000×1000. In terms of training, the classification accuracy can be guaranteed, but for large-scale data this kind of training is too slow. In order to speed up the image training with ensuring the accuracy, we resize the captured image to 500×500, the vascular lesions unit can be seen in the retina image under this kind of resolution. Suppose original image is $Raw(W_r, H_r)$, H_r denotes the height of the corresponding edge of the intercepted image, then the intercepted and zoomed out region of interest image $ROI(W_0, H_0)$ can be calculated using the following formula.

$$ROI(W_0, H_0) = G_{trans}(F_{scaling}(Raw(W_r, H_r) * M_{scaling})) \tag{1}$$

where

$$M_{scaling} = \begin{bmatrix} 0 \cdots 0 & 1 \cdots 0 & 0 \cdots 0 \\ \vdots \ddots \vdots & \vdots \ddots \vdots & 0 \ddots 0 \\ 0 \vdots 0 & 0 \cdots 1 & 0 \cdots 0 \end{bmatrix}^T_{W_r, H_r} \tag{2}$$

$$F_{scaling_{i,j}}(Raw) = \frac{1}{(TH_{high} - TH_{low})^2} \sum_{m=TH_{low}, n=TH_{low}}^{TH_{high}, TH_{high}} Raw_{m,n} \tag{3}$$

$$G_{trans}(Raw) = Raw_{image} * \begin{bmatrix} 1 \cdots 0 \\ \vdots \ddots \vdots \\ 0 \cdots 1 \end{bmatrix}_{K,K} * (\frac{e^{\frac{Raw_{i,j}}{255}} - 1}{e - 1}) \tag{4}$$

In the formula above, $M_{scaling}$ denotes the scaling matrix, we can obtain region of interest from original image. Function $F_{scaling}$ can resize ROI region to right size for training, and Function G_{trans} denotes an exponential form mapping, this function can reduce image contrast and give more details of extracted object. The internal parameters can be found below.

$$TH_{low} = \lfloor \frac{H_0}{K} \rfloor * K \tag{5}$$

$$TH_{high} = \lceil \frac{H_0}{K} \rceil * K \tag{6}$$

$$K = 500 \tag{7}$$

Processed image contains the desired region of interest and these images are scaled to the size of the 500×500.

3.2 Multi-layer Feature Sensing and Extraction

General FCN framework only contains convolution layers except pooling layers. As shown in Fig. 2, the system puts the original image into the convolution layer, and after multiple convolution and sub-sampling layer, the final result maps the two-dimensional image to one-dimensional space. Input layer to C1 is one step convolution operation. As shown in Fig. 2, the pixel points in a certain neighborhood can be mapped to the same points in the classification, indicating that all pixels within this neighborhood belong to the same class. Convolution layer is the core step of FCN, local connection and weight sharing are realized through convolution kernel. The convolution kernel acts as a filter and receptive field. The spatial relationship of the image obeys the principle that local pixels are closely related and those pixels far away have weak correlation. Therefore, the next convolution kernel only needs to perceive the local information of the current layer, and this will greatly reduce the training parameters and the training complexity. The influence convolution layer to image feature extraction includes two factors, the number of convolution kernel and the size of convolution kernel. Each convolution kernel can learn one feature of the current image, if the first layer convolution kernel size is 500 × 500, obviously feature extraction is not sufficient. The solution is to add multiple convolution kernels, for example, Lenet-5 uses six convolution kernels, which can learn 6 features from the upper image. For complex images such as retinal images, more convolution kernels are needed. In addition, the size of the convolution kernel is also critical, it decides how many pixels within the receptive fields share the same weights, too big will make different types of pixels have the same characteristics, too small extracting feature will not be sufficient.

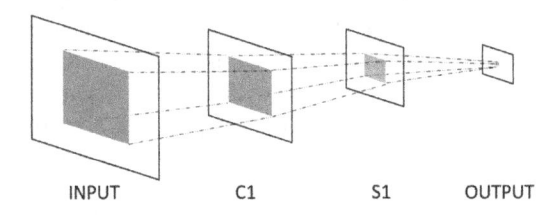

INPUT   C1   S1   OUTPUT

Fig. 2. Simple structure for deep learning using convolution network, basic elements include input layer, convolution layer, pooling layer and output layer.

FCN deals with the two-dimensional image signal, as for convolution, there are

$$f(m,n) * g(m,n) = \sum_{u}^{\infty} \sum_{v}^{\infty} f(u,v)g(m-u,n-v) \tag{8}$$

In a convolution operation, suppose the size of the original image or feature map is $M \times M$, given that there are A convolution kernels, these convolution kernels' size is $N \times N$, which we can know that $N < M$. So as for the convolution feature map using k–convolution kernel, the value of every pixel can be calculated from the following formula.

$$h_{i,j}^{k} = F_{non-linear}(F_{conv}) \tag{9}$$

where

$$F_{non-linear}(x) = tanh(x) \tag{10}$$

$$F_{conv} = \sum_{u=0}^{2} \sum_{v=0}^{2} w_{2-u,2-v} x_{u+i,v+j} + b_{i,j}^{k} \tag{11}$$

In the formula above, the parameter b denotes the bias constant of every convolution kernel, a total of A training parameters. w is the weight of each convolution kernel representation, each convolution kernel has $N \times N$ data. Therefore, there are $N * N * A$ training parameters in addition. From the above formula, the convolution operation of two-dimensional image is to convolute the weight matrix and the input feature map, the convolution results add the bias of the neurons in the corresponding position of the input layer, after a non-linear transformation, we can find the output of the corresponding neurons.

3.3   Local Redundant Data Reduction

The down sampling layer, also known as down pooling layer, is one key step in processing course. Its main purpose is to reduce the feature map, slightly improve transformation invariance. The visual cortex has a similar lateral inhibitory effect, it can reduce parameters to prevent overfitting. Usually sampling size is 2×2, commonly used methods include maximum pooling, mean pooling, Gauss pooling and trainable pool. Maximum pooling takes the maximum value of 4 adjacent pixels as the value of the corresponding output unit. Mean pooling uses the average of 4 adjacent pixels, and Gauss pool uses the same method as Gauss blur. Trainable pool is a function with training parameters. The inputs are the values of 4 adjacent pixels, and the outputs are the corresponding unit values. However, the side length of the feature map is not necessarily a multiple of 2, in this situation, there are two ways to deal with object edges. One way is to ignore the edge, this method directly eliminates redundant edges. The second way is to preserve the object edge, fill the side of the feature map using 0 to reach an integer multiple of 2, then put it into the sampling operation. The main reason of using the down sampling layer rather than increasing the size of the convolution kernel is that the latter will increase the number of training parameters, and lose some of the characteristics of detected objects. Down sampling layer will lose some information, but can retain the characteristic information of object edge.

As shown in Fig. 3, the size of the input image is $K \times K$, every time after sampling, the original image is reduced by half. Down-sampling can be achieves by the following four ways.

$$DownSampling_{max} = \max_{i,j \in win(K_{sampling})} Pixel_{i,j} \tag{12}$$

$$DownSampling_{mean} = \frac{1}{K_{sampling}^{2}} \sum_{i,j \in win(K_{sampling})} Pixel_{i,j} \tag{13}$$

$$DownSampling_{weight} = \sum_{i,j \in win(K_{sampling})} Pixel_{i,j} * W_{Pixel_{i,j}} \tag{14}$$

$$DownSampling_{weight} = \sum_{i,j \in win(K_{sampling})} Pixel_{i,j} * F_{weight_{i,j}} \tag{15}$$

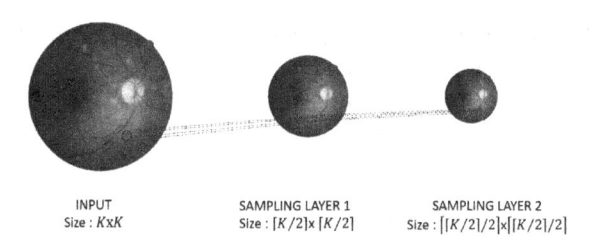

INPUT
Size : KxK

SAMPLING LAYER 1
Size : $[K/2]$x$[K/2]$

SAMPLING LAYER 2
Size : $[[K/2]/2]$x$[[K/2]/2]$

Fig. 3. Simplified down-sampling structure, after each sampling, previous image is reduced by half

where
$$K_{sampling} = 2 \tag{16}$$

In the formula above, (13) is max down-sampling, and the second one denotes mean down-sampling. (14) and (15) are similar, but in (14) the weights are fixed, in (15) weights are trained out. We use the fourth function as the sampling mode. This process will add some parameters, but can improve the classification accuracy in the training process.

3.4   End-to-End Classification Output

FCN is an end-to-end training type, its output can reach state-of-art status. FCN abandons the traditional CNN whose last two layers are full connection structure, and uses two convolution layers. The neurons in the convolution layer are only connected to the local data in the input data, and the neurons share the same parameters in convolution sequence, the rest are 0, this structure greatly reduces the number of parameters to be trained.

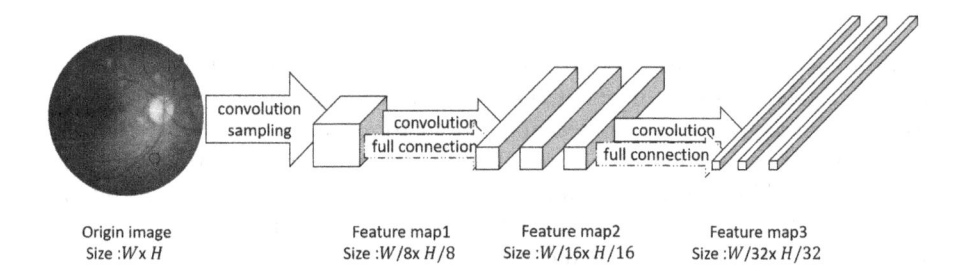

convolution sampling

convolution
full connection

convolution
full connection

Origin image
Size :Wx H

Feature map1
Size :$W/8$x $H/8$

Feature map2
Size :$W/16$x $H/16$

Feature map3
Size :$W/32$x $H/32$

Fig. 4. Output structure for RI-FCN, the dashed arrow denotes a general CNN structure.

In the Fig. 4, in the process of origin image to the first feature map, there are several feature layers, including some convolution and down sampling operations. This process is the same as that of general convolutional neural network, what is different is the output layer. The first feature layer to the third feature layer, CNN includes two full connections, shown as the dotted arrow in Fig. 4. However, RI-FCN uses two convolution layers as the solid line arrow shows. As can be seen above, RI-FCN can accept any size of the original image.

3.5   Trainable Feature Backtracking

Feature backtracking includes two parts, up-sampling and transposedal layer. When the output image is reduced to $\frac{1}{32^2}$ of the original image size, we can obtain the category of each pixel, the output image needs feature backtracking to restore the space position to the original image. There are many ways to achieve the up-sampling. In our RI-FCN model, we use the three convolution interpolation algorithm as the up-sampling method with the edge enhancement effect. Target pixel value can be calculated as follows.

$$f(i + u, j + v) = [A] \cdot [B] \cdot [C] \tag{17}$$

where

$$[A] = [S(u + 1)S(u + 0)S(u - 1)S(u - 2)] \tag{18}$$

$$[B] \begin{bmatrix} f(i-1,j-1) & f(i-1,j+0) & f(i-1,j+1) & f(i-1,j+2) \\ f(i-0,j-1) & f(i-0,j+0) & f(i-0,j+1) & f(i-0,j+2) \\ f(i+1,j-1) & f(i+1,j+0) & f(i+1,j+1) & f(i+1,j+2) \\ f(i+2,j-1) & f(i+2,j+0) & f(i+2,j+1) & f(i+2,j+2) \end{bmatrix} \tag{19}$$

$$[C] \begin{bmatrix} S(v + 1) \\ S(v + 0) \\ S(v - 1) \\ S(v - 2) \end{bmatrix} \tag{20}$$

$$S(x) = \begin{cases} 1 - (\lambda + 3) \cdot |x|^2 + (\lambda + 2) \cdot |x|^3 & |x| < 1 \\ -(4 \cdot \lambda) + (8 \cdot \lambda) \cdot |x| - (5 \cdot \lambda) \cdot x^2 + \lambda \cdot |x|^3 & 1 \le |x| \le 2 \\ 0 & 2 \le |x| \end{cases} \tag{21}$$

The convolution back operation is performed in order to calculate the loss parameters and input gradients of the roll up layer. The negative gradient represents the steepest descent direction, in order to make the function value (i.e., Loss) as small as possible. It is also called fractionally stride convolutions, and works by switching the forward and backward passes of a step of convolution. One approach denotes that the kernel defines a convolution, but whether it is a direct convolution or a transposed convolution is determined by how the forward and backward passes are computed.

4   Experiments

In this part, we mainly introduce the experimental setup, the strategy of the experiment, and at the next section, we present our experimental results.

4.1. Strategy

In our RI-FCN model, in the process of obtaining all the pixels of the original image, we use 5 convolution layers and 5 down-sampling layers. In general, as we have introduced, the last two convolutions of RI-FCN is unique. The kernel of the first three convolution layers and the kernel of the latter two convolution layers are different when extracting object pixel feature. In order to get more accurate classification results, we set up a series of control experiments, the main difference of the experiment is that the size and number of each convolution layer is different. RI-FCN core processes are illustrated in Fig. 5.

We split the algorithm into three parts, step1 is similar to convolutional neural network, step2 is the core of the RI-FCN algorithm and in step3 we restore classified characteristics. First, we import the image into the system, after a set of pretreatment, we carry out the first convolution. In our RI-FCN model diagram, we set that the convolution kernel of the first layer is 5, the size is also 5, which can be modified in the subsequent operations, then the number of feature maps after convolution is 5. Convolution operation does not ignore edges, those parts of the convolution kernel overflow fill with 0, then the convolution feature maps C1 have the same size with the input image. After getting C1, we progress the first down-sampling operation. We set the kernel of down-sampling 2, demonstrating that each adjacent 4 pixels corresponds to the same dynamic weight function operation, and we can obtain the first down-sampling feature map S1. Then, there are a total of 10 subsampling maps, the 1/4 size of the original image, the subsequent operations of Step1 are similar to these two operations. After getting S3, we still use the convolution and down-sampling from S3 to S5, rather than full connection. Such structure can further extract features, whose process is similar to step1. In step3, we have got the classification of all pixels, what needs to be done is to display the spatial information of the features on the original image, this process consists of up-sampling and transposed convolution. First, after an up-sampling, a pixel is mapped into the 4×4 region, and then through the transpose of original convolution kernel, we get the feature map C6. Repeat this process once we can get the final feature layer C8. After an up-sample of 2×2, we get the final result image.

4.2   Experimental Setup

We use the retina dataset on kaggle, the retinal images of the right eye and the left eye are 40000 respectively, 80000 in total. 60000 of them are used as training set and the rest as test set. Detailed data are shown in the Table 1, the total number of "Normal", "extrusion" and "lesion" are larger than 80k, this is because one abnormal picture may contains both extrusion and lesion. Each picture is marked in advance, and put them into the RI-FCN network to train our model. We set up a series of comparative experiments, including varying the RI-FCN internal parameters, as well as comparison with the CNN classifier.

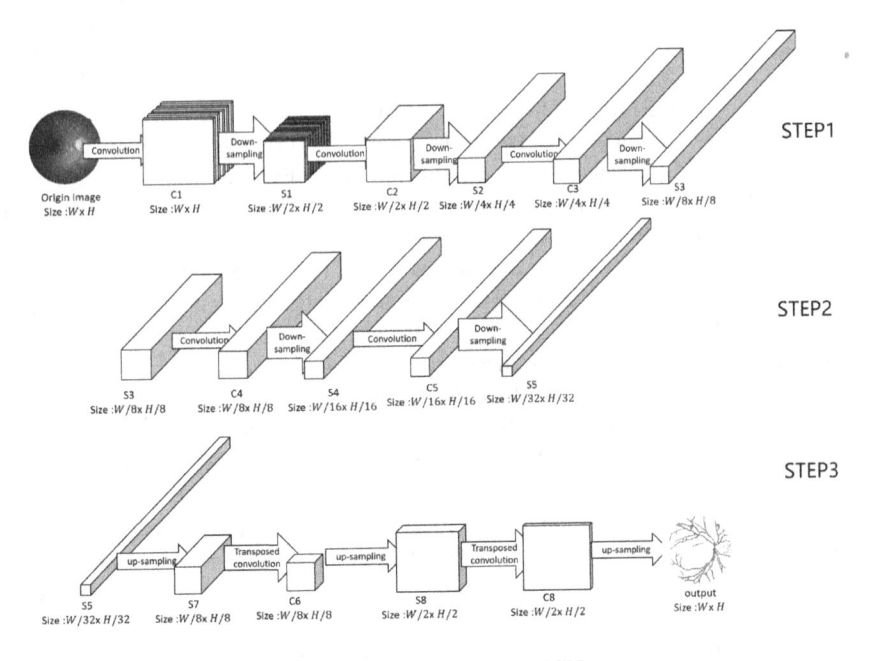

Fig. 5. Whole structure for RI-FCN system.

We set the RI-FCN model with RI-FCN($\alpha_1, \alpha_2, \alpha_3$), α_1, α_2 indicate the size of the convolution kernel in step1 and Step2 respectively, α_3 represents the convolution kernel number overall. CNN uses the best structural parameters in the RI-FCN experiment, so as to contrast the experimental effect. Here we have $\alpha_1 \in \{4, 5, 6\}, \alpha_2 \in \{5, 6\}, \alpha_3 \in \{5, 6\}$.

Table 1. Basic information about the data set

Type	Number	Training set	Test set
Normal	21450	14350	7100
Extrusion	28751	19167	9584
Lesion	32122	21414	10708

5   Results and Analysis

5.1   Image Segmentation Results

Figure 6 illustrates the results of our experiments using the proposed method RI-FCN, and we pick out three distinct feature maps. In the picture, (a)(b)(c) denote the original input image, (d)(e)(f) denote the corresponding segmented feature map. Red, blue, green and yellow represent vein, artery, the lesion region and the extrusion region respectively. From the Fig. 6, we can see that our method can effectively mark the target region. In the feature extraction of an original image, the morphological features and position features of pixel points and their surrounding points can be mapped to the final feature map according to the trained model. One more thing can be seen from the graph is that the blood vessels do not necessarily have the same width as the original image, because it is difficult to mark a particularly fine blood vessel in the process of marking the original image training set. But the overall location information is preserved, this information plays a key role in medical judgment, such as vascular misplacement, and three-dimensional reconstruction. Also, we reach a very high accuracy for extracting the lesion region. In the labeling process of the original training set, we use the method of doctor assisted marking to determine the boundary of the lesion region and the background, so as to obtain the relatively accurate mark region. As can be seen from the be contrast map (b)(e), most of the lesions can be marked out, only a small part of the regions that are not obvious or obtaining little difference between the ground color are not split out, but it does not affect the condition judgment. From (c) to (f), our method uses yellow dots to indicate the region of the arteriovenous crossing. Vascular extrusion position is mostly concentrated in some locations, the feature of the extrusion region can be extracted from the training set, and find the location of the maximum probability of detection of the extrusion region and marked out according to trained parameters. The following table is the experimental probability of segmentation and detection as well as the contrast data of CNN and original FCN detection.

5.2   Accuracy Comparison

The data in Table 2 are the results obtained from 20000 test data. Lesion detection accuracy denotes the ratio of the number of images that can correctly detect the lesion region to the total image number of test set. Extrusion detection accuracy denotes the ratio of the number of detected arteriovenous extrusion region to the total images. We suppose whether the ratio of the width of the artery and vein is within the normal range or not as the basis of the retinopathy. Correct prediction accuracy of retinopathy indicates the probability to predict retina disease correctly. The latter two indexes are related to the position information of pixels. Position sensitivity indicates the ratio of the number of pixels that can be correctly detected and segmented to the total number pixels of the current image. Pixel specificity indicates the ratio of the number of pixels marked correctly to the overall pixels. Given that CNN and FCN are the best results under the same conditions, the optimal results of these two methods is directly compared with our method RI-FCN.

CNN can be used for classification, but cannot achieve pixel level operation. As can be seen from Table 2, the accuracy of CNN in retinal image classification is relatively high. In the detection of lesions, vascular compression region and retinopathy prediction experiments, as for the first three indicators, CNN has

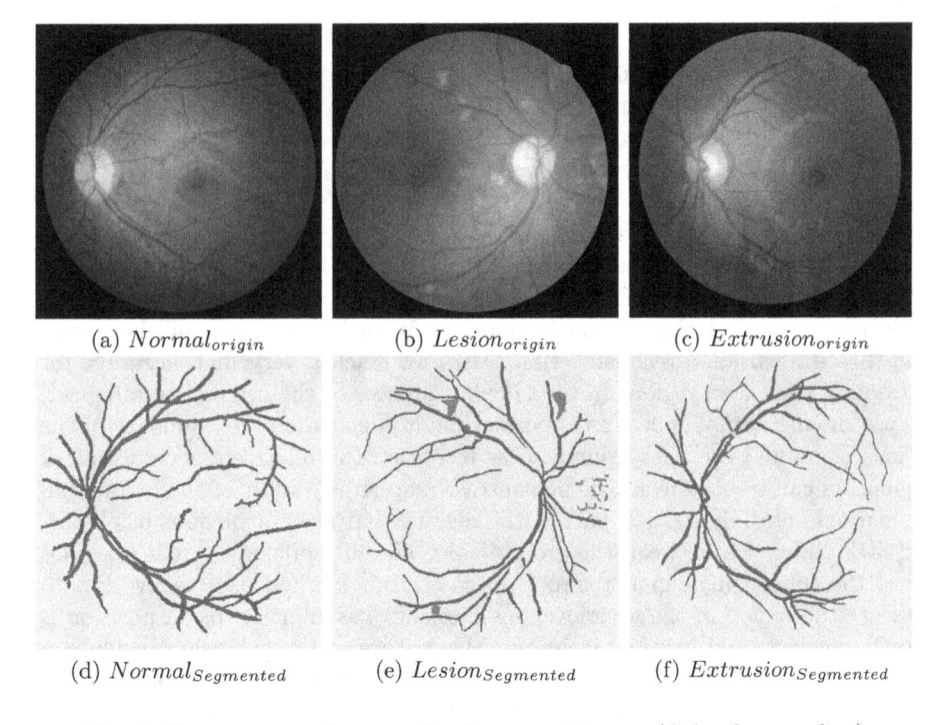

(a) $Normal_{origin}$ (b) $Lesion_{origin}$ (c) $Extrusion_{origin}$

(d) $Normal_{Segmented}$ (e) $Lesion_{Segmented}$ (f) $Extrusion_{Segmented}$

Fig. 6. Feature extraction map for three special cases (Color figure online)

better performance than the accuracy of some of experiments based on RI-FCN, but still fails to reach the best performance of FCN and RI-FCN. This is because CNN only contains the training data categories, but FCN and RI-FCN can further improve the accuracy of segmentation and detection based on the spatial relative position of the pixel. In addition, FCN is better than CNN in the detection accuracy, but still cannot compare the performance of the optimal RI-FCN results under the same conditions. The key point is that on the basis of FCN, we perform some preprocessing for the specific retinal images, and improve part of the sampling and convolution operation, this improvement can achieve higher accuracy. Appropriate processing can reduce the redundant information of the pixel spatial position, and map the original image information to the final feature map better.

5.3   Performance Comparison

As shown in Fig. 7, we compare the classification and prediction performance of RI-FCN, CNN, and SVM. It can be seen from (a) and (b) that when there is little amount of training samples, the accuracy of CNN and SVM is very low and there is not much difference between the precision of the three methods. With the increase of training samples, the accuracy of classification increases gradually. Compared with CNN and SVM, the performance of RI-FCN is getting better.

Table 2. Accuracy comparison using different methods

	Lesion detection accuracy	Extrusion detection accuracy	Correct prediction accuracy of retinopathy	Position sensitivity	pixel specificity
RI-FCN(4, 5, 5)	0.8927	0.8059	0.8738	0.8757	0.8597
RI-FCN(4, 5, 6)	0.9153	0.8145	0.8750	0.8646	0.8517
RI-FCN(4, 6, 5)	0.9241	0.8031	0.8690	0.8807	0.8603
RI-FCN(4, 6, 6)	0.9212	0.8230	0.8911	0.8825	0.8974
RI-FCN(5, 5, 5)	0.9311	0.8393	0.9053	0.9053	0.9124
RI-FCN(5, 5, 6)	0.9370	0.8418	0.9144	0.8545	0.8962
RI-FCN(5, 6, 5)	0.9584	0.8599	0.9086	0.9061	0.9168
RI-FCN(5, 6, 6)	0.9813	0.8794	0.9223	0.9155	0.9109
RI-FCN(6, 5, 5)	0.9759	0.9099	0.9110	0.8671	0.8657
RI-FCN(6, 5, 6)	0.9623	0.8607	0.8927	0.8546	0.8528
RI-FCN(6, 6, 5)	0.9605	0.8418	0.8878	0.9068	0.8711
RI-FCN(6, 6, 6)	0.9654	0.8545	0.8530	0.8928	0.8708
CNN(6, x, 6)	0.8716	0.8616	0.8625	*	*
FCN(6, 5, 5)	0.9145	0.8879	0.8681	0.8526	0.8526

(c) illustrates the error of the three methods in predicting retinopathy. When the number of training samples is increased to 5000, the prediction error can be reduced to about 30%. By increasing the number of samples, the prediction error is further reduced, and our method has greater probability in reducing prediction error than other two methods and hence has better performance. CNN and SVM do not consider the spatial location specificity, therefore, in (d), we only represent RI-FCN performance. It can be seen that increasing the training sample can increase the probability of the pixel position in the final mapping near the original pixel location.

5.4   Simple 3D Reconstruction

As the Fig. 8 illustrates, we present a simple 3D reconstruction for segmented results in Fig. 8. Due to the complexity of reconstruction. We do not give specific segmentation of different regions. However, from the overall framework, our segmented images can provide great support for 3D reconstruction.

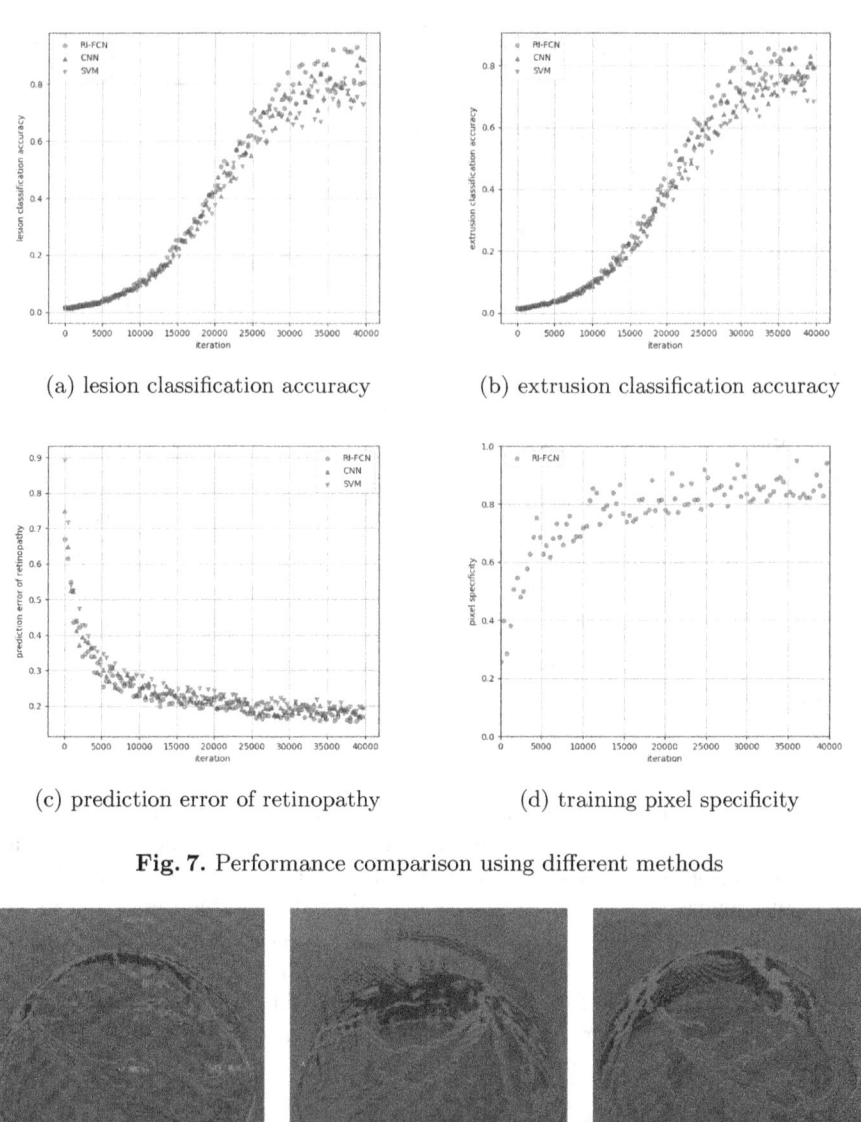

(a) lesion classification accuracy

(b) extrusion classification accuracy

(c) prediction error of retinopathy

(d) training pixel specificity

Fig. 7. Performance comparison using different methods

(a) $3D - Normal_{Seg}$

(b) $3D - Lesion_{Seg}$

(c) $3D - Extrusion_{Seg}$

Fig. 8. Simple 3D reconstruction for segmented results

6   Conclusion

In this paper, we propose a new method for semantic segmentation for retinal image, RI-FCN. We train an optimal end-to-end model to extract the lesion region, arteriovenous extrusion region and whether the arteriovenous ratio is in the normal range, and map the pixel of the original image to the feature map. On the basis of the general FCN framework, we derive a customized pretreatment function, adopt multi-layer feature sensing and extraction, and improve the operation of partial sampling and convolution, these improvement can achieve higher accuracy and more accurate pixel mapping. Compared to CNN, the classification error of our method is reduced by more than 10%. This method overcomes the shortcomings of traditional deep learning approaches that only focus on classification, also solves the problem that the pure image processing is very difficult to detect the small extrusion region.

There are still some improvements to continue in our method, such the identification of some blood vessels in the retina light spot, and most of the errors occur in this position. Also, there are a little cases that our method performs no better than FCN and CNN, our future work will focus on solving this. The next step should be to increase the processing of the original training set and try to extend the blood vessel detection to other parts of the human body where the contrast is not obvious.

Acknowledgements. This work was supported in part by The National Key Research and Development Program of China (Grant No. 2016YFB1001404) and National Natural Science Foundation of China (No. 61572075).

References

1. Lam, B.S., Gao, Y., Liew, A.W.: General retinal vessel segmentation using regularization-based multiconcavity modeling. IEEE Trans. Med. Imaging **29**(7), 1369–81 (2010)
2. Fraz, M.M., Remagnino, P., Hoppe, A., et al.: Blood vessel segmentation methodologies in retinal images – a survey. Comput. Methods Progr. Biomed. **108**(1), 407–433 (2012)
3. Lam, B.Y., Yan, H.: A novel vessel segmentation algorithm for pathological retina images based on the divergence of vector fields. IEEE Trans. Med. Imaging **27**(2), 237–246 (2008)
4. Mendonça, A.M., Campilho, A.: Segmentation of retinal blood vessels by combining the detection of centerlines and morphological reconstruction. IEEE Trans. Med. Imaging **25**(9), 1200–1213 (2006)
5. Seoud, L., Hurtut, T., Chelbi, J., et al.: Red lesion detection using dynamic shape features for diabetic retinopathy screening. IEEE Trans. Med. Imaging **35**(4), 1116–1126 (2016)
6. Hoover, A., Kouznetsova, V., Goldbaum, M.: Locating blood vessels in retinal images by piece-wise threshold probing of a matched filter response. IEEE Trans. Med. Imaging **19**(3), 931 (1998)
7. Fraz, M.M., Barman, S.A., Remagnino, P., et al.: An approach to localize the retinal blood vessels using bit planes and centerline detection. Comput. Methods Progr. Biomed. **108**(2), 600–16 (2012)
8. Nguyen, U.T.V., Bhuiyan, A., Park, L.A.F., et al.: An effective retinal blood vessel segmentation method using multi-scale line detection. Pattern Recogn. **46**(3), 703–715 (2013)

9. Foracchia, M., Grisan, E., Ruggeri, A.: Detection of optic disc in retinal images by means of a geometrical model of vessel structure. IEEE Trans. Med. Imaging **23**(10), 1189–1195 (2004)

10. Akram, U.M., Khan, S.A.: Automated detection of dark and bright lesions in retinal images for early detection of diabetic retinopathy. J. Med. Syst. **36**(5), 3151 (2012)

11. Jiang, X., Mojon, D.: Adaptive local thresholding by verification-based multi-threshold probing with application to vessel detection in retinal images. IEEE Trans. Pattern Anal. Mach. Intell. **25**(1), 131–137 (2003)

12. Agurto, C., Murray, V., Barriga, E., et al.: Multiscale AM-FM methods for diabetic retinopathy lesion detection. IEEE Trans. Med. Imaging **29**(2), 502–512 (2010)

13. Köse, C., Evik, U.U., Kiba, C., et al.: Simple methods for segmentation and measurement of diabetic retinopathy lesions in retinal fundus images. Comput. Methods Progr. Biomed. **107**(2), 274–293 (2012)

14. Tariq, A., Akram. M.U.: An automated system for colored retinal image background and noise segmentation. In: Industrial Electronics and Applications, pp. 423–427. IEEE (2010)

15. Antal, B., Hajdu, A.: An ensemble-based system for microaneurysm detection and diabetic retinopathy grading. IEEE Trans. Biomed. Eng. **59**(6), 1720–1726 (2012)

16. Ramlugun, G.S., Nagarajan, V.K., Chakraborty, C.: Small retinal vessels extraction towards proliferative diabetic retinopathy screening. Expert Syst. Appl. **39**(1), 1141–1146 (2012)

17. Shanmugam V, Banu, R.S.D.W.: Retinal blood vessel segmentation using an extreme learning machine approach. In: Point-of-Care Healthcare Technologies (PHT), pp. 318–321. IEEE (2013)

18. Narasimhan, K., Neha, V.C., Vijayarekha, K.: An efficient automated system for detection of diabetic retinopathy from fundus images using support vector machine and bayesian classifiers. In: 2012 International Conference on Computing, Electronics and Electrical Technologies (ICCEET), pp. 964–969. IEEE (2012)

19. Lachure, J., Deorankar, A.V., Lachure, S., et al.: Diabetic Retinopathy using morphological operations and machine learning. In: IEEE International Advance Computing Conference (IACC), pp. 617–622. IEEE (2015)

20. Ricci, E., Perfetti, R.: Retinal blood vessel segmentation using line operators and support vector classification. IEEE Trans. Med. Imaging **26**(10), 1357–1365 (2007)

21. You, X., Peng, Q., Yuan, Y., et al.: Segmentation of retinal blood vessels using the radial projection and semi-supervised approach. Pattern Recogn. **44**(10–11), 2314–2324 (2011)

22. Sopharak, A., Dailey, M.N., Uyyanonvara, B., et al.: Machine learning approach to automatic exudate detection in retinal images from diabetic patients. J. Mod. Opt. **57**(2), 124–135 (2010)

23. Roychowdhury, S., Koozekanani, D.D., Parhi, K.K.: DREAM: diabetic retinopathy analysis using machine learning. IEEE J. Biomed. Health Inf. **18**(5), 1717–1728 (2014)

24. Li, Q., Feng, B., Xie, L.P., et al.: A cross-modality learning approach for vessel segmentation in retinal images. IEEE Trans. Med. Imaging **35**(1), 109–118 (2016)

25. Holbura, C., Gordan, M., Vlaicu, A., et al.: Retinal vessels segmentation using supervised classifiers decisions fusion. In: 2012 IEEE International Conference on Automation Quality and Testing Robotics (AQTR), pp. 185–190. IEEE (2012)

26. Long, J., Shelhamer, E., Darrell, T.: Fully convolutional networks for semantic segmentation. In: Proceedings of the IEEE Conference on Computer Vision and Pattern Recognition, pp. 3431–3440 (2015)

27. Bertasius, G., Shi, J., Torresani, L.: Semantic segmentation with boundary neural fields. In: Proceedings of the IEEE Conference on Computer Vision and Pattern Recognition, pp. 3602–3610 (2016)
28. Ganin, Y., Lempitsky, V.: N^4-fields: neural network nearest neighbor fields for image transforms. In: Cremers, D., Reid, I., Saito, H., Yang, M.-H. (eds.) ACCV 2014 Part II. LNCS, vol. 9004, pp. 536–551. Springer, Cham (2015). https://doi.org/10.1007/978-3-319-16808-1_36
29. Wang, S., Yin, Y., Cao, G., et al.: Hierarchical retinal blood vessel segmentation based on feature and ensemble learning. Neurocomputing **149**, 708–717 (2015)

Formal Analysis and Verification for Three-Party Authentication Protocol of RFID

Jia Chen[1(✉)] [iD], Meihua Xiao[1(✉)] [iD], Ke Yang[1(✉)] [iD], Wei Li[2(✉)] [iD],
and Xiaomei Zhong[1(✉)] [iD]

[1] School of Software, East China Jiaotong University,
Nanchang 330013, People's Republic of China
chenjia_guan@163.com, landexplorer@163.com,
{xiaomh,zhongxm}@ecjtu.edu.cn
[2] Intelligent Network Research and Development Department,
CRRC Zhuzhou Locomotive Co., Ltd.,
Zhuzhou 412001, Hunan, People's Republic of China
vic.me@foxmail.com

Abstract. RFID three-party authentication protocol based on NTRU cryptosystem is a type of multi-entities authentication protocol. Unlike other RFID mutual authentication protocols, this protocol realizes mutual authentication of Server to Reader, and Server to Tag. Model checking is a formal method to check the correctness specifications hold in each state on concurrent and distributed systems, which can be used to verify the security of network protocol. A multi-channels constructing method is proposed to build this protocol model for formal analysis, then authentication property of the protocol is verified by model checker SPIN. Formal verification result reveals that an attack exists in this protocol, hence the protocol cannot guarantee the security of the three-party authentication protocol. The modeling method proposed above has great significance on security analysis for such three-party authentication protocols.

Keywords: RFID three-party authentication protocol · Model checking
Multi-channel modeling

1 Introduction

Radio frequency identification (RFID) technology is a non-contact communication technology that can identify specific targets, and read or write related data through radio signals. RFID is widely used in various areas such as warehousing, logistics, supermarkets, automatic road toll collection, library management, and healthcare [1]. To achieve automatic object recognition, wireless communication is adopted between Reader, Tag and Server. Therefore, it is more vulnerable to malicious attacks during information exchange phase, which might causes huge economic losses in its application fields [2]. The authentication protocol is a pre-protocol for an encrypted session, once the authentication protocol has a vulnerability, the conversation initiator with the honest subject may be an attacker, as making important information leaked. Formal method is an important means to improve the security and reliability of software system, and it can be provided a strong support for the construction of a secure and reliable RFID system.

© Springer Nature Singapore Pte Ltd. 2018
L. Li et al. (Eds.): NCTCS 2018, CCIS 882, pp. 46–60, 2018.
https://doi.org/10.1007/978-981-13-2712-4_4

RFID system is consists of Server, Reader and Tag. According to the numbers of entity, authentication protocols can be divided into two-party authentication and three-party authentication. Research works [3, 4] aim at mutual authentication of Server and Tag, but lack authentication of Server and Reader, therefore, intruder can potentially steal random numbers from Server. Research works [5, 6] focus on mutual authentication of Reader and Tag, but lack authentication between Reader and Server. As a result, intruder can steal information from the Reader.

Research work [7] has been expanded on the basis of [8], Deng [7] claims that the protocol they proposed can improve the efficiency of encryption and decryption, and reduce the consumption of resources. However, this paper [7] only analyzed the security of cryptosystem, without considering the security of protocol interaction.

Formal methods are divided into modal logic, theorem proving and model checking [9]. There are three some model checker such as SMV, Murphi SPIN and etc. SPIN (Simple Promela Interpreter) [10] is a well-known model detection tool and is awarded with the "Soft System Award" by ACM. Maggi et al. [11] proposes a security protocol modeling method based on the Dolev-Yao attacker model [12], and has found the N-S public key protocol vulnerability with SPIN. This paper extends the Maggi's modeling method, and the proposed method can be used to verify RFID three-party authentication protocol.

2 Related Work

In [8], the author proposed a three-party unidirectional authentication protocol, but tags do not authenticate Reader and Server. The random number generated by the reader and server is not updated, which is easily to cause Denial of Service (DoS) attack. In [13], Wang presents a three-party authentication protocol between the Tag, Reader and Server. However, their work only uses the security of the BAN logic analysis protocol. In [14], Li used model checking to analyze the RFID authentication protocol. But he only analyzed the mutual authentication protocol, and did not analyze the three-party authentication protocol.

Unlike most two-party authentication protocols, RFID three-party authentication protocol based on NTRU public key cryptosystem can complete the mutual authentication between Server and Reader, Server and Tag. However, the research works of the three-party authentication protocol in model checking are still insufficient. Most scholars use modal logic [15] (BAN logic, GNY logic, etc.) to verify the security of three-party authentication protocols but it is difficult to achieve automation.

This paper explores the security of the three-party authentication protocol by using model checking and formal methods. After a reasonable abstraction of the RFID three-party authentication protocol with multi-channels constructing method, an RFID three-party authentication protocol model is constructed. We describe protocol behavior and convert the protocol model to Promela code. Then we use SPIN to verify the authentication of the protocol. Formal verification result reveals that an attack is existed in the protocol, and SPIN gives out the attack sequence.

The structure of this paper is as follows: Sect. 3 abstracts the RFID three-party authentication protocol based on NTRU cryptosystem, and builds a protocol model; Sect. 4 describes the Promela modeling process of the protocol; Sect. 5 analyze and verify the protocol with SPIN; Sect. 6 concludes.

3   Three-Party Authentication Protocol and Formal Representation

In this three-party authentication protocol, Tag, Reader, and Server are treated as independent three parties. The data stored in each Tag is (key_i, ID_t, h_t); the data stored in Reader is (ID_r, h_r); the data stored in Server is $(key_i, ID_t, ID_{new}, ID_{old}, h_t, h_r, y_r, y_t)$. The three-party authentication protocol works as follows:

The Reader first sends a random number $R1$ and an authentication request message $Query$ to the Tag. After receiving the message, the Tag generates a shared secret key key_i and pubic key h_t to compute secret information T_s, and then Tag sent the secret information to the Reader as the response of authentication request. (Note: XOR () is an exclusive or operation function)

$$1.Reader \rightarrow Tag: \ R1 \&\& Query$$
$$2.Tag \rightarrow Reader: \ T\_s$$

$$T\_s = Xor(R1 \ key\_i)$$

Upon the Reader receiving T_s, the Reader verifies the correctness of the message through the decryption operation. If succeeds, the Reader generates $R2$ and ID_r to compute secret message R_s and send to the Server for authentication. (Note: $\coprod$ () is a connection operation, and $\oint$ () is an Interception operation)

$$3.Reader \rightarrow Servers: \ R1 \&\& R\_s$$
$$4.Servers \rightarrow Reader: \ S\_r \&\& S\_t$$

$$R\_s = (ID_r \coprod R2), (R2 \coprod ID_r), PID_1$$
$$S\_r = Xor(R2 \oplus Xor(R1 \oplus ID_t))$$
$$S\_t = Xor(Xor(R1 \oplus ID_t) \oplus (R2 \coprod R1))$$

After receiving the messages $R1$ and R_s, the Server decrypts R_s with the private key pair K_r and K_t respectively, and then uses the interception operation to obtain the shared key K_i' and ID_r, and compares them with the stored data. If the shared key K_i' is the same as the key K_i stored in the Server, Tag is successfully authenticated by the Server. If the ID_r is the same as the ID_{new} or ID_{old} stored in the Server, Reader is successfully authenticated by the Server. The Server then continue to calculate the message $S\_r \&\& S\_t$ and send it to the Reader.

$$5.Reader \rightarrow Tag: \ R\_t$$

$$R\_t = Xor(R1 \oplus ID_t)$$

After the Reader receives the message $(S\_r \&\& S\_t)$, Reader obtains data $R2$ through connection operation and XOR operation. Then Reader verifies the correctness of the data. If the data is correct, the Server is successfully authenticated by the Reader.

At this point, the Server and Reader have completed mutual authentication, and then the Reader sends the message R_t to the Tag. Then Tag calculates the received data and verifies its correctness. If the data is correct, the Server passes the authentication of Tag. At this point, the Tag and the Server complete the mutual authentication.

Due to the complexity of cryptographic operations, it is difficult to directly use formal methods for analysis. Before the formal analysis of the three-party RFID authentication protocol, it is necessary to abstract the protocol. Following work [14], the protocol abstraction is based on the following principles:

(1) Assume that the cryptosystem of the protocol is perfect, that is, there is no flaws in cryptographic operations. Therefore, all the cryptographic operations in the protocol are abstracted into E_k functions. In this way, the defects analysed by the formal method are the defects of protocol itself, rather than the vulnerabilities of the cryptosystem.

(2) After the two parties share the key encrypted message, only the two parties can decrypt. For convenience of presentation, the public key K_T, K_R and the shared key K_i in the protocol are recorded as the key tuple Key, i.e., Key = $\{K_T, K_R, K_i\}$;

Then, following the above two principles and using the modelling method, an abstract model for the RFID three-party authentication protocol can be constructed, as shown in Fig. 1.

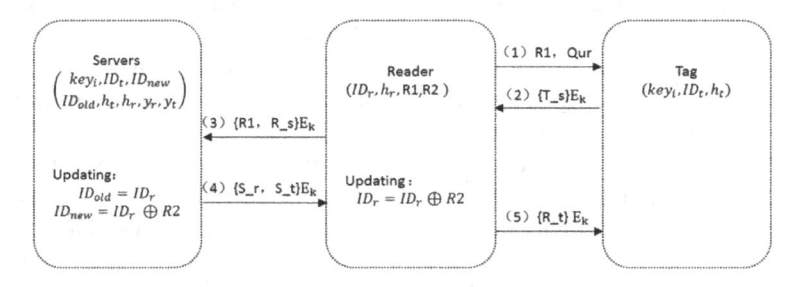

Fig. 1. The abstract model of the three-party authentication protocol

According to the RFID three-party authentication protocol model in Fig. 1, the protocol can be formalized and simplified as follows:

1.Reader→Tag: R1, Query

2.Tag→ Reader: {T_s}E_k

3.Reader→Servers: {R1, R_s}E_k

4.Servers→Reader: {S_r, S_t}E_k

5.Reader→Tag: {R_t}E_k

Here, *R1* is a random number generated by the Reader, *Query* is an authentication request sent by the Reader to the Tag, and E_k is an encryption function.

4 Modeling Three-Party Authentication Protocol with Promela

After formalizing the RFID three-party authentication protocol, the protocol needs to be converted into Promela language. The modeling of RFID three-party authentication protocol can be divided into two parts: honest principal modeling and attacker modeling. Because of the protocol has three instances, three main processes must be constructed. Attacker modelling is guided by the Dolev-Yao model. when using the PROMELA language to build honest subject models and attacker model, we should follow the principles: ①There is no defects in the encryption and decryption process of the three-party authentication protocol; ②The attacker is powerful enough to impersonate any legal entity; ③Messages encrypted through the NTRU cryptosystem can be decrypted only by three parties.

4.1 Honest Principal Modelling

The RFID three-party authentication protocol mainly includes three honest entities: Server, Reader, and Tag. Therefore, it is necessary to define the respective processes for these three entities, which are named *proctype PS ()*, *proctype PR ()*, and *proctype PT ()*. In the language of Promela, message transmission needs to be realized by means of the data structure of the message channel chan. For this purpose, messages in three-party RFID authentication protocol needs to be classified, and the same type of messages are transmitted using the same message channels.

Before starting the session, the Reader does not encrypt the random number *R1* and the authentication request *Query*. However, this message cannot be regarded as the message (*Hello*) in the RFID mutual authentication protocol. In the RFID three-party authentication protocol, the attacker needs to intercept the message and learn the random number *R1*. In addition, due to the increased number of authentication parties, there will be a problem of repeating sub message items and multi round session parallel. Therefore, in order to solve these two types of problems, this paper proposed multi-channel modelling to describe the ability of participants. According to the type of three-party authentication protocol, Message channel transmission is defined as an encrypted channel and an unencrypted channel as follows:

$$chan\ ca = [0]\ of\ \{mtype, mtype, mtype, mtype\};$$
$$chan\ cb = [0]\ of\ \{mtype, mtype, mtype\};$$
$$chan\ cc = [0]\ of\ \{mtype, mtype, mtype\};$$

The *ca* and *cb* channels are encrypted channels, and the *cc* channel is an unencrypted channel. Messages (3) and (4) from the model are transmitted by channel *ca*, messages (2) and (5) are transmitted by channel *cb*, and message (1) is transmitted by channel *cc*. Take the message channel *ca* as an example, the encrypted channel is defined as follows: If the party wants to send a secret message, the format of the send statement should be *Ca! x1, x2, x3, x4*. In this statement, *x1* is the receiver of the message, *x2* and *x3* is the data items, *x4* represents encryption key; Take the message channel *cc* as an example, the unencrypted channel is defined as follows: If the party wants to send a public message, the format of the send statement should be *Ca! x1, x2, x3*. In this statement, *x1* is the receiver of the message, *x2* and *x3* is the data items.

The ultimate goal of protocol modeling is to transform a protocol into a concurrent system. Therefore, the state transitions generated by the cross-operation between processes are very enormous, and may even produce a state explosion problem [16]. For this purpose, it is necessary to reduce the number of state transitions. In the receiving statement, *Eval* can be used to determine whether each item is consistent with expectations. Judging from left to right, if an item is inconsistent, the receiver will directly reject the message. Discarding messages that are not expected can effectively reduce the state migration of concurrency systems. For example, statement *ca? eval (x1), x2, x3, eval(x4)*, The receiver and key are important conditions for receiver that whether the receiver receives the message.

The modeling of Reader is as shown in the detailed code of the following proctype PR:

```
proctype PR(mtype self;mtype party1;mtype nonce;mtype mes;mtype party2){
        mtype g1;mtype g2;mtype g3;
        atomic{
        IniRunningR_T(self,party1);
        cc ! self, nonce, mes;
        }
        atomic{
        cb ? eval(self),g1,eval(party1);
        IniRunningR_S(self, party2);
        ca ! self,nonce,g1,self;
        }
        atomic{
        ca ? eval(self),g2,g3,eval(party1);
        IniCommitR_S(self, party2);
        cb ! self,R_t,party1;
        IniCommitR_T(self,party1);
        }
}
```

In the Reader process, self represents the initiator of the messages; *party1* and *party2* all represent the receivers of the information; *g1*, *g2*, and *g3* represent generic variables for receiving unknown data. Atomic can make local calculations atomized to reduce the number of intersecting processes.

Each properties of the model is represented by a Promela global variable. The initialization operation is as follows:

```
bit IniRunningRT = 0;bit IniCommitRT = 0;bit ResRunningRT = 0;
bit ResCommitRT = 0;bit IniRunningRS = 0;bit IniCommitRS = 0;
bit ResRunningRS = 0;bit ResCommitRS = 0;
```

IniRunning and *IniCommit* are defined for macros and are used to update the value of the atomic predicate variables. *IniRunningR_T(R, T)* indicates that the Reader initiated a conversation with the Tag. *IniCommitR_T(R, T)* indicates that the Reader submitted a conversation with the Tag. While the session state changes, the value of its corresponding atomic predicate will change from the initial value 0 to 1. Therefore, these atomic predicate variables can be used to describe the properties of the protocol. In order to describe the security nature of the protocol as an acceptable language for SPIN, LTL (Linear Temporal Logic) [17] needs to be used to characterize the protocol. This paper uses the LTL formula to describe the security properties of the RFID three-party authentication protocol as follows:

Mutual authentication between Server and Reader:

$$[]((([] !IniCommitRS) || (!IniCommitRS \ U \ ResRunningRS))$$
$$[]((([] !ResCommitRS) || (!ResCommitRS \ U \ IniRunningRS))$$

Mutual authentication between Server and Tag:

$$[]((([] !IniCommitRT) || (!IniCommitRT \ U \ ResRunningRT))$$
$$[]((([] !ResCommitRT) || (!ResCommitRT \ U \ IniRunningRT))$$

Sequence of the protocol (1):

$$[]((([] ! IniRunningRS) || (!IniRunningRS \ U \ ResRunningRT))$$

The Sequence of the protocol (1) is used to ensure that the Reader can start a session with the Server after the Tag responds to the Reader's session.

Sequence of the protocol (2):

$$[]((([] !ResCommitRS) || (!ResCommitRS \ U \ ResCommitRT))$$

The sequentially of the protocol (2) is used to ensure that the Server continues to authenticate with the Tag after completing the mutual authentication of the Reader.

That is, before the Reader starts a session with the Server, the Tag needs to respond; the Reader needs to respond before the Server submits a session with the Reader; before the Reader submits a session with the Tag, the Reader needs to submit a session with the Server.

According to the same modelling rules, the process PT of the principal Tag and the process PS of the principal Server are similarly defined. After defining the various honest subjects, we need to define the initialization process, which is defined as follows.

init{

   atomic{

      run PR(R, T, R1,Qur,S)

      run PT(T, R,T_s);

      run PS(S,R,T,S_r,S_t);

      run PI();

     }

   }

PI is the attacker's process. The attacker is powerful enough to intercept arbitrary messages from the message channel.

4.2   Attacker Modelling

In this paper, the Dolve-Yao model is used to model the attacker of the RFID three party authentication protocol. The attacker has a powerful ability to intercept, reassemble, and forward any messages in the channel. But this capability is limited without knowing the session key. If the attacker has limited knowledge, they can learn new knowledge items through interception and eavesdropping, thereby strengthening the attacker's capability to attack.

Attacker modelling first needs to solve the knowledge base of attackers, then describes the process of knowledge learning by attackers, and finally designs attackers' sending statements. The attacker knowledge base is mainly composed of two parts of knowledge items. In addition to the original knowledge possessed by attackers, attackers can expand knowledge base by intercepting messages. If the intercepted message is not encrypted, all of its knowledge items will be stored in the knowledge base directly. If the message is encrypted, the attacker uses the existing knowledge to decrypt the message, and if the message cannot be decrypted, the message will be completely stored in the repository for reserve.

In order to reduce the invalid system state, it is necessary to simplify the representation of the attacker's knowledge item. In attacker modelling, the message that an attacker cannot learn or the message that the honest party refuses to receive is not expressed. Based on the above principles, we can calculate the knowledge that an attacker needs to express, as shown in Fig. 2:

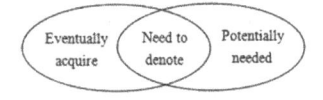

Fig. 2. The actual knowledge set which needs to be denoted

The knowledge that an attacker can learn is to decrypt and analyze it by intercepting the honest party and storing it completely. The knowledge that an attacker can learn is obtained by intercepting, deciphering and storing the messages from the parties of honestly. The messages captured by an attacker and the knowledge elements that can be obtained are specifically shown in Table 1:

Table 1. Knowledge elements that the intruder can acquire

Received messages	Learnt item	Received messages	Learnt item
R1,Qur	R1	{ S_r,R1}PK(T)	{ S_r, R1}PK(T)
{R1, T_s}PK(R)	{R1, T_s}PK(R)	{ S_r,T_s}PK(T)	{ S_r, T_s}PK(T)
{T_s ,T_s}PK(R)	{T_s ,T_s}PK(R)	{ S_r,S_r}PK(T)	{S_r, S_r }PK(T)
{S_r, T_s}PK(R)	{S_r, T_s}PK(R)	{ S_r,R_t}PK(T)	{ S_r, R_t }PK(T)
{S_t, T_s}PK(R)	{S_t, T_s}PK(R)	{ S_r,gD}PK(T)	{ S_r, gD }PK(T)
{R_t, T_s}PK(R)	{R_t, T_s}PK(R)	{R1, S_t}PK(H)	R1, S_t
{gD, T_s}PK(R)	{gD, T_s}PK(R)	{T_s,S_t}PK(H)	T_s,S_t
{R1,R1}PK(R)		{S_r, S_t}PK(H)	S_r, S_t
{R1,S_r}PK(R)	{R1,S_r}PK(R)	{S_t,S_t}PK(H)	S_t
{R1,S_t}PK(R)	{R1,S_t}PK(R)	{R_t,S_t}PK(H)	R_t,S_t
{R1,R_t}PK(R)	{R1,R_t}PK(R)	{gD,S_t}PK(H)	gD,S_t
{R1,gD}PK(R)	{R1,gD}PK(R)	{ S_r,R1}PK(H)	S_r,R1
{R1, T_s}PK(H)	R1, T_s	{ S_r,T_s}PK(H)	S_r,T_s
{T_s ,T_s}PK(H)	T_s	{ S_r,S_r}PK(H)	S_r
{S_r, T_s}PK(H)	S_r, T_s	{ S_r,R_t}PK(H)	S_r,R_t
{S_t, T_s}PK(H)	S_t, T_s	{ S_r,gD}PK(H)	S_r
{R_t, T_s}PK(H)	R_t, T_s	{R1}PK(T)	
{gD, T_s}PK(H)	gD, T_s	{T_s}PK(T)	{T_s}PK(T)
{R1,R1}PK(H)		{S_r}PK(T)	{S_r}PK(T)
{R1,S_r}PK(H)	R1,S_r	{S_t}PK(T)	{S_t}PK(T)
{R1,S_t}PK(H)	R1,S_t	{R_t}PK(T)	{R_t}PK(T)
{R1,R_t}PK(H)	R1,R_t	{gD}PK(T)	
{R1,gD}PK(H)	R1	{R1}PK(H)	R1
{R1, S_t}PK(T)	{R1, S_t }PK(T)	{T_s}PK(H)	T_s
{T_s,S_t}PK(T)	{T_s,S_t }PK(T)	{S_r}PK(H)	S_r
{S_r, S_t}PK(T)	{S_r, S_t }PK(T)	{S_t}PK(H)	S_t
{S_t,S_t}PK(T)	{S_t, S_t }PK(T)	{R_t}PK(H)	R_t
{R_t,S_t}PK(T)	{R_t, S_t }PK(T)	{gD}PK(H)	
{gD,S_t}PK(T)	{gD,S_t }PK(T)		

The next step is to analyse the knowledge that an attacker needs to learn. That is, a message that an attacker can send to the legal principals and be received by legal principals. This message can be obtained by analysing the messages that the honest principal can receive. As shown in Table 2, the attacker needs to learn the knowledge elements.

Table 2. Knowledge elements that the intruder potentially needs

Messages	Needed Knowledge
R1,Qur	R1
{T_s}PK(T)	T_s or {T_s}PK(T)
{R1}PK(T)	R1 or {R1}PK(T)
{S_r}PK(T)	S_r or {S_r}PK(T)
{S_t}PK(T)	S_t or {S_t}PK(T)
{R_t}PK(T)	R_t or {R_t}PK(T)
{gD}PK(T)	
{R1, T_s}PK(R)	R1, T_s or {R1, T_s}PK(R)
{T_s, T_s}PK(R)	T_s, T_s or {T_s, T_s}PK(R)
{S_r, T_s}PK(R)	S_r, T_s or {S_r, T_s}PK(R)
{S_t, T_s}PK(R)	S_t, T_s or {S_t, T_s}PK(R)
{R_t, T_s}PK(R)	R_t, T_s or {R_t, T_s}PK(R)
{gD, T_s}PK(R)	T_s or {gD, T_s}PK(R)
{R1, R1}PK(R)	R1 or {R1, R1}PK(R)
{R1, S_r}PK(R)	R1, S_r or {R1, S_r}PK(R)
{R1, S_t}PK(R)	R1, S_t or {R1, S_t}PK(R)
{R1, R_t}PK(R)	R1, R_t or {R1, R_t}PK(R)
{R1,gD}PK(R)	R1 or {R1,gD}PK(R)
{S_r, S_t}PK(T)	S_r, S_t or {S_r, S_t}PK(T)
{ R1, S_t}PK(T)	R1, S_t or { R1, S_t}PK(T)
{ T_s, S_t}PK(T)	T_s, S_t or { T_s, S_t}PK(T)
{ S_t, S_t}PK(T)	S_t, S_t or { S_t, S_t}PK(T)
{ R_t, S_t}PK(T)	R_t, S_t or { R_t, S_t}PK(T)
{gD, S_t}PK(T)	S_t or {gD, S_t}PK(T)
{S_r, R1}PK(T)	S_r, R1 or {S_r, R1}PK(T)
{S_r, T_s }PK(T)	S_r, T_s or {S_r, T_s }PK(T)
{S_r, S_r }PK(T)	S_r or {S_r, S_r }PK(T)
{S_r, R_t }PK(T)	S_r, R_t or {S_r, R_t }PK(T)
{S_r, gD}PK(T)	S_r or {S_r, gD}PK(T)

The knowledge items which the attacker needs to denote are the intersection of the right column of Tables 1 and 2, and results are shown as follows:

$\{R1, Qur\};$ $\{T\_s\}E_k$; $\{R1, R\_s\}E_k;$ $\{S\_r, S\_t\}E_k;$ $\{R\_t\}E_k$

Based on the above analysis results, the attacker model code can be written, and the writing framework is shown as follows:

```
proctype PI(){
        mtype x1=0;mtype x2=0;mtype x3=0;
        bit K_Na = 0; /* knowledge items that need to denote*/
        bit K_Qur = 0;bit K_Ts = 0;bit K_Sr = 0;bit K_St = 0;
        bit K_Rt = 0;bit K_Na_Qur = 0;bit K_Ts_T =0;
        bit K_Srt_T = 0;bit K_Rt_T = 0;bit K_Na_Ts_R = 0;
        do
        ::    cc ! ((K_Na&&K_Qur)||K_Na_Qur -> T:A),R1,Qur
        ::    cb ! (K_Ts||K_Ts_T -> R:A),T_s,T
        ::    ca ! (K_Na_Ts_R -> S:A),R1,T_s,R
        ::    ca ! ((K_Sr&&K_St)|| K_Srt_T -> R:A),S_r,S_t,T
        ::    cb ! (K_Rt || K_Rt_T -> T:A),R_t,T
        ::    d_step {ca ? _,x1,x2,x3; ···}/*intercepting messages from    channel ca*/
        ::    d_step{cb ? _,x1,x2; ···}/*intercepting messages from    channel cb*/
    ::   d_step{cc ? _,x1,x2; ···}
        od
}
```

Simulation experiments were conducted in a Windows 7 64-bit system, Cygwin 2.510.2.2, and SPIN 5.2.0 environment, and the attack sequence as shown in the Fig. 3 was found.

5   Analysis of Verification Results

In this experiment, the SPIN tool is used to detect the above model, and an attack vulnerability is found. The attack sequence shown in Fig. 3 is obtained.

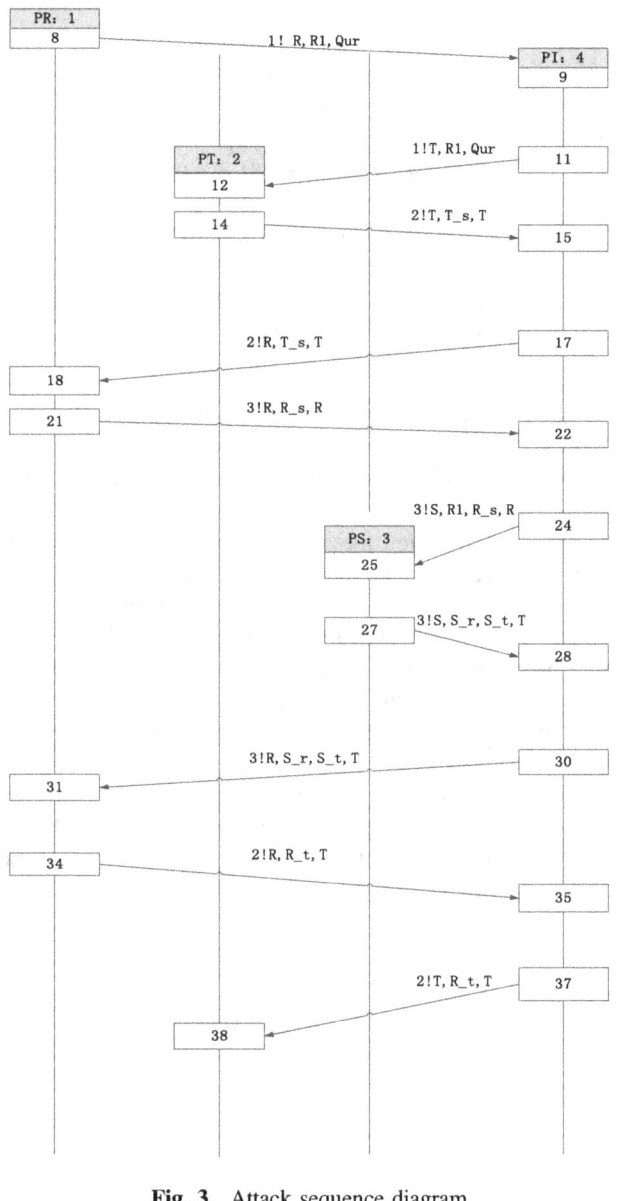

Fig. 3. Attack sequence diagram

And got the following attack process:

(1)Reader→Intruder: {R1, Qur};
Intruder→Tag: {R1, Qur}
(2)Tag→Intruder: {T_s}E_T;
Intruder→Reader: {T_s}E_T
(3)Reader→Intruder: {R1, R_s}E_R;
Intruder→Server: {R1, R_s}E_R
(4)Server→Intruder: {S_r, S_t}E_T;
Intruder→Reader: {S_r, S_t}E_T
(5)Reader→Intruder: {R_t}E_T;
Intruder→Tag: {R_t}E_T

At the beginning of protocol operation, Reader sends the random number and the authentication request to the attacker. Because the message is not encrypted, any subject can directly obtain the authentication request and random number. So the attacker has mastered the relevant information of the authentication request, and then the attacker sends the authentication message to the Tag. The tag sends the message T_s to the attacker after receiving the authentication request message. The first error trail showing the attack is reported in Fig. 3. During the operation of the protocol, the attacker impersonates the initiator and the respondent to send and receive messages (Break the known message and forward the unknown message). However, Reader, Server, and Tag do not know that the attackers are talking to them. They mistook the attacker as a legitimate subject and sent important messages to it, which indicates that the protocol is fraught with danger.

The result of the property violation is shown in Fig. 4. The experimental results show that, after the protocol is completed, the two variables of IniCommitRS and IniRunningRS are still 0. It shows that the protocol violates the corresponding safety property, and the legal subject has no normal participation in the interaction of information.

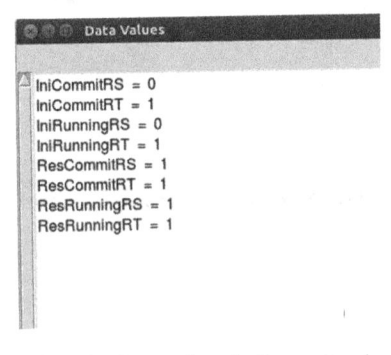

Fig. 4. Data values in the protocol

6   Conclusion and Future Work

In this paper, we explore formal method to perform analysis on RIFD three-party authentication protocol. However, the three-party authentication protocol based on NTRU cryptosystem is different from the general two-party authentication protocol, so that multi-party of the protocol brings some difficulty to analyse security properties with formal method. In order to apply formal method into analysing three-party authentication protocol, a multi-channel modelling method is used to model the protocol. Using SPIN, a malicious attack is successfully found, and the corresponding attack sequence is given. In the next step, we will dedicate to improving the three-party authentication protocol and verifying security of the improved protocol.

Acknowledgements. The work supported by National Natural Science Foundation of China (61562026, 61163005), in part by the Jiangxi Province Key Subject Academic and Technical Leader Funding Project (2017XSDTR0105), in part by the National Natural Science Foundation of Jiangxi Province of China (20161BAB202063), in part by the Science and Technology Research Project of Education Department in Jiangxi Province (GJJ170384).

References

1. Wang, Z., Yan, X., Sun, B., et al.: Review and outlook of studies on application of RFID technology. Logist. Technol. **33**(09), 1–5 (2014). https://doi.org/10.3969/j.issn.1005-152x. 2014.05.001
2. Li, B.: Overview of RFID security authentication protocol. Sci. Technol. Innov. Her. **2015** (32), 17–19 (2015)
3. Shi, Z., Xia, Y., Yu, C.: A strong RFID mutual authentication protocol based on a lightweight public-key cryptosystem. Inst. Adv. Eng. Sci. **12**(3). http://dx.doi.org/10.11591/ telkomnika.v12i3.4517
4. Cai, Q., Zhan, Y., Yu, S., et al.: RFID communication security protocol based on NTRU public key cryptosystem. Acta Scientiarum Naturalium Universitatis Sunyatseni **48**(5), 6–11 (2009)
5. Yao, H., Liu, C.: Authentication protocol based on AES and NTRU for RFID. Comput. Eng. Appl. **48**(35), 80–84 (2012). https://doi.org/10.3778/j.issn.1002-8331.1105-0409
6. Li, B.: An NTRU public key encryption system based RFID authentication protocol. Comput. Appl. Softw. **29**(4), 271–278 (2012)
7. Deng, Q., Yang, S.: Research on RFID three-way mutual authentication protocol based on public key cryptosystem. Comput. Appl. Softw. **32**(12), 298–301 (2015). https://doi.org/10. 3969/j.issn.1000-386x.2015.12.070
8. Hao, X., Yang, P., Kun, L.: NTRU-based RFID three-party authentication protocol. Comput. Eng. Appl. (2014). https://doi.org/10.3778/j.issn.1002-8331.1305-0201
9. Xiao, M., Ma, C., Deng, C., et al.: A novel approach to automatic security protocol analysis based on authentication event logic. Chin. J. Electron. **24**(1), 187–192 (2015). https://doi. org/10.1049/cje.2015.01.031
10. Holzmann, G.J.: The model checker SPIN. IEEE Trans. Softw. Eng. **23**(5), 279–295 (1997)
11. Maggi, P., Sisto, R.: Using SPIN to verify security properties of cryptographic protocols. In: SPIN, vol. 2, pp. 187–204 (2002). https://doi.org/10.1007/3-540-46017-9_14

12. Dolev, D., Yao, A.: On the security of public key protocols. IEEE Trans. Inf. Theor. **29**(2), 198–208 (1983)
13. Wang, L., Peng, S.: Research on RFID multi-authentication protocol and security analysis. J. Comput. Appl. **33**(S2), 136–138 (2013)
14. Li, W., Xiao, M., Li, Y., Mei, Y., Zhong, X., Tu, J.: Formal analysis and verification for an ultralightweight authentication protocol RAPP of RFID. In: Du, D., Li, L., Zhu, E., He, K. (eds.) NCTCS 2017. CCIS, vol. 768, pp. 119–132. Springer, Singapore (2017). https://doi.org/10.1007/978-981-10-6893-5_9
15. Bruce, N., Kim, H., Kang, Y., Lee, Y., Lee, H.: On modeling protocol-based clustering tag in RFID systems with formal security analysis. In: IEEE, International Conference on Advanced Information NETWORKING and Applications, pp. 498–505 (2015). https://doi.org/10.1109/aina.2015.227
16. Hou, G.: Survey of state explosion problem in model checking. Comput. Sci. **40**(06A), 77–86 (2013). https://doi.org/10.3969/j.issn.1002-137X.2013.z1.018
17. Xiao, M., Xue, J.: Formal description of properties of concurrency system by temporal logic. J. Nav. Univ. Eng. **05**, 10–13 (2004). https://doi.org/10.3969/j.issn.1009-3486.2004.05.003

Security Proof of KerNeeS Protocol Based on Logic of Events

Ke Yang$^{(\boxtimes)}$, Meihua Xiao, and Jia Chen

School of Software, East China Jiaotong University,
Nanchang 330013, People's Republic of China
landexplorer@163.com, xiaomh@ecjtu.edu.cn,
chenjia_guan@163.com

Abstract. The Near Filed Communication (NFC) is widely used on mobile devices and make it possible to take advantage of NFC system to complete mobile payment. But with the development of NFC, its problem are increasingly exposed, especially the security and privacy of authentication. Logic of events is a formal method to describe the protocol state transition and algorithm in concurrent and distributed systems, which can be used to prove the security of network protocols. Based on logic of events, we propose migration rule and derive inheritability to reduce redundancy and complexity of protocol analysis procedure, and improve efficiency of protocol analysis. We study the KerNeeS protocol which providing mutual authentication between POS and NFC phone, and conclude that the protocol can guarantee authentication between entities involved in the payment for secure payment transactions. The logic of events can be applied to the formal analysis of similar mobile payment protocols.

Keywords: NFC · Mobile payment protocol · Logic of events
Mutual authentication

1 Introduction

The continuously increasing growth of developments in mobile technologies opened new opportunities to maximize the benefits of using mobile on a daily basis. Nowadays, mobile phones have great capabilities for the development of new applications, which are engaged in our daily lives. Moreover, mobile phones provide a new style of life, where the availability of many applications such as Internet browsing, sending and receiving e-mails, and mobile payment is one of the most important applications. The NFC technology [1, 2] has features of convenience and fast, which makes the mobile devices with NFC function increase greatly, more and more users choose mobile phones with NFC function as payment tools, and the mobile payment market based on this is increasing year by year. In 2014, Apple Corp issued its first NFC payment tool Apple Pay. In March 2016, Samsung Pay, the Samsung NFC payment tool, officially launched. In August of the same year, Huawei also formally launched its own NFC payment tool Huawei Pay. The scale of China's mobile payment market is showing an explosive growth, it's estimated that by 2019, China's mobile payment market will reach the scale of 104 trillion yuan.

© Springer Nature Singapore Pte Ltd. 2018
L. Li et al. (Eds.): NCTCS 2018, CCIS 882, pp. 61–79, 2018.
https://doi.org/10.1007/978-981-13-2712-4_5

Since NFC is used to make payments in mobile phones, security issues raise more concerns among consumers. As a near filed communication technology, the communication transmission process is completely exposed an open and uncontrollable communication environment. So in the payment system NFC technology is used to transfer sensitive data between a card and a reader with limited security standards provided by NFC specifications, this makes NFC a common target to a number of attacks such as eavesdropping, data corruption, data tampering, man in the middle attack and so on [3, 4]. Moreover, due to the similarity between RFID and NFC, most of the attacks on RFID are applicable on the NFC [5]. In 2012, two American researchers found that there were serious security vulnerabilities in NFC payment, they can take subway for free after it being cracked. In 2013, *Journal of Engineering* released a research report from the University of Survey's research group in UK, where researchers used special equipment to intercept sensitive data without contact. These series of incidents reflect the security issues of NFC technology, which threaten the mobile payment based on NFC technology and restrict the development of mobile e-commerce.

Formal methods are based on strict mathematical concepts and languages with clear semantics and unambiguous expression, it can discover the vulnerability of mobile payment protocols that other methods are not easy to find [6]. Modal logic is the most widely used formal method in protocol analysis, including BAN logic and BAN class logic [7]. The grammatical definition of various logical methods has its own features, the protocol security property is proved by logical reasoning, which is consistent with logic of events. Take BAN logic as an example, BAN logic relies too much on analyzer's intuition for the idealization of protocol, and the idealization process will cause some problem, which makes the idealized protocol have a little difference with the original protocol. In addition, BAN logic uses strict reasoning rules to prove protocol security step by step, but the semantic description of BAN logic is not clear enough, and the result of proof procedures can't be convincing [8]. Theorems and derivation rules defined by logic of events [9] are clear and unambiguous, so that the reliability of proof procedures can be guaranteed and protocol security are more credible.

Logic of events is a formal method to describe state migration in distributed system, which can be used to formally describe security protocols. It formalizes generating new nonces, sending messages, receiving messages, encryption, decryption, digital signature and verification actions, as well as formalization of keys and protocol messages [10, 11]. Compared with other formal methods like BAN logic and BAN class logic, proving protocol security based on logic of events which has obvious advantages, so this paper formally analyzes a mutual authentication protocol between POS and NFC phone based on logic of events, trying to prove the security of mutual authentication protocol and process of transmitting session keys.

The rest of this paper is organized as follows. In Sect. 2 the KerNeeS protocol will be introduced. In Sect. 3, we introduce logic of events theory, propose migration rule and derive *inheritability* to reduce redundancy and complexity of protocol analysis procedure based on logic of events, expound properties that need to be met in the procedure of identity authentication analysis. In Sect. 4, security proof of KerNeeS protocol will be elaborated in detail. In Sect. 5, our conclusions and future work are given.

2 KerNeeS Protocol

2.1 Protocol Introduction

KerNeeS [12] is proposed by Ceipidor from Sapineza University of Rome in 2012, which is intended to provide mutual authentication between an NFC phone (N) in card emulation mode and a POS (P), allowing phone and POS the share a session key to use to perform secure transactions. This mechanism is possible by means of a trusted third entity, more specifically an Authentication Server (AS), able to verify the reliability of the entities involved in the money transaction, thus allowing not only the authentication of the smart card towards the POS, but also the authentication of the POS towards the smart card, This protocol only makes use of symmetric keys: POS and smart cards both are provided with an identifier (ID) and a symmetric key, shared with the Authentication Server. AS contains the association between device ID and shared key, as well as other information such as the trusted level of entities. The server has the same function of a Certification Authority but it works in real time and this is necessary to overcome the limitations of the smart cards. The abbreviations used in the protocol description can be seen in [12].

2.2 Protocol Description

This protocol was designed inside the RFID Laboratory of CATTID, Sapienza University of Rome, for mutual authentication between POS and smart cards.

Steps of the protocol are listed as follows:

(1) Authentication request:

$$P \rightarrow N : \{R_1, TS\}K_p \tag{1}$$

In the first step, the POS sends to the NFC phone a command containing a payload with a random value and a timestamp, both encrypted with the secret key of the POS, this message marks the beginning of a session by means of the timestamp.

(2) Request confirmation

$$N \rightarrow P : ID_N, \{R_2, \{R_1, TS\}K_P\}K_N \tag{2}$$

In the second step, the NFC phone replies to the POS with a message that contains the ID of the NFC phone without encryption, together with the random value concatenated to the message of the step (1), encrypted with K_N. The random value R_2 acts as timestamp, in fact even if the NFC secure element cannot access to a system clock, it is able to distinguish sessions by means of R_2.

(3) Session request

$$P \rightarrow AS : ID_P, ID_N, \{R_2, \{R_1, TS\}K_P\}K_N \tag{3}$$

The POS adds its ID to the message of the step (2) and delivers it to the authentication server. After the receipt of this message, AS analyzes it and if ID_P and ID_N are known, it fetches their keys, decrypts $\{R_2, \{R_1, TS\}K_P\}K_N$ and then checks for the timestamp validity. If the timestamp is not valid, the Authentication Server doesn't reply, otherwise it generates a session key K and builds two tickets, one for the NFC phone and one for the POS.

(4) Session confirmation

$$AS \rightarrow P : \{K, ID_N, TS\}K_P, \{K, ID_P, R_2\}K_N \tag{4}$$

The Authentication Server sends the two tickets to the POS, that can't read or modify $\{K, ID_P, R_2\}K_N$ but it can fetch its own ticket and it is the only one (in addition to AS) able to decrypt $\{K, ID_N, TS\}K_P$. The POS decrypts $\{K, ID_N, TS\}K_P$, checks for the timestamp and the ID: if they are incorrect, it means that an error occurred and the POS has close the session, otherwise it fetches the session key, build a random value and encrypt the random value with the session key.

(5) Verify request

$$P \rightarrow N : \{K, ID_P, R_2\}K_N, \{R_3\}K \tag{5}$$

In the step (5), P sent its ticket and the random value encrypted with the session key to N. At the receipt of the ticket, the phone is able decrypt it, because it is the only one to know the secret key K_N (in addition to AS). Once decryption is complete, the phone checks for R_2 value, if it is not equal to the random value generated in the step (2) it will finish the session, otherwise the phone fetches the K value and decrypts $\{R_3\}K$, it calculates a simple function R (for example $R_3 - 1$), it generates a random value R_4 and it encrypts R_3 and R_4 with the K value.

(6) Verify confirmation from NFC phone

$$N \rightarrow P : \{R_3 - 1, R_4\}K \tag{6}$$

Having the session key, the POS is able to decrypt the message in (6). Then it checks for $R_3 - 1$, if it is a correct value it calculates $R_4 - 1$ value and encrypt it with K in order to give N a confirmation for knowing the session key. Else P finishes the session.

(7) Verify confirmation from POS
After the receipt of the step (6) command, the phone decrypts it and checks for the validity of R_4 value. If R_4 value is wrong, then N will finishes the session.

3 Logic of Events

Logic of events [10, 11] is a theorem proving method proposed by Bickford et al. of Cornell University in 2003, it's a logic that describes protocols and algorithms in distributed system, and can formalize the basic primitives of security protocols.

3.1 Symbol Description

This section describes symbols and operators [13] involved in specifying mutual authentication protocol KerNeeS using logic of events. The basic symbols and its semantics are given in Table 1.

Table 1. Basic symbols and semantics of event logic

Basic symbols	Semantics
ID	Identity
$Data$	All of message and plaintext
$Atom$	Secret message
e	A event e
n	Random number in event nonce
$Key(e)$	Secret key of entity in event e
$Loc(e)$	The location of event e
$Nonce$	The set of random number
$New(e)$	A nonce in event e
$e_1 < e_2$	Event e_2 happened after event e_1
$Send(e)$	Sending $Data$ type message in event e
$Rcv(e)$	Receiving $Data$ type message in event e
$Encrypt(e) = \langle x, K, c \rangle$	Encrypt plaintext c using secret key K to get ciphertext x
$Decrypt(e') = \langle x, K', c \rangle$	Decrypt ciphertext x using secret key K' to get plaintext c
$Sign(e) = \langle x, A, s \rangle$	Signing plaintext x to get ciphertext s in entity A of event e
$Verify(e') = \langle x, A, s \rangle$	Verifying signed message s to get plaintext x in entity A of event e'
$\langle E, loc, <, info \rangle$	Event language
$\parallel$	Logic relationship "independent"
$\leq$	Locally-finite partial order (every e has finitely many predecessors)

3.2 Event Classes

Our formal theory of authentication uses the language of event-orderings and another key concept—event classes. We describe protocols by classifying the events in the protocol. In authentication protocols there are send, receive, nonce, sign, verify, encrypt and decrypt events. Events in each class have associated information, and the type of this information depends on the class of the event. For example, a nonce event e will be a member of class New and its associated information $New(e)$ will have type $Atom$ because it is the nonce chosen at event e. A send or receive event e_0 is a member of class *Send* or *Rcv* and its associated information, *Send(e_0)* or *Rcv(e_0)* is the message sent or received at event e_0 and has type *Data* (Fig. 1).

$$New : EClass(Atom)$$
$$Send, Rcv : EClass(Data)$$
$$Encrypt, Decrypt : Eclass(Data \times Key \times Atom)$$
$$Sign, Verify : EClass(Data \times Id \times Atom)$$

Fig. 1. Event classes of the authentication theory

3.3   Axiomatic System

(1) Casual axioms

Three axioms that we call *AxiomR*, *AxiomV*, and *AxiomD* relate events in classes *Rcv*, *Verify*, and *Decrypt* to corresponding, causally earlier, events in classes *Send*, *Sign*, and *Encrypt*. *AxiomR* and *AxiomV* are similar and say that for any receive or verify event there must be a causally prior send or sign event with the same associated information.

$$\left\{ \begin{array}{c} AxiomR : \forall e : E(Rcv).\exists e' : E(Send).(e' < e)\wedge \\ Rcv(e) = Send(e') \end{array} \right\}$$
$$\left\{ \begin{array}{c} AxiomV : \forall e : E(Verify).\exists e' : E(Sign).(e' < e)\wedge \\ Verify(e) = Sign(e') \end{array} \right\}$$

AxiomD is similar except that for a decrypt event, the prior encrypt event has the same associated information except for the key, which, rather than being the same is a matching key.

$$\left\{ \begin{array}{c} AxiomD : \forall e : E(Decrypt).\exists e' : E(Encrypt)(e' < e)\wedge \\ DEMatch(e, e') \end{array} \right\}$$
$$\left\{ \begin{array}{c} DEMatch(e, e') \equiv {}_{def} plaintext(e) = plaintext(e')\wedge \\ cipheretext(e) = cipheretext(e')\wedge \\ MatchingKeys(key(e) : key(e')) \end{array} \right\}$$

(2) Honesty axiom

Our theory includes a function Honest: $Id \rightarrow \mathbb{R}$ that allows us to express assumptions about honest agents. In particular, honest agents do not release their private keys, so sign events with an honest signer; and encryption or decryption events that use the private key of an honest agent must occur at that agent. We call this axiom *AxiomS* (because it includes the properties of honest signers).

$$\left\{ \begin{array}{l} AxiomS : \forall A : Id. \forall s : E(Sign). \forall e : E(Encrypt). \\ \qquad \forall d : E(Decrypt).Honest(A) \Rightarrow \\ \left\{ \begin{array}{l} signers(s) = A \Rightarrow (loc(A)) \\ key(e) = PrivateKey(A) \Rightarrow loc(e) = A \wedge \\ key(d) = PrivateKey(A) \Rightarrow loc(d) = A \end{array} \right\} \end{array} \right\}$$

(3) Nonce axiom

The assertion about nonces, one part of the axiom we call *AxiomF* (the flow property), is

$$\left\{ \begin{array}{l} AxiomF_1 : \forall e_1 : E(New). \forall e_2 : E. \\ e_2 \ has \ New(e_1) \Rightarrow e_1 \xrightarrow{New(e_1)} e_2 \end{array} \right\}$$

This part of *AxiomF* implies that nonces are associated with unique events:

Lemma 1 *(unique nonces)*.

$$\text{If } e_1, e_2 \in E(New) \text{ and } New(e_1) = New(e_2) \text{ then } e_1 = e_2.$$

The two other parts of *AxiomF* assert a similar relation between signatures and ciphertexts and events that have them. The difference is that we do not assume that signatures and encryptions are always associated with unique events, so if an action has a signature or ciphertext we can only infer that for some sign or encrypt action with the same information, the flow relation holds:

$$\left\{ \begin{array}{l} AxiomF_2 : \forall e_1 : E(Sign). \forall e_2 : E. \\ e_2 \ has \ signature(e) \Rightarrow \\ \exists e' : E(Sign).Sign(e') = \\ Sign(e_1) \wedge e' \xrightarrow{signature(e)} e_2 \end{array} \right\}$$

$$\left\{ \begin{array}{l} AxiomF_3 : \forall e_1 : E(Encrypt). \forall e_2 : E. \\ e_2 \ has \ cipheretext(e_1) \Rightarrow \\ \exists e' : E(Encrypt).Encrypt(e') = \\ Encrypt(e_1) \wedge e' \xrightarrow{cipheretext(e_1)} e_2 \end{array} \right\}$$

(4) Flow relation

The final axiom of Authentication Event Logic concerns the causal ordering between events that contain nonces. This is the most complex axiom, and to state it we need some auxiliary definitions. The type *Act* contains the events in any of the seven special classes—we call these actions. The relation (*e* has *a*) is true when action *e* has atom *a*. Its definition has the seven obvious cases:

$$e \; has \; a \equiv_{def}$$
$$(e \in E(New) \land New(e) \; has \; a) \lor$$
$$(e \in E(Send) \land Send(e) \; has \; a) \lor \cdots$$

We define the flow relation $e_1 \xrightarrow{a} e_2$ to mean that atom a flows from action e_1 to action e_2. This can happen only in limited ways; either the actions e_1 or e_2 is at the same location, or there are intervening send and receive events that send atom a "in the clear", or atom a is in the plaintext of an encryption event, and the ciphertext flows to a matching decryption event. The formal, recursive definition of the flow relation is

$$e_1 \xrightarrow{a} e_2 =_{rec}$$
$$(e_1 \; has \; a \land e_1 \; has \; a \land e_1 \leq_{loc} e_2)$$
$$\land$$
$$(\exists s : E(Send).\exists r : E(Rcv).e_1 \leq s < r)$$
$$\land \; Send(s) = Rcv(r) \land e_1 \xrightarrow{a} s \land r \xrightarrow{a} e_2)$$
$$\land$$
$$(\exists e : E(Encrypt).\exists d : E(Decrypt)).$$
$$e_1 < e < d \leq e_2 \land DEMatch(d, e) \land$$
$$key(d) \neq Symma(a) \land$$
$$e_1 \xrightarrow{a} e \land e \xrightarrow{ciphertext} d \land d \xrightarrow{a} e_2)$$

Lemma 2 *(releasing nonce).*
A send event s that potentially has atom a releases the atom because an agent or group of agents that receives the sent message and has all the necessary decryption keys could get the atom. If event e_1 at location A generates a nonce n and an action e_2 has n, then e_1 must causally precede e_2; and if e_2 takes place at a location other than A, it must be preceded by an event at A that sends n or an encrypted version of n. To express this, we define the release relation:

$$release(n, e_1, e_2) \equiv_{def}$$
$$e_1 \leq_{loc} e_2 \lor$$
$$\exists s : E(Send).(e_1 <_{loc} s < e_2) \land s \; has^* n$$

3.4   Relating Properties

Property 1: No Overlapping
In the proof procedure of protocol analysis, for the action that have been verified in the matching conversation, the result can be directly used in new round of analysis to reduce redundancy.

$$\forall A : Id.\forall e_1, e_2 : e_1 < e_2 \Rightarrow \forall e_2 : A| \equiv E(e_1)$$

Property 2: Time-Matching

In these seven events, the event class that initiator A and responder B participate in must be two parties and multiparty under the premise of obeying *protocol(bss)*, thus ensuring the effectiveness of events.

$$\forall A : Id.\forall e_1, e_2 : e_1 < e_2 \Rightarrow \forall e_2 : A| \equiv E(e_1)$$
$$\forall A, B : (A \neq B).\forall e_1, e_2 : ((e_1 \in A, e_2 \in B) \wedge (e_1 < e_2)) \vee$$
$$Send(e_1) = Rcv(e_2) \vee Sign(e_1) = Verify(e_2) \vee$$
$$Decrypt(e_1) = Encrypt(e_2)$$

Property 3: No Repeating

In the proof procedure of event matching, if multiple events need to be verified at the same time, it's analyzed on the basic of from top to bottom to reduce repeated operations in proof procedures.

Property 4: Not Considering Future Actions

In the procedure of considering matching actions, we don't consider actions that did not happen afterwards only based on current events, so as to reduce proof complexity.

The security of Neuman-Stubblebine protocol and wireless mesh network authentication protocol are proved using logic of events in paper [14–17], however the interaction process of proven protocols are not complex. The KerNeeS protocol we want to analyze in this paper has three entities, and KerNeeS protocol has more interaction steps. In order to overcome this challenge, *migration rule* has been proposed based on logic of events, *property inheritability* were derived to further reduce the redundancy and complexity in protocol analysis procedure, and improve the efficiency of protocol analysis.

Migration Rule

Thread *thr* is one of a basic sequence bss in A, written as *thr = oneof (bss, A)*, where there are many subsequences in *bss*, written as $bss_i \in bss$, as well as we have $bss_1 \subseteq bss_2 \cdots \subseteq bss_n$. If the subsequence bss_i possess event e, so bss_i can migrates into next subsequence bss_{i+1}, which can be expressed formally as

$$\forall e \in Eclass(x) \subset bss_i \vee loc(e) = A$$
$$\Rightarrow e \in Event(x) \subset bss_{i+1} \vee loc(e) = A(1 \leq i < n)$$

Property 5: Inheritability

We can deduce the *inheritability* based on *migration rule*, it can be expressed formally as

$$\forall e_i, e_{i+1} \in Eclass(x) \lor Event(e_i) = Event(e_{i+1}) \subset bss_i$$
$$\Leftrightarrow Event(e_i) = Event(e_{i+1}) \subset bss_{i+1}(1 \leq i < n)$$

Proof:

If $e_i, e_{i+1} \in Eclass(x)$ and $Event(e_i) = Event(e_{i+1}) \subset bss_i$, obviously, e_i, e_{i+1} $\subset bss_i \subset bss_{i+1}$, according to Axiom *flow relation* and *inheritability*, $Event(e_i) = Event(e_{i+1}) \subset bss_{i+1}$, then we can get

$$\forall e_i, e_{i+1} \in Eclass(x) \lor Event(e_i) = Event(e_{i+1}) \subset bss_i$$
$$\Rightarrow Event(e_i) = Event(e_{i+1}) \subset bss_{i+1}(1 \leq i < n)$$

If $e_i, e_{i+1} \in Eclass(x)$ and $Event(e_i) = Event(e_{i+1}) \subset bss_i$, obviously, e_i, e_{i+1} $\subset bss_{i+1}$, according to *AxiomS* and *inheritability*, there are no events $Event(e_i) = Event(e_{i+1})$ in other threads, then we can get

$$Event(e_i) = Event(e_{i+1}) \subset bss_{i+1} \Rightarrow$$
$$\forall e_i, e_{i+1} \in Eclass(x) \lor Event(e_i) = Event(e_{i+1}) \subset bss_i(1 \leq i < n)$$

4 Security Analysis of KerNeeS Protocol

4.1 Proof Procedures

Proving security of protocol based on logic of events, specific steps are as follows:

1. The logic of events is used to formally describe the security protocol, including specific actions of initiator and responder, standardizing basic sequence of the protocol, and confirming strong authentication property of protocol that need to be proved.
2. The subject is defined to be honest and abide by protocol, assuming that a thread is an instance of protocol's basic sequence, defining actions on the thread and determining matching events on protocol. Analyzing matching events, confirming whether there is a matching session and whether there is a matching event inside the matching session that requires further proof.
3. Analyzing whether the matching event is consistent with the matching session, if the consistence can be concluded and then proving matching session from the inside to the outside. If not, performing the screening verification of the next matching event to confirm whether whole matching events satisfy the weak matching.
4. Confirming that the matching session belongs to weak matching, analyzing the length of matching session in protocol interaction process, and confirming strong matching session according to axiomatic system.
5. After the establishment of one-way proof, the proof of two-way strong authentication will be carried out. If proof is proved to be established, it means that the protocol is secure. In the whole proof procedures, if matching events can't meet weak matching, the protocol can't meet strong authentication and can't guarantee

mutual authentication in authentication stage. The protocol is easily attacked by an attacker who disguised as a legitimated subject, and the protocol is not secure.

The steps mentioned above can be represented by the following flow chart in Fig. 2.

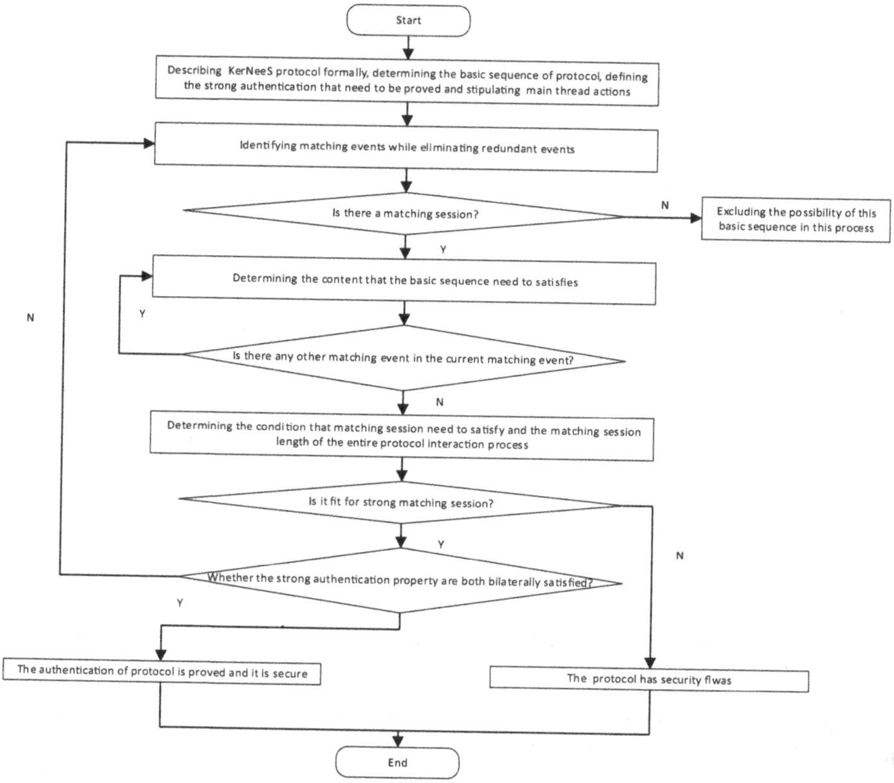

Fig. 2. The flow chart of logic of event to prove protocol authentication

4.2 Detailed Security Analysis

We use logic of events to sort out the basic interaction sequences of KerNeeS protocol, the description of protocol is shown in Fig. 3. s_1–s_7 are corresponding ciphertext generated by plaintext in encryption. P_1–P_7, N_1–N_6 and A_1–A_2 are actions generated by POS, NFC phone and Authentication Server during protocol interaction.

Then, we formalize the expected properties using logic of events to analyze security of KerNeeS protocol. The basic sequence of KerNeeS protocol is shown in Fig. 4.

In KerNeeS protocol, the function of Authentication Server (AS) is to provides session key K for POS (P) and NFC phone (N). As sends encrypted message (s_3, s_4) to P, where $s_3 = \{K, ID_N, TS\}K_P$ and $s_4 = \{K, ID_P, R_2\}K_N$, the important messages TS and R_2 can be decrypted from s_1 and s_2. To ensure the confidentiality of session key K,

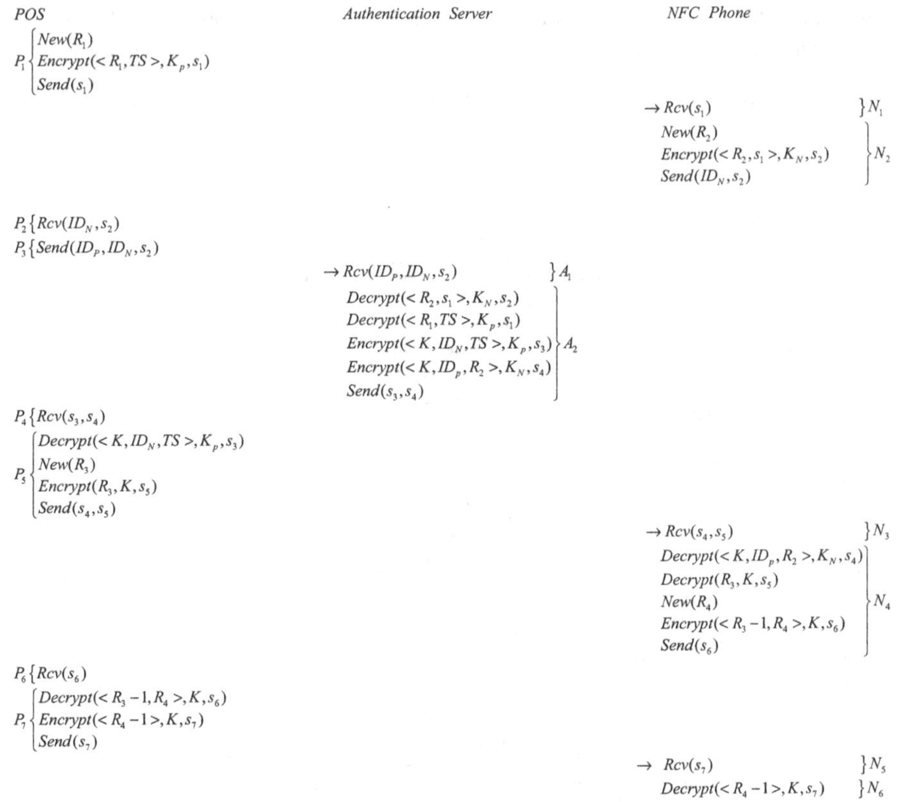

POS   Authentication Server   NFC Phone

$P_1 \begin{cases} New(R_1) \\ Encrypt(<R_1,TS>,K_p,s_1) \\ Send(s_1) \end{cases}$

$\rightarrow Rcv(s_1)$ $\}N_1$

$\begin{cases} New(R_2) \\ Encrypt(<R_2,s_1>,K_N,s_2) \\ Send(ID_N,s_2) \end{cases} \}N_2$

$P_2\{Rcv(ID_N,s_2)$
$P_3\{Send(ID_P,ID_N,s_2)$

$\rightarrow Rcv(ID_P,ID_N,s_2)$ $\}A_1$

$\begin{cases} Decrypt(<R_2,s_1>,K_N,s_2) \\ Decrypt(<R_1,TS>,K_p,s_1) \\ Encrypt(<K,ID_N,TS>,K_p,s_3) \\ Encrypt(<K,ID_p,R_2>,K_N,s_4) \\ Send(s_3,s_4) \end{cases} \}A_2$

$P_4\{Rcv(s_3,s_4)$
$P_5 \begin{cases} Decrypt(<K,ID_N,TS>,K_p,s_3) \\ New(R_3) \\ Encrypt(R_3,K,s_5) \\ Send(s_4,s_5) \end{cases}$

$\rightarrow Rcv(s_4,s_5)$ $\}N_3$

$\begin{cases} Decrypt(<K,ID_p,R_2>,K_N,s_4) \\ Decrypt(R_3,K,s_5) \\ New(R_4) \\ Encrypt(<R_3-1,R_4>,K,s_6) \\ Send(s_6) \end{cases} \}N_4$

$P_6\{Rcv(s_6)$
$P_7 \begin{cases} Decrypt(<R_3-1,R_4>,K,s_6) \\ Encrypt(<R_4-1>,K,s_7) \\ Send(s_7) \end{cases}$

$\rightarrow Rcv(s_7)$ $\}N_5$
$Decrypt(<R_4-1>,K,s_7)$ $\}N_6$

Fig. 3. The basic sequence description of mutual authentication and negotiation of session key

the reliability of s_1 and s_2 must be proved, where s_1 and s_2 exist in $Send(s_1)$ and $Rcv(s_1)$, $Send(ID_N,s_2)$ and $Rcv(ID_N,s_2)$. So in the first, we need to prove $Send(s_1) = Rcv(s_1)$ and $Send(ID_N,s_2) = Rcv(ID_N,s_2)$.

Suppose $P \neq N \neq AS$ are both honest and obey KerNeeS protocol, thread thr_1 is an instance of P_7. Let $e_0 <_{loc} e_1 < \cdots <_{loc} e_{13}$, so the location of $e_0, e_1, e_2, \cdots, e_{13}$ is P. For some atoms $R_1, TS, s_1, s_2, s_3, s_4$ we have

$$\left.\begin{array}{l} New(e_0) = R_1 \wedge Encrypt(e_1) = \langle <R_1,TS>, K_p,s_1 \rangle \wedge \\ Send(e_2) = s_1 \wedge Rcv(e_3) = \langle ID_N,s_2 \rangle \wedge Send(e_4) = \\ \langle ID_P,ID_N,s_2 \rangle \wedge Rcv(e_5) = \langle s_3,s_4 \rangle \wedge Decrypt(e_6) = \\ \langle <K,ID_N,TS>, K_p,s_3 \rangle \wedge New(e_7) = R_3 \wedge Encrypt(e_8) = \\ \langle R_3,K,s_5 \rangle \wedge Send(e_9) = (s_4,s_5) \wedge Rcv(e_{10}) = s_6 \wedge \\ Decrypt(e_{12}) = \langle <R_3-1,R_4>, K,s_6 \rangle \end{array}\right\} \quad (7)$$

By *AxiomS* and *AxiomD*, there is an event e' such that

$$\begin{cases} P_1 = New(R_1), Encrypt(< R_1, TS >, K_p, s_1), Send(s_1) \\ P_2 = P_1, Rcv(ID_N, s_2) \\ P_3 = P_2, Send(ID_p, ID_N, s_2) \\ P_4 = P_3, Rcv(s_3, s_4) \\ P_5 = P_4, Decrypt(< K, ID_N, TS >, K_p, s_3), New(R_3), \\ \qquad Encrypt(R_3, K, s_5), Send(s_4, s_5) \\ P_6 = P_5, Rcv(s_6) \\ P_7 = P_6, Decrypt(< R_3 - 1, R_4 >, K, s_6), \\ \qquad Encrypt(< R_4 - 1 >, K, s_7), Send(s_7) \\ N_1 = Rcv(s_1) \\ N_2 = New(R_2), Encrypt(< R_2, s_1 >, K_N, s_2) \\ \qquad Send(ID_N, s_2) \\ N_3 = N_2, Rcv(s_4, s_5) \\ N_4 = N_3, Decrypt(< K, ID_p, R_2 >, K_N, s_4), Decrypt(R_3, K, s_5) \\ \qquad New(R_4), Encrypt(< R_3 - 1, R_4 >, K, s_6), Send(s_6) \\ N_5 = N_4, Rcv(s_7) \\ N_6 = N_5, Decrypt(< R_4 - 1 >, K, s_7) \\ A_1 = Rcv(ID_p, ID_N, s_2) \\ A_2 = A_1, Decrypt(< R_2, s_1 >, K_N, s_2), Decrypt(< R_1, TS >, K_p, s_1) \\ \qquad Encrypt(< K, ID_N, TS >, K_p, s_3) \\ \qquad Encrypt(< K, ID_p, R_2 >, K_N, s_4), Send(s_3, s_4) \end{cases}$$

Fig. 4. Basic sequence of mutual authentication protocol

$$e' < e_6 \wedge DEMatch(e_6, e') \wedge loc(e') = N \wedge loc(e') = A$$

So we can conclude

$$Encrypt(e') = \big\langle <K, ID_N, TS > , K_p, s_3 \big\rangle$$

First, we take event e' as the research object. Because AS obeys KerNeeS, action e' must be a member of an instance belonging to one of the basic sequence of KerNeeS. The only one that include an $Encrypt(\_)$ action is $P_1, P_2, P_3, P_4, P_5, P_6, P_7, N_2, N_3,$ N_4, N_5, N_6, A_2. Next, we need to exclude each other and choose the action that matches event e'.

According to *Property* 4 and *Property* 1, actions N_5, N_6 occurs after P_7, so N_5, N_6 can be ruled out. According *Property* 2, under the prerequisite of compliance with *Protocol(bss)*, events that the initiator or the responder participates in must be two parties or multiparty, so actions $P_1, P_2, P_3, P_4, P_5, P_6, P_7$ should be excluded, and actions N_2, N_3, N_4, A_2 are left.

If e' is an instance of N_2, then for some atoms s_1', R_2', K_N', s_2', there is an $e_1' < {}_{loc} e'$ such that

$$New(e_1') = R_2 \wedge Encrypt(e_2') = \langle <R_2', s_1'> , K_N', s_2' \rangle$$

Comparing $Encrypt(e_2')$ with $Encrypt(e')$, it's found that the requirement is obviously not satisfied, so action N_2 can be excluded. According to *Property* 5, there is no encryption event in N_3 and N_3 occurs after N_2, so action N_3 can be excluded.

For N_4, we have

$$N_4 = N_3, Decrypt(<K, ID_p, R_2> , K_N, s_4), Decrypt(R_3, K, s_5),$$
$$New(R_4), Encrypt(<R_3 - 1, R_4> , K, s_6), Send(s_6)$$

It's easy to observe that the first part of N_4 is inherited from N_3, according to *Property* 5, the first part of N_4 could be excluded, so we only need to consider the rest of N_4 to simply complexity of proof. If e' is an instance of N_4, then for some atoms R_4, $<R_3 - 1, R_4>''$, K'', s_6', there is an $e_2'' < e'$ such that

$$New(e_2'') = R_4'' \wedge Encrypt(e_3'') = \langle <R_3 - 1, R_4>'', K'', s_6'' \rangle$$

Compared $Encrypt(e_3'')$ with $Encrypt(e') = \langle <K, ID_N, TS> , KP, s_3 \rangle$, we can found that their format of encrypted message are different, so N_4 can be excluded.

If e' is an instance of A_2, according to *replacement rule* [14], the U can replace POS and V can replace NFC phone. For U and atoms $ID_U, ID_V, {}_1s_1, {}_1s_2, {}_1s_3, {}_1s_4, {}_1R_1, {}_1R_2, {}_1TS, K_U, K_V, {}_1K$, there are events $e_0', e_1', e_2', e_3', e_4', e_5'$ in POS, we can conclude

$$e_0' <_{loc} e_1' <_{loc} e_2' <_{loc} e_3' <_{loc} e_4' <_{loc} e_5' \wedge Rcv(e_0') = <ID_U, ID_v, {}_1s_2 >$$
$$\wedge Decrypt(e_1') = \langle <{}_1R_2, {}_1s_1> , K_V, {}_1s_2 \rangle \wedge Decrypt(e_2') =$$
$$\langle <{}_1R_1, TS> , K_U, {}_1s_1 \rangle \wedge Encrypt(e_3') = \langle <{}_1K, ID_V, {}_1TS> , K_U, {}_1s_3 \rangle \qquad (8)$$
$$\wedge Encrypt(e_4') = \langle <{}_1K, ID_U, {}_1R_2> , K_V, {}_1s_4 \rangle \wedge Send(e_5') = \langle {}_1s_3, {}_1s_4 \rangle$$

In formula (8), encryption event e_3' need to satisfy the following requirement

$$Encrypt(e_3') = \langle <{}_1K, ID_V, {}_1TS> , K_U, s_3 \rangle = Encrypt(e') \langle <K, ID_N, TS> , K_p, s_3 \rangle$$

We can conclude that $e_3' = e'$, so we have ${}_1K = K, ID_V = ID_N, {}_1TS = TS, K_U = K_P, {}_1s_3 = s_3$. Equations $U = P$, $V = N$ can be derived from $ID_V = ID_N$ and $K_U = K_P$, it's drawn the following formula by substituting result into formula (8).

$$e_0' <_{loc} e_1' <_{loc} e_2' <_{loc} e_3' <_{loc} e_4' <_{loc} e_5' \wedge Rcv(e_0') = \langle ID_P, ID_N, {}_1s_2 \rangle$$
$$\wedge Decrypt(e_1') = \langle <_1 R_2, {}_1s_1 >, K_N, {}_1s_2 \rangle \wedge Decrypt(e_2') =$$
$$\langle <_1 R_2, TS >, K_P, {}_1s_1 \rangle \wedge Encrypt(e_3') = \langle <K, ID_N, TS >, K_P, s_3 \rangle \qquad (9)$$
$$\wedge Encrypt(e_4') = \langle <K, ID_P, {}_1R_2 >, K_N, {}_1s_4 \rangle \wedge Send(e_5') = \langle s_3, {}_1s_4 \rangle$$

By *AxiomD* and *AxiomS*, the presence of event e'' and e''' enable action A_2 to satisfy the following formula.

(1) $\exists e'', e'' <e_2' \wedge DEmatch(e_2', e'') \wedge loc(e'') = P \wedge loc(e'') = N$
(2) $\exists e''', e''' <e_2' \wedge DEmatch(e_2', e''') \wedge loc(e''') = P \wedge loc(e''') = N$

According to *Property* 3, we consider e'' as research object in the first. *AS* obeys KerNeeS protocol. Event e'' is an instance of basic sequence, the only one that includes *Encrypt(_)* action are $P_1, P_2, P_3, P_4, P_5, P_6, P_7, N_2, N_3, N_4, N_5, N_6, A_2$, actions $P_3, P_4, P_5, P_6, P_7, N_3, N_4, N_5, N_6$ can be excluded with similar method when we selected N_4 as the suitable action.

If e'' is an instance of N_2, then for atoms ${}_2s_1, {}_2R_2, {}_2s_2$, there are $e_0'', e_1'', e_2'', e_3''$ in N such that

$$\left. \begin{array}{l} e_0'' <_{loc} e_2'' <_{loc} e_2'' <_{loc} e_3'' \wedge Rcv(e_0'') = {}_1s_1 \wedge New(e_1'') = {}_1R_2 \wedge \\ Encrypt(e_2'') = \langle <_1 R_2, {}_1s_1 >, K_N, {}_1s_2 \rangle \wedge Send(e_3'') = (ID_N, {}_1s_2) \end{array} \right\} \quad (10)$$

So, the formula $Encrypt(e'') = \langle <_1 R_2, {}_1s_1 >, K_N, {}_1s_2 \rangle = \langle <_2 R_2, {}_2s_1 >, K_N, {}_2s_2 \rangle = Encrypt(e_2'')$ need to be satisfied, it can be drawn that ${}_1R_2 = {}_2R_2$, ${}_1s_1 = {}_2s_1, {}_1s_2 = {}_2s_2$. We can conclude the following formula by substituting result into formula (8).

$$\left. \begin{array}{l} Rcv(e_0'') = {}_1s_1 \wedge New(e_1'') = {}_1R_2 \wedge Encrypt(e_2'') = \\ \langle <_1 R_2, {}_1s_1 >, K_N, {}_1s_2 \rangle \wedge Send(e_3'') = \langle ID_N, {}_1s_2 \rangle \end{array} \right\} \quad (11)$$

Now, looking back to event e''', If e''' is an instance of P_1, for some atoms ${}_3R_1, {}_3s_1$, there are events e_0''', e_1''', e_2''' such that

$$\left. \begin{array}{l} e_0''' <_{loc} e_1''' <_{loc} e_2''' \wedge New(e_0''') = {}_3R_1 \wedge \\ Encrypt(e_1''') = \langle <_3 R_1, {}_3TS >, K_p, {}_3s_1 \rangle \wedge \\ Send(e_2''') = {}_3s_1 \end{array} \right\} \quad (12)$$

Formula $Encrypt(e''') = \langle <_1 R_1, TS >, K_P, {}_1s_1 \rangle = \langle <_3 R_1, {}_3TS >, K_P, {}_3s_1 \rangle = Encrypt(e''')$ need to be satisfied, so it can be easily drawn that ${}_1R_1 = {}_3R_1, {}_3TS = TS$, ${}_1s_1 = {}_3s_1$. We can conclude the following formula by substituting result into formula (12).

$$\left. \begin{array}{l} e_0''' <_{loc} e_1''' <_{loc} e_2''' \wedge New(e_0''') = {}_1R_1 \wedge Encrypt(e_1''') = \\ \langle <_1 R_1, TS >, K_p, {}_1s_1 \rangle \wedge Send(e_2''') = {}_1s_1 \end{array} \right\} \quad (13)$$

According to *Lemma* 1 (unique nonce) and *Lemma* 2 (nonce release), there are equations $_1R_1 = R_1$ and $_1R_2 = R_2$. In addition, we can derive equations $_1s_1 = s_1$ and $_1s_2 = s_2$ from $s_1 = \{R_1, TS\}K_P$, $s_2 = \{R_2, s_1\}K_N$ in KerNeeS protocol, we have

$$
\left. \begin{array}{l}
Rcv(e_0'') = s_1 \land New(e_1'') = R_2 \land Encrypt(e_2'') = \\
\langle <_1 R_2, s_1 >, K_N, s_2 \rangle \land Send(e_3'') = \langle ID_N, s_2 \rangle
\end{array} \right\} \tag{14}
$$

$$
\left. \begin{array}{l}
e_0''' <_{loc} e_1''' <_{loc} e_2''' \land New(e_0''') = R_1 \land \\
Encrypt(e_1''') = \langle <R_1, TS >, K_p, s_1 \rangle \land \\
Send(e_2''') = s_1
\end{array} \right\} \tag{15}
$$

So we can conclude that $Send(e_2) = s_1 = Rcv(e_0'')$ and $Send(e_3'') = (ID, s_2) = Rcv(e_4)$. These two send-receive actions include message s_1, s_2, therefore AS got plaintext R_2 and TS by decrypting s_1, s_2. We can believe the reliability of s_3, s_4, K by *AxiomS*.

When P received the session key K from AS, the rest part of KerNeeS is a process of exchanging K between P and N. Since the reliability s_3, s_4, K in first part of protocol have been proved, in order to simply proving procedures, s_3, s_4, K will not consider in rest part.

Suppose $P \neq N \neq AS$ are both honest and obey KerNeeS, and suppose that thread thr_2 is an instance of P_7. Let $e_0^{(4)} <_{loc} e_1^{(4)} <_{loc} e_2^{(4)} <_{loc} e_3^{(4)} <_{loc} e_4^{(4)} <_{loc} e_5^{(4)} <_{loc} e_6^{(4)}$ be the actions in thr_2, then $e_0^{(4)}, e_1^{(4)}, \cdots, e_6^{(4)}$ have location P, and for some atoms $R_3, R_4, K, s_4, s_5, s_6$ and s_7 we have

$$
\left. \begin{array}{l}
New(e_0^{(4)}) = R_3 \land Encrypt(e_1^{(4)}) = <R_3, K, s_5 > \land \\
Send(e_2^{(4)}) = <s_4, s_5 > \land Rcv(e_3^{(4)}) = s_6 \land \\
Decrypt(e_4^{(4)}) = \langle <R_3 - 1, R_4 >, K, s_6 \rangle \land \\
Encrypt(e_5^{(5)}) = \langle <R_4 - 1 >, K, s_7 \rangle \land Send(e_6^{(7)}) = s_7
\end{array} \right\} \tag{16}
$$

By *AxiomS* and *AxiomD*, there is an event $e^{(4)}$ such that

$$
e^{(4)} < e_4^{(4)} \land DEmatch(e_4^{(4)}, e^{(4)}) \land loc(e^{(4)}) = N \land loc(e^{(4)}) = AS
$$

So we can conclude $Encrypt(e^{(4)}) = \langle <R_3 - 1, R_4 >, K, s_6 \rangle$.

Because AS and N obey KerNeeS, actions $e^{(4)}$ must be a member of an instance of one of the basic sequence of KerNeeS. The only ones that include $Encrypt(\_)$ actions are $P_5, P_6, P_7, N_4, N_5, N_6$. According to *Property* 2 and *Property* 5, P_5, P_6, P_7, N_5, N_6 can be ruled out and N_4 implies a matching conversation

If $e^{(4)}$ is in an instance of N_4, then for some atoms $_5R_3, _5R_4, _5K, _5s_4, _5s_6, _5s_7$ and some location N, there are events $e_0^{(5)}, e_1^{(5)}, \cdots, e_6^{(5)}$ such that

$$\left.\begin{array}{l} e_0^{(5)} <_{loc} e_1^{(5)} <_{loc} e_2^{(5)} <_{loc} e_3^{(5)} <_{loc} e_4^{(5)} <_{loc} e_5^{(5)} <_{loc} e_6^{(5)} \wedge \\ Rcv(e_0^{(5)}) = <_5 s_4, _5 s_5 > \wedge Decrypt(e_1^{(5)}) = <_5 R_3, _5 K, _5 s_5 > \wedge \\ New(e_2^{(5)}) = _5 R_4 \wedge Encrypt(e_3^{(5)}) = \langle <_5 R_3 - 1, _5 R_4 >, _5 K, _5 s_6 \rangle \wedge \\ Send(e_4^{(5)}) = _5 s_6 \wedge Rcv(e_5^{(5)}) = _6 s_6 \wedge Decrypt(e_6^{(6)}) = \\ \langle <_5 R_4 - 1 >, _5 K, _5 s_7 \rangle \end{array}\right\} \quad (17)$$

It can be easily found that a decryption event $Decrypt\left(e_0^{(5)}\right) = <R_3, K, _5 s_5 >$ exists in formula (17), by *AxiomD* and *AxiomS*, there is an event $e^{(5)}$ such that

$$e^{(5)} < e_1^{(5)} \wedge DEmatch(e_4^{(5)}, e^{(5)}) \wedge loc(e^{(5)}) = AS \vee loc(e^{(5)}) = N$$

So, it must satisfies $Encrypt(e^{(5)}) = <R_3, K, _5 s_5 > .$

If $e^{(5)}$ is an instance of P_5, then for some atoms $_6 R_3, _6 K, _6 s_4, _6 s_5$ and some location P, there are events $e_0^{(6)}, e_1^{(6)}, e_2^{(6)}$ such that

$$\left.\begin{array}{l} e_0^{(6)} <_{loc} e_1^{(6)} <_{loc} e_2^{(6)} \wedge New(e_0^{(6)}) = _6 R_3 \wedge \\ Encrypt(e_1^{(6)}) = \langle _6 R_3, _6 K, _6 s_5 \rangle \wedge \\ Send(e_2^{(6)}) = \langle _6 s_4, _6 s_5 \rangle \end{array}\right\} \quad (18)$$

It need to satisfy $Encrypt(e^{(5)}) = <R_3, K, _5 s_5 > = < _6 R_3, _6 K, _6 s_5 > = Encrypt\left(e_1^{(6)}\right)$, so we have $R_3 = _6 R_3, _6 K = K$ and $_5 s_5 = _6 s_5$. We can conclude the following formula by substituting result into formula (18).

$$\left.\begin{array}{l} e_0^{(6)} <_{loc} e_1^{(6)} <_{loc} e_2^{(6)} \wedge New(e_0^{(6)}) = R_3 \wedge \\ Encrypt(e_1^{(6)}) = \langle R_3, K, _5 s_5 \rangle \wedge \\ Send(e_2^{(6)}) = \langle _6 s_4, _5 s_5 \rangle \end{array}\right\} \quad (19)$$

There are two equations $Send\left(e_2^{(6)}\right) = <_6 s_4, _5 s_5 >$ and $Rcv\left(e_0^{(5)}\right) = <_5 s_4, _5 s_5 >$ in formula (17), (19). In the previous proof we have proved that s_4 is reliable, so we can conclude that $_5 s_4 = _6 s_4 = s_4$ and $Send\left(e_2^{(6)}\right) = <s_4, _5 s_5 > = Rcv\left(e_0^{(5)}\right)$ according to *Property 5(Inheritability)*. In formula (16), (18) we have $Rcv\left(e_3^{(4)}\right) = s_6$ and $Send(e_4^{(5)}) = s_6$ as well as actions $Rcv\left(e_3^{(4)}\right)$ is equal to $Send\left(e_4^{(5)}\right)$, therefore we get two pairs of matching conversations.

To prove $KNS| = auth(P_7, 6)$, we need to get six pairs of strong matching conversations. To prove strong matching conversation, we must first have strong matching. In the above proof procedure, we get six pairs of weak matching conservations as follows.

$$\left.\begin{array}{l}
Send(e_2) = s_1 = Rcv(e_0'') \\
Send(e_3'') = (ID, s_2) = Rcv(e_3) \\
Send(e_4) = \langle ID_p, ID_N, s_2 \rangle = Rcv(e_0') \\
Send(e_5') = \langle s_3, s_4 \rangle = Rcv(e_5) \\
Send(e_2^{(6)}) = \langle s_4, 5s_5 \rangle = Rcv(e_0^{(5)}) \\
Send(e_4^{(5)}) = s_6 = Rcv(e_3^{(4)})
\end{array}\right\}$$

In order to prove that KerNeeS satisfies strong matching conversation, we must prove $e_2 < e_0'', e_3'' < e_3, e_4 < e_0', e_5' < e_5, e_2^{(6)} < e_0^{(5)}, e_3^{(4)} < e_4^{(5)}$, let taking events $e_3^{(4)}, e_4^{(5)}$ as an example to illustrate.

Suppose $P \neq N \neq AS$ are both honest and obey KerNeeS, according to *AxiomF* and *flow relation*, there is an event s releasing R between $e_3^{(4)}$ and $e_3^{(5)}$. If $e_3^{(5)} \leq s$, the sorting result $e_3^{(4)} < e_3^{(5)}$ can be obtained. In the next step we rule out $e_3^{(4)} <_{loc} j <_{loc} e_4^{(5)}$, if the relationship $e_3^{(4)} <_{loc} j <_{loc} e_4^{(5)}$ holds, the event s must be a membership of P, however we know that there is no sending action between $e_3^{(4)}$ and $e_4^{(5)}$ in thread thr_2 by *Lemma 2(nonce release)*, which means that R will be not released before event $e_4^{(5)}$. By using similar method, we also can prove $e_2 < e_0'', e_3'' < e_3, e_4 < e_0', e_5' < e_5$ and $e_2^{(6)} < e_0^{(5)}$.

According to the above proof procedure, there are six pairs of strong matching conversations at location P in KerNeeS, it means that we can prove $KNS| = auth(P_7, 6)$.

Similarly, $KNS| = auth(N_6, 5)$ can be proved.

The KerNeeS protocol satisfies strong authentication property, the security of KerNeeS protocol is proved and the session key is confirmed during the interaction of entities, it means that mutual authentication can be guaranteed between POS and NFC phone. The KerNeeS protocol is secure and the attacker can't carry on replay attack by disguising as a legitimate user.

5   Conclusions and Future Work

Mobile payment based on NFC technology brings great conveniences to people's lives, but the security issues existing in NFC technology threaten the development of mobile payment. Based on logic of events, this paper proposed migration rule and then derived inheritability from the rule of axiom cluster in order to optimize the application of logic of events. These reasoning rules and properties are mainly used to reduce complexity and redundancy in the process of protocol analysis, optimize security protocol analysis method based on logic of events, and use axiomatic system and reasoning rules to conduct formal analysis of KerNeeS protocol, and conclude that the protocol can guarantee mutual authentication between POS and NFC phone. The next step of this paper is to formalize the confidentiality and integrity of sensitive data in the process of protocol interaction.

Acknowledgements. This work was supported in part by the National Natural Science Foundation of China under Grant 61163005 and 61562026, the Jiangxi Province Key Subject Academic and Technical Leader Funding Project (2017XSDTR0105), the National Natural Science Foundation of Jiangxi Province of China (20161BAB202063).

References

1. Odelu, V., Das, A.K., Goswami, A.: SEAP: secure and efficient authentication protocol for NFC applications using pseudonyms. IEEE Trans. Consum. Electron. **62**(1), 3–38 (2016)
2. Badra, M., Badra, R.B.: A lightweight security protocol for NFC-based mobile phone. Proc. Comput. Sci. **83**, 705–711 (2016)
3. Dong, M., Ota, K., Yang, L.T., Liu, A., Guo, M.: LSCD: a low storage clone protocol for cyber-physical systems. IEEE Trans. Comput. Aided Des. Integr. Circ. Syst. **35**(5), 712–723 (2016)
4. Zhang, L., Wei, L., Huang, D., Zhang, K., Dong, M., Ota, K.: MEDAPs: secure multi-entities delegated authentication protocols for mobile cloud computing. Secur. Commun. Netw. **9**(16), 3777–3789 (2016)
5. Zhang, Y., Wang, Z., Li, Q., Lou, J., Yao, D.: Research progress and trends on the security of near field communication. Chin. J. Comput. **39**(06), 1190–1207 (2016)
6. Datta, A., Derek, A., Mitchell, J.C., et al.: Protocol composition logic (PCL). Electron. Notes Theor. Comput. Sci. **172**, 311–358 (2007)
7. Gao, S., Hu, A.Q., Shi, L., Chen, X.B.: A survey on formal analysis of security protocols. J. Cryptol. Res. **1**(5), 504–512 (2014)
8. Wang, Z., Xu, D., Wang, X., Tang, Z., Wei, L.: Reliability analysis and improvement of BAN logic. Comput. Eng. **38**(17), 110–115 (2012)
9. Xiao, M., Bickford, M.: Logic of events for proving security properties of protocols. In: Proceedings of IEEE International Conference on Web Information System and Mining (WISM 2009), pp. 519–523 (2009)
10. Bickford, M.: Unguessable atoms: a logic foundation for security. In: Proceedings of VSTTE 2008, pp. 30–53 (2008)
11. Bickford, M., Constable, R.L.: Automated proof of authentication protocols in logic of events. In: Proceedings of 6th International Verification Workshop, pp. 13–30 (2010)
12. Ceipher, U.B., Medaglia, C.M., Marino, A., Sposto, S., Moronli, A.: KerNeeS: a protocol for mutual authentication between NFC phones and POS terminals for secure payment transactions. In: 2012 9th International ISC Conference on Information Security and Cryptology (ISCISC). IEEE, pp. 115–120 (2012)
13. Xiao, M., Ma, C., Deng, C.: A novel approach to automatic security protocol analysis based on authentication event logic. Chin. J. Electron. **24**(1), 187–192 (2015)
14. Li, Y., Xiao, M., Li, W.: Security proof of wireless mesh network authentication protocol based on logic of events. Comput. Eng. Sci. **39**(12), 2236–2244 (2017)
15. Xiao, M., Deng, C., Ma, C., et al.: Proving authentication property of modified Needham-Schroder protocol with logic of events. In: Proceedings of International Conference on Computer Information System and Industrial Applications, pp. 379–383 (2015)
16. Liu, X., Xiao, M., Cheng, D., et al.: Security authentication property of the modified Needham-Schroder protocol based on logic of event. Comput. Eng. Sci. **37**(10), 1850–1855 (2015)
17. Xiao, M., Liu, X., Li, Y., et al.: Security certification of three-party network protocols based on strong authentication theory. J. Front. Comput. Sci. Technol. **10**(12), 1701–1710 (2016)

An Interest-Matrix-Based Mechanism for Selfish Bin Packing

Xia Chen, Xin Chen$^{(\boxtimes)}$, and Qizhi Fang

School of Mathematical Sciences, Ocean University of China, Qingdao 266100, Shandong, People's Republic of China
cxin0307@163.com

Abstract. Selfish bin packing considers a cost-sharing system of the classical bin packing problem, where each item is controlled by a selfish agent and aims to minimize the sharing cost. In this paper we study an incentive mechanism: Interest-Matrix-based (IM-based) mechanism, a new perspective that focuses on the interest or the satisfaction between any pair of items rather than personal sharing cost. Under the IM-based mechanism, we show that $PoA \leq 1.7$ for general instances with item size inside $(1/n_0, 1]$, where n_0 is an arbitrary large integer. In special, when $n_0 = 4$, the PoA of the IM-based mechanism does not exceed 1.5.

Keywords: Selfish bin packing · Mechanism · Nash equilibrium

1 Introduction

Selfish bin packing, originating from bin packing problem [6,13], previously considers a cost-sharing game system. Given a set of items and sufficiently unit-capacity bins. Each item has its size inside the interval $(0, 1]$ and it is controlled by a selfish agent who chooses bins actively and aims to minimize the sharing cost rather than the social cost (the number of consumed bins in total). Note that each bin has unit cost 1, which is shared by all items packed in it. In order to minimize the social cost in this game circumstance, designing incentive mechanisms to lead the agent's actions is necessary. The quality of the mechanism is commonly evaluated by the price of anarchy (PoA), which is the ratio between the social welfare that derives from the worst Nash equilibrium and that of the social optimum.

Selfish bin packing was first introduced in 2006 by Bilò [1] with the first mechanism, proportional weight mechanism. He showed that a pure Nash equilibrium always exists and the PoA is between 1.6 and 1.6667. Epstein et al. [4] did further research of proportional weight mechanism, they proved that the PoA fell into $[1.6416; 1.6428]$, which is the currently best result of proportional weight mechanism.

Until 2013, Han et al. [8] present another mechanism for selfish bin packing, unit weight mechanism. Dosà and Epstein [3] proved that for this mechanism, $PoA \in [1.6966, 1.6994]$. It is the best-known result of unit weight mechanism.

This work is supported by NSFC (No. 11271341).

Recently, a novel mechanism proposed by Wang et al. [14] for selfish bin packing was proposed which is a generalization of several well-known mechanisms, such as, proportional-weight and unit-weight mechanisms. This new mechanism introduces an interest matrix and it focuses on various interests between any pair of items while they shares the same bin. In fact, the motivation of this new mechanism for selfish bin packing is to express that items choose bins not only considering packing-cost, but they always care about the interest or the satisfaction of current situations (sharing bins with items). Therefore, it is a natural idea to take into account the interest between any two items, i.e. interest matrix, in selfish bin packing [14], Wang et al. showed that (1) there exists Nash equilibrium when the matrix is symmetric; (2) the PoA is bounded in several special matrices while in general it can be arbitrary large.

Under the framework of the interest-matrix-based mechanism proposed by Wang et al. [14], we construct a new interest matrix based on the idea: leading the agent to choose bins with the most possible number of items and the largest possible total size.

The organization of the paper is as follows. In Sect. 2, we introduce the related definitions. In Sect. 3, we present the new mechanism, Interest-Matrix-based Mechanism (IM-based mechanism), and give some properties. Section 4 is dedicated to the analysis of PoA of the IM-based mechanism for a special kind of instances, where the size of the items belongs to $(1/4, 1]$. In Sect. 5, we extend the analysis in Sect. 4 to general instances where the size of the items belongs to $(1/n_0, 1]$, and show that the PoA of the IM-based mechanism falls into $[1.623, 1.7]$.

2 Preliminaries

2.1 Selfish Bin Packing and Previous Mechanisms

Selfish bin packing considers a cost-sharing game system [10]. An instance of this game, denoted as $\mathcal{I} = \{L, S\}$, consists of a list $L = \{a_1, \ldots, a_n\}$ of items and the sizes of the items $S = \{s(a_1), \ldots, s(a_n)\}$, $s(a_i) \in (0, 1]$. Assume that each item is controlled by a selfish agent whose strategy is to choose bins under the capacity constraint and aims to minimize the sharing cost rather than the social cost, i.e., the number of consumed bins. In order to minimize the social cost in this game system, designing reasonable payoff rules, i.e., mechanisms is a valid method.

Denote by B a unit-capacity bin that contains a set of items. For a consumed bin B, denote by $s(B)$ the total size of items, $|B|$ the number of items. Some known mechanisms, such as proportional weight mechanism and unit weight mechanism, are extensively studied [2,5,11,15].

- Proportional weight mechanism: item a_i's payoff is proportional to the total size of items sharing the same bin, i.e.,

$$p(a_i) = s(a_i)/s(B), \forall a_i \in B.$$

– Unit weight mechanism: item a_i's payoff is proportional to the number of items sharing the same bin, i.e.,

$$p(a_i) = 1/|B|, \forall a_i \in B.$$

– General weight mechanism: item a_i's payoff is proportional to the total weight of items sharing the same bin, i.e.,

$$p(a_i) = w(a_i)/w(B), \forall a_i \in B,$$

which is the generalization of proportional and unit weight mechanisms.

2.2 Nash Equilibrium and Price of Anarchy

Given any instance of selfish bin packing and a specific mechanism, selfish items actively choose bins or constantly change strategies for minimizing their costs. A Nash equilibrium (NE) [9] is a feasible packing and a stable state in this game system that (1) No item can benefit (decrease its cost) by changing only its own strategy (moving to anther bin) while the other items keep their unchanged. (2) A Nash equilibrium is not necessarily a optimal packing.

The price of anarchy (PoA) [7,12] is a metric to measure the quality of mechanisms, which is defined the ratio between the social cost of the worst NE and that of the optimal solution. Formally, given an instance of selfish bin packing $\mathcal{I}$ and a specific mechanism $\mathcal{M}$, denote by $NE(\mathcal{M_I})$ the social cost of an NE under the mechanism $\mathcal{M}$ and denote by $OPT(\mathcal{I})$ the social cost of the optimal solution. The PoA of mechanism $\mathcal{M}$ is defined as

$$PoA(\mathcal{M_I}) = \limsup_{OPT(\mathcal{I}) \to \infty} \max_{\forall NE} \left\{ \frac{NE(\mathcal{M_I})}{OPT(\mathcal{I})} \right\}.$$

3 Interest-Matrix-Based (IM-Based) Mechanism

In this section, we present an interest-matrix-based mechanism for selfish bin packing. We define the interests between each pair of items as the sum of the sizes of both items. The personal goal of each item is to maximize the total interest that derives from other items packed in the same bin.

Given an instance of selfish bin packing $\mathcal{I} = \{L, S\}$: $L = \{a_1, \cdots, a_n\}$, $S = \{s(a_1), \cdots, s(a_n)\}$ and given an interest matrix $A_{n \times n} = [a_{ij}]$, a_{ij} is defined as $a_{ij} = s(a_i) + s(a_j)$.

Our mechanism $\mathcal{M}^\flat$ is as following:

Interest-Matrix-Based (IM-Based) Mechanism $\mathcal{M}^\flat$

For any item a_i in the instance $\mathcal{I}$, assume that a_i chooses the bin B in the current situation. The payoff of item a_i is

$$p(a_i) = \sum_{j \in B} a_{ij} = \sum_{j \in B} (s(a_i) + s(a_j)) = |B| \cdot s(a_i) + s(B).$$

Remark. Under the IM-based mechanism, each item would like to choose the bin that contains the most possible items and the largest possible total size. However it is difficult to decide, between the number of items and the total size of the items in a bin, which is more influential for item's strategy.

We first show that, under the IM-based mechanism, a Nash equilibrium always exists and it can be obtained in finite steps from any packing.

Lemma 1. *Under the IM-based mechanism $\mathcal{M}^b$, an NE always exists and it can be obtained in finite steps from any feasible packing.*

The proof of the lemma is omitted, which follows directly from the result in [14] by making use of the method of potential functions.

The following proposition describes an important property of IM-based mechanism. Denote by $\mathcal{B}^i = \{B | B \in NE, |B| = i\}$.

Proposition 1. *Under the IM-based mechanism, there exists at most one bin $B_0^i \in \mathcal{B}^i$ in an NE packing such that $s(B_0^i) \leq \frac{i}{i+1}$.*

Proof. For an NE packing induced by IM-based mechanism, if there exists two bins $B_1, B_2 \in \mathcal{B}^i$ such that $s(B_k) \leq \frac{i}{i+1}$, $k = 1, 2$, we will show the contradiction at the end. Without loss of generality, assume that $s(B_1) \geq s(B_2)$. Consider the smallest item $a_{2\min}$ in the bin B_2, we have

$$ s(a_{2\min}) \leq \frac{s(B_2)}{|B_2|} \leq \frac{\frac{i}{i+1}}{i} = \frac{1}{i+1} \leq (1 - s(B_1)), $$

implying that item $a_{2\min}$ can move to the bin B_1. Observe that item $a_{2\min}$'s payoff is

$$ p(a_{2\min}) = |B_2| \cdot s(a_{2\min}) + s(B_2) $$
$$ = i \cdot s(a_{2\min}) + s(B_2), \qquad [a_{2\min} \text{ is packed in } B_2] $$

and if $a_{2\min}$ moves to the bin B_1, the payoff will be

$$ p'(a_{2\min}) = (|B_1| + 1) \cdot s(a_{2\min}) + s(B_1) + s(a_{2\min}) $$
$$ = (i + 2) \cdot s(a_{2\min}) + s(B_1) $$
$$ > i \cdot s(a_{2\min}) + s(B_2) $$
$$ = p(a_{2\min}), \qquad [a_{2\min} \text{ moves to } B_1] $$

Therefore item $a_{2\min}$ has an incentive to move from B_2 to B_1, which contradicts the property of NE. The proof is complete. $\qquad\qquad \square$

4   The Bounds of PoA While $s(a_{\min}) > 1/4$

In this section, we consider a special case $\mathcal{I}_s = \{L, S\}$ with $s(a_{\min}) > 1/4$, where $a_{\min}$ is the item of smallest size. We show that under the IM-based mechanism, the PoA falls into the interval $[1.333, 1.5]$.

4.1   Upper Bound of the PoA

Given an instance $\mathcal{I}_s = \{L, S\}$ where $L = \{a_1, \cdots, a_n\}$, $S = \{s(a_1), \cdots, s(a_n)\}$ and an interest matrix $A_{n \times n} = [a_{ij}]$ where $a_{ij} = s(a_i) + s(a_j)$. We first discuss the upper bound of the PoA.

Theorem 1. *Given a special instance $\mathcal{I}_s$ with $s(a_{\min}) > 1/4$. Under the IM-based mechanism for selfish bin packing, we have*

$$PoA(\mathcal{M}_{\mathcal{I}_s}) \leq \frac{3}{2}.$$

Proof. Consider an NE packing $NE = \mathcal{B}^1 \cup \mathcal{B}^2 \cup \mathcal{B}^3$ for the instance $\mathcal{I}_s$, where

$$\mathcal{B}^1 = \{B \mid B \in NE, |B| = 1\};$$
$$\mathcal{B}^2 = \{B \mid B \in NE, |B| = 2\};$$
$$\mathcal{B}^3 = \{B \mid B \in NE, |B| = 3\}.$$

Note that there exists no bins with four or more items in any feasible packing since $s(a_{\min}) > 1/4$ and the capacity constraint of bins. Denote by $NE(\mathcal{M}_{\mathcal{I}_s})$ and $OPT(\mathcal{I}_s)$ the number of bins in an NE packing and the optimal packing. The following will show the relation between $NE(\mathcal{M}_{\mathcal{I}_s})$ and $OPT(\mathcal{I}_s)$ by the bridge $S(\mathcal{I}_s) = \sum_{i \in \mathcal{I}_s} s(a_i)$, the total size of items in the instance.

We consider $\mathcal{B}^2 = \mathcal{B}_\ell^2 \cup \mathcal{B}_s^2$, where

$$\mathcal{B}_\ell^2 = \{B | B \in \mathcal{B}^2, \exists a_i \in B, s(a_i) > \frac{1}{2}\};$$

$$\mathcal{B}_s^2 = \{B | B \in \mathcal{B}^2, \forall a_i \in B, s(a_i) \leq \frac{1}{2}\}.$$

Observe that there exists $3|\mathcal{B}^3| + 2|\mathcal{B}_s^2| + |\mathcal{B}_\ell^2|$ small items (with size smaller than $1/2$) in the item list. The following discusses whether all these small items can share bins with the large items (with size strictly larger than $1/2$).

(1) If $3|\mathcal{B}^3| + 2|\mathcal{B}_s^2| \leq |\mathcal{B}^1|$, then $|\mathcal{B}^3| + |\mathcal{B}_s^2| \leq \frac{1}{2}|\mathcal{B}^1|$. Thus we obtain

$$\frac{NE(\mathcal{M}_{\mathcal{I}_s}^b)}{OPT(\mathcal{I}_s)} \leq \frac{\frac{3}{2}|\mathcal{B}^1| + |\mathcal{B}_\ell^2|}{|\mathcal{B}^1| + |\mathcal{B}_\ell^2|} < \frac{3}{2},$$

which implies that $PoA \leq 3/2$.

(2) If $3|\mathcal{B}^3| + 2|\mathcal{B}_s^2| > |\mathcal{B}^1|$, we assume that $3|\mathcal{B}^3| + 2|\mathcal{B}_s^2| = |\mathcal{B}^1| + x, (x > 0)$. Since there are $|\mathcal{B}^1| + x + |\mathcal{B}_\ell^2|$ small items in the list, they need at least another $x/3$ bins besides sharing bins with large items. Then we obtain

$$OPT(\mathcal{I}_s) \geq |\mathcal{B}^1| + |\mathcal{B}_\ell^2| + \frac{1}{3} \cdot x,$$

$$NE(\mathcal{M}_{\mathcal{I}_s}^b) = |\mathcal{B}^1| + |\mathcal{B}_\ell^2| + |\mathcal{B}_s^2| + |\mathcal{B}^3| \leq \frac{3}{2}(|\mathcal{B}^1| + \frac{2}{3}|\mathcal{B}_\ell^2| + \frac{1}{3} \cdot x).$$

Thus

$$\frac{NE(\mathcal{M}_{\mathcal{I}_s}^b)}{OPT(\mathcal{I}_s)} \leq \frac{\frac{3}{2}(|\mathcal{B}^1| + |\mathcal{B}_\ell^2| + \frac{1}{3} \cdot x)}{|\mathcal{B}^1| + |\mathcal{B}_\ell^2| + \frac{1}{3} \cdot x} \leq \frac{3}{2},$$

implying that $PoA \leq 3/2$. $\qquad\square$

4.2   Lower Bound of the PoA

In this subsection, we construct a worst case example for the IM-based mechanism $\mathcal{M}^{\flat}$ to give the lower bound of PoA.

Theorem 2. *Under the IM-based mechanism, for the special case $s(a_{\min}) > 1/4$, we have*

$$PoA(\mathcal{M}^{\flat}) \geq \frac{4}{3} > 1.333.$$

Proof. We construct an instance as follows. Let N be an arbitrary large integer and let $\varepsilon = 1/N$. There are N large items with size $1/2 + \varepsilon$ and N small items with size $1/4 + \varepsilon$.

We present an NE packing that consists of $4/3 \cdot N$ bins as illustrated in Fig. 1, where each large item monopoly occupies one bin and every three small items share one bin. It is clear that no item can benefit from moving alone:

1. Each large item can not move to other bins since the capacity constraint;
2. Each small item can not move to other three-item bins since the capacity constraint and each small item would not like to move to monopoly bins since its payoff will change from $6/4 + 6\varepsilon$ to $5/4 + 4\varepsilon$ (decreasing).

However, the optimal packing (showed in Fig. 1) only consumes N bins, one large item is packed with one small item in each bin. Therefore,

$$PoA(\mathcal{M}^{\flat}) \geq \frac{4}{3}.$$

$\square$

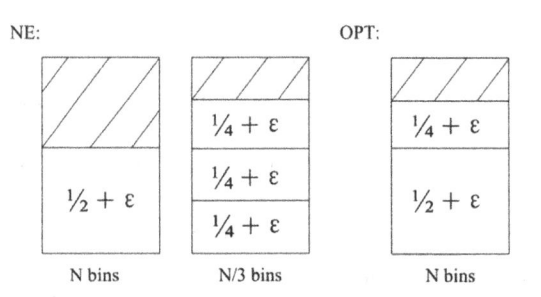

Fig. 1. A worst case of IM-based mechanism $\mathcal{M}^{\flat}$ while $s(a_{\min}) > 1/4$.

5   The Bounds of PoA While $s(a_{\min}) > 1/n_0$

In this section, we consider more general instances of selfish bin packing problem. Given an instance $\mathcal{I}$ of selfish bin packing, $\mathcal{I} = \{L, S\}$, where $L = \{a_1, \cdots, a_n\}$, $S = \{s(a_1), \cdots, s(a_n)\}$ and an interest matrix $A_{n \times n} = [a_{ij}]$ where $a_{ij} = s(a_i) + s(a_j)$. Note that $s(a_i) > 1/n_0$, $\forall a_i \in L$ and n_0 is an arbitrary large integer. We show that under the IM-based mechanism, the PoA falls into the interval $[1.623, 1.7]$.

5.1 Upper Bound of PoA

The following theorem illustrates that under the IM-based mechanism $\mathcal{M}^b$, the upper bound of the PoA is $17/10$.

Theorem 3. *For any instance $\mathcal{I}$ with $s(a_{\min}) > 1/n_0$, we show that under the IM-based mechanism $\mathcal{M}_\mathcal{I}$,*

$$PoA(\mathcal{M}_\mathcal{I}) \leq \frac{17}{10}.$$

For the purpose of showing the upper bound of PoA, we introduce a weight function to be the bridge connecting the number of bins in optimal packing and an NE packing. For each item $a \in \mathcal{I}$, the weight $w(a)$ is defined as

$$w(a) = \frac{6}{5}s(a) + v(a),$$

where

$$v(a) = \begin{cases} 0, & 0 < s(a) \leq \frac{1}{6}; \\[2mm] \frac{3}{5}(s(a) - \frac{1}{6}), & \frac{1}{6} < s(a) \leq \frac{1}{3}; \\[2mm] \frac{1}{10}, & \frac{1}{3} < s(a) \leq \frac{1}{2}; \\[2mm] \frac{4}{10}, & \frac{1}{2} < s(a) \leq 1. \end{cases}$$

Denote by $w(\mathcal{I}) = \sum_{a \in \mathcal{I}} w(a)$ the total weight of all items in the instance. Recall that $NE(\mathcal{M}_\mathcal{I})$ and $OPT(\mathcal{I})$ are the number of bins in an NE packing and the optimal packing respectively.

Sketch of the Proof of Theorem 3. For any instance $\mathcal{I}$ and any NE packing, based on the weight function, we focus on illustrating both inequalities:

$$w(\mathcal{I}) \leq \frac{17}{10} \cdot OPT(\mathcal{I}) \quad \text{[total weight \& the optimal packing]} \qquad (1)$$

$$w(\mathcal{I}) \geq NE(\mathcal{M}_\mathcal{I}^b) - n_0 \quad \text{[total weight \& an NE packing]} \qquad (2)$$

If these two inequalities hold, we obtain

$$\frac{NE(\mathcal{M}_\mathcal{I}^b) - n_0}{OPT(\mathcal{I})} \leq \frac{17}{10}. \quad \text{[n_0 is a constant]}$$

When $OPT(\mathcal{I}) \to \infty$,

$$PoA(\mathcal{M}_\mathcal{I}) \leq \frac{17}{10}.$$

In the rest of section we will show the both inequalities (1) and (2).

Lemma 2. *For any instance $\mathcal{I}$ with $s(a_{\min}) > 1/n_0$, we show that*

$$w(\mathcal{I}) \leq \frac{17}{10} \cdot OPT(\mathcal{I}).$$

Proof. To show the lemma, it is sufficient to show the following conclusion:

$$w(B) = \sum_{i=1}^{m} w(a_i) \leq \frac{17}{10}, \quad \forall B \in OPT(\mathcal{I}),$$

where $B = \{a_1, \cdots, a_m\}$ is an arbitrary bin in the optimal packing. Without loss of generality, assume that $s(a_1) \geq \cdots \geq s(a_m)$.

Case 1. If $s(a_1) \in (\frac{1}{2}, 1], s(a_2) \in (\frac{1}{3}, \frac{1}{2}], s(a_3), \cdots, s(a_m) \in (0, \frac{1}{6}]$. Based on the weight function, we have

$$w(B) = \frac{6}{5}s(B) + v(B) \leq \frac{6}{5} \cdot 1 + \frac{4}{10} + \frac{1}{10} = \frac{17}{10}.$$

Case 2. If $s(a_1) \in (\frac{1}{2}, 1], s(a_2), s(a_3) \in (\frac{1}{6}, \frac{1}{3}], s(a_4), \cdots, s(a_m) \in (0, \frac{1}{6}]$, then we obtain

$$w(B) = \frac{6}{5}s(B) + v(B) = \frac{6}{5}s(B) + \frac{4}{10} + \frac{3}{5}\left[s(a_2) + s(a_3) - \frac{2}{6}\right]$$

$$\leq \frac{6}{5} + \frac{4}{10} + \frac{3}{5}\left(\frac{1}{2} - \frac{2}{6}\right) = \frac{17}{10}.$$

Case 3. If $s(a_1) \in (\frac{1}{2}, 1], s(a_2) \in (\frac{1}{6}, \frac{1}{3}], s(a_3), \cdots, s(a_m) \in (0, \frac{1}{6}]$, then

$$w(B) = \frac{6}{5}s(B) + v(B) = \frac{6}{5}s(B) + \frac{4}{10} + \frac{3}{5}\left[s(a_2) - \frac{1}{6}\right]$$

$$\leq \frac{6}{5} + \frac{4}{10} + \frac{3}{5}\left(\frac{1}{3} - \frac{1}{6}\right) = \frac{17}{10}.$$

Case 4. If $s(a_1) \in (\frac{1}{2}, 1], s(a_2), \cdots, s(a_m) \in (0, \frac{1}{6}]$, then we obtain

$$w(B) = \frac{6}{5}s(B) + v(B) \leq \frac{6}{5} \cdot 1 + \frac{4}{10} = \frac{8}{5}.$$

Case 5. If $s(a_i) \in (0, \frac{1}{2}], \forall a_i \in B$. Observe that there exists at most five items with size inside $(1/6, 1]$ in B since capacity constraint. That is B contains at most five items with $v(a_i) > 0$ and $v(a_i) \leq 1/10$. Thus,

$$w(B) = \frac{6}{5}s(B) + v(B) \leq \frac{6}{5} \cdot 1 + \frac{1}{10} \cdot 5 = \frac{17}{10}.$$

Thus, the lemma is proved. □

Lemma 3. *For any instance $\mathcal{I}$ with $s(a_{\min}) > 1/n_0$, under IM-based mechanism $\mathcal{M}^b$, we show that*

$$w(\mathcal{I}) \geq NE(\mathcal{M}_{\mathcal{I}}^b) - n_0.$$

Proof. Consider any NE packing contains bins $\mathcal{B}^1 \cup \mathcal{B}^2 \cup \cdots \cup \mathcal{B}^{n_0-1}$, where

$$\mathcal{B}^1 = \{B \mid B \in NE, |B| = 1\};$$
$$\mathcal{B}^2 = \{B \mid B \in NE, |B| = 2\};$$
$$\cdots$$
$$\mathcal{B}^{n_0-1} = \{B \mid B \in NE, |B| = n_0 - 1\}.$$

Note that there exists no bins with n_0 or more items since $s(a_{\min}) > 1/n_0$. To clearly illustrate the property of NE, we give an order of bins in the NE: sorting bins in non-decreasing order by the number of items in a bin.

Case 1. For one-item bins $\mathcal{B}^1$. Based on Proposition 1, there exists at most one bin B_0^1 belonging to $\mathcal{B}^1$ such that $s(B_0^1) \leq 1/2$. Thus,

$$w(B) = \frac{6}{5} \cdot s(B) + v(B) > \frac{6}{5} \cdot \frac{1}{2} + \frac{4}{10} = 1, \quad \forall B \in \mathcal{B}^1 \backslash B_0^1,$$

implying that

$$w(\mathcal{B}^1) = \sum_{B \in \mathcal{B}^1} w(B) \geq |\mathcal{B}^1| - 1.$$

Case 2. For two-item bins $\mathcal{B}^2$. Based on Proposition 1, there exists at most one bin B_0^2 belonging to $\mathcal{B}^2$ such that $s(B_0^2) \leq 2/3$. Let $B_1, B_2 = \{a_1, a_2\}$ be two bins in $\mathcal{B}^2 \backslash B_0^2$. Without loss of generality, assume that B_1 is arranged before B_2 in the order of NE and $s(B_1) \geq s(B_2)$. Note that $s(B_1), s(B_2) > 2/3$.

(1) If $s(B_1) \geq 5/6$, then we have

$$\frac{6}{5} s(B_1) + v(B_2) \geq \frac{6}{5} \cdot \frac{5}{6} = 1.$$

(2) If $s(B_1) < 5/6$, assume that $s(B_1) = 5/6 - x$, $x \in (0, 1/6)$. By Proposition 1, we obtain

$$s(a_1), s(a_2) > 1 - s(B_1) = \frac{1}{6} + x.$$

Then

$$v(a_i) \geq \frac{3}{5}\left(s(a_i) - \frac{1}{6}\right) > \frac{3}{5}\left(\frac{1}{6} + x - \frac{1}{6}\right) = \frac{3}{5} \cdot x, \quad i = 1, 2.$$

Thus we have

$$\frac{6}{5} s(B_1) + v(B_2) \geq \frac{6}{5}\left(\frac{5}{6} - x\right) + \frac{3}{5} \cdot x \cdot 2 = 1,$$

implying that

$$w(\mathcal{B}^2) = \sum_{B \in \mathcal{B}^2} s(B) + v(B) \geq \sum_{i=1, B_i \in \mathcal{B}^2}^{|\mathcal{B}^2|-1} s(B_i) + v(B_{i+1}) \geq |\mathcal{B}^2| - 2.$$

Case 3. For three-item bins $\mathcal{B}^3$. Based on Proposition 1, there exists at most one bin B_0^3 belonging to $\mathcal{B}^3$ such that $s(B_0^3) \leq 3/4$. Let $B = \{a_1, a_2, a_3\}$ be any bin belonging to $\mathcal{B}^3 \backslash B_0^3$. Note that $s(B) > 3/4$.

Based on the case-by-case analysis analogous to the proof of Lemma 2, we obtain that $w(B) \geq 1$.

Thus, we obtain

$$w(\mathcal{B}^3) \geq |\mathcal{B}^3| - 1.$$

Case 4. For four-item bins $\mathcal{B}^4$. Based on Proposition 1, there exists at most one bin B_0^4 belonging to $\mathcal{B}^4$ such that $s(B_0^4) \leq 4/5$. Let $B = \{a_1, a_2, a_3, a_4\}$ be any bin belonging to $\mathcal{B}^4 \backslash B_0^4$. Note that $s(B) > 4/5$.

Also by similar analysis as in Case 3, we have $w(B) \geq 1$.

Thus, we obtain

$$w(\mathcal{B}^4) \geq |\mathcal{B}^4| - 1.$$

Case 5. For five-plus-item bins $\mathcal{B}^j$, $5 \leq j \leq n_0 - 1$. Based on Proposition 1, there exists at most one bin B_0^j belonging to $\mathcal{B}^j$ such that $s(B_0^j) \leq j/(j+1)$. Let $B = \{a_1, \cdots, a_j\}$ be any bin belonging to $\mathcal{B}^j \backslash B_0^j$. Note that $s(B) > j/(j+1) \geq 5/6$. We have

$$w(B) = \frac{6}{5}s(B) + v(B) > \frac{6}{5} \cdot \frac{5}{6} = 1.$$

Then

$$w(\mathcal{B}^j) \geq |\mathcal{B}^j| - 1, \quad 5 \leq j \leq n_0 - 1.$$

In summary,

$$w(\mathcal{I}) = \sum_{i=1}^{n_0-1} w(\mathcal{B}^i) \geq \sum_{i=1}^{n_0-1} |\mathcal{B}^i| - n_0 = NE(\mathcal{M}_\mathcal{I}^\flat) - n_0.$$

$\square$

5.2   Lower Bound of PoA

Given an instance of selfish bin packing with $s(a_i) \in (1/n_0, 1] (i = 1, 2, \cdots, n)$, where n_0 is an arbitrary large integer. In this subsection, we discuss the lower bound of *PoA* for the IM-based mechanism.

Theorem 4. *For any instance $\mathcal{I}$ with $s(a_{\min}) > 1/n_0$, we show that under the IM-based mechanism $\mathcal{M}^\flat$,*

$$PoA(\mathcal{M}^\flat) \geq \frac{211}{130} > 1.623.$$

Proof. Consider the following instance: let N be an arbitrary large integer and let $\varepsilon = 1/N$,

$$\mathcal{I} = \left(\frac{1}{2} + \varepsilon, N\right), \left(\frac{1}{4} + \varepsilon, N\right), \left(\frac{1}{6} + \varepsilon, N\right), \left(\frac{1}{13} + \varepsilon, N\right), \left(\frac{1}{156} - 4\varepsilon, N\right),$$

which corresponding to five types of items: type I, II, III, IV, and V. Note that the first number in (,) is the size, second one is the number of items occurred.

NE:

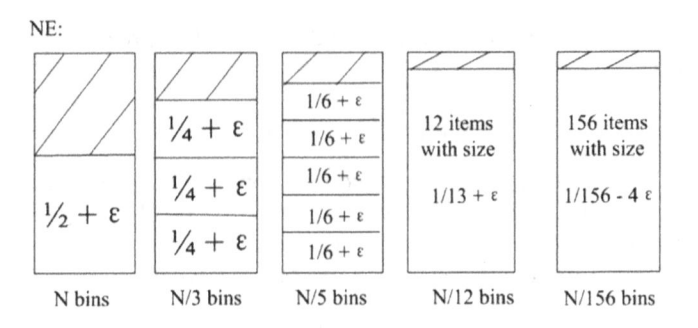

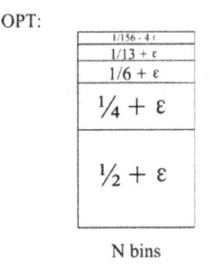

Fig. 2. A worst case of IM-based mechanism $\mathcal{M}^\flat$ while $s(a_{\min}) > 1/n_0$.

We present an NE packing that consists of $211/130 \cdot N$ bins as illustrated in Fig. 2. All these bins can be divided into five types: type 1, 2, 3, 4, and 5. More exactly, Each type-I item monopoly occupies one bin; Every three type-II items share one same bin; Every five type-III items share one same bin; Every 12 type-IV items share one same bin; Every 156 type-V items share one same bin. Clearly, no item can benefit by moving alone under this packing:

(1) Each type-I item can not move to other bins since the capacity constraint;
(2) Each type-II item can not move to other type 2–5 bins since the capacity constraint and each type-II item would not like to move to type-1 bins since its payoff will change from $6/4 + 6\varepsilon$ to $5/4 + 5\varepsilon$ (decreasing);
(3) Each type-III item can not move to other type 3–5 bins since the capacity constraint and type-III item would not like to move to type-1 or type-2 bins since its payoff will change from $20/12 + 10\varepsilon$ to at most $19/12 + 8\varepsilon$ (decreasing);
(4) Each type-IV item can not move to other type 4 or type 5 bins since the capacity constraint and type-IV item would not like to move to type 1–3 bins since its payoff will change from $144/78 + 24\varepsilon$ to at most $107/78 + 12\varepsilon$ (decreasing);
(5) Each type-V item would not like to move to other bins since it currently stays in the bin with the largest size and the most number of items.

However, the optimal packing (showed in Fig. 2), only consumes N bins, in which each bin is full and consists of five items that belongs to five different types. Therefore,

$$PoA(\mathcal{M}^b) \geq \frac{211}{130} > 1.623.$$

$\square$

6 Conclusion and Extension

In this paper, we present an interest-matrix-based mechanism for selfish bin packing that focuses on the interest or the satisfaction between each pair of items rather than the sharing cost. Under this mechanism, we show that for a general case where $s(a_{\min}) > 1/n_0$ (n_0 is an larger integer), the PoA falls into the interval $[1.623, 1.7]$. Specially, when $n_0 = 4$, the $PoA \in [1.333, 1.5]$. Based on our discussion, there are still several open problems.

1. When the smallest item's size tends to zero, i.e., $n_0 \to \infty$ is not a fixed number, is the upper bound of PoA still 1.7?
2. Does there exist any more incentive mechanism with interest matrix for selfish bin packing?
3. Is it possible to consider a new social goal, such as the total interest of all items? Correspondingly, is it desirable to discuss the PoA that is the ratio between the total interest that derives from the worst NE and the optimal solution?

References

1. Bilò, V.: On the packing of selfish items. In: Proceedings 20th IEEE International Parallel & Distributed Processing Symposium. IEEE (2006)
2. Chen, X., Nong, Q., Fang, Q.: An improved mechanism for selfish bin packing. In: Gao, X., Du, H., Han, M. (eds.) COCOA 2017. LNCS, vol. 10628, pp. 241–257. Springer, Cham (2017). https://doi.org/10.1007/978-3-319-71147-8_17
3. Dósa, G., Epstein, L.: Generalized selfish bin packing. arXiv preprint arXiv:1202.4080 (2012)
4. Epstein, L., Kleiman, E.: Selfish bin packing. Algorithmica 60(2), 368–394 (2011)
5. Epstein, L., Kleiman, E., Mestre, J.: Parametric packing of selfish items and the subset sum algorithm. Algorithmica 74(1), 177–207 (2016)
6. Johnson, D.S., Demers, A., Ullman, J.D.: Worst-case performance bounds for simple one-dimensional packing algorithms. SIAM J. Comput. 3(4), 299–325 (1974)
7. Koutsoupias, E., Papadimitriou, C.: Worst-case equilibria. In: Meinel, C., Tison, S. (eds.) STACS 1999. LNCS, vol. 1563, pp. 404–413. Springer, Heidelberg (1999). https://doi.org/10.1007/3-540-49116-3_38
8. Ma, R., Dósa, G., Han, X.: A note on a selfish bin packing problem. J. Glob. Optim. 56(4), 1457–1462 (2013)
9. Nash, J.: Non-cooperative games. Ann. Math. 286–295 (1951)
10. Nisan, N., Roughgarden, T., Tardos, E., Vazirani, V.V.: Algorithmic Game Theory. Cambridge University Press, Cambridge (2007)

11. Nong, Q.Q., Sun, T., Cheng, T.C.E., Fang, Q.Z.: Bin packing game with a price of anarchy 3/2. J. Comb. Optim. **35**(2), 632–640 (2018)
12. Roughgarden, T.: Selfish Routing and the Price of Anarchy. MIT Press, Cambridge (2005)
13. Ulman, J.D.: The performance of a memory allocation algorithm. Technical report 100, Princeton University, Princeton NJ (1971)
14. Wang, Z., Han, X., Dósa, G., et al.: A general bin packing game: interest taken into account. Algorithmica 1–22 (2017)
15. Yu, G., Zhang, G.: Bin packing of selfish items. In: Papadimitriou, C., Zhang, S. (eds.) WINE 2008. LNCS, vol. 5385, pp. 446–453. Springer, Heidelberg (2008). https://doi.org/10.1007/978-3-540-92185-1_50

Connected [1,2]-Sets in Graphs

Chao Zhang[2] [ID] and Chengye Zhao[1]([✉]) [ID]

[1] College of Science, China Jiliang University, Hangzhou 310018, China
cyzhao@cjlu.edu.cn
[2] Department of Basic Courses, Nanjing Tech University Pujiang Institute,
Nanjing 211134, China

Abstract. A subset $S \subseteq V(G)$ in a graph $G = (V, E)$ is a connected $[j, k]$-set, if it satisfies that $G[S]$ is a connected subgraph of G and every vertex $v \in V \setminus S$, $j \leq |N(v) \cap S| \leq k$ for non-negative integers $j < k$. In this paper, we study the connected [1, 2]-domination number of graph G, which denoted $\gamma_{c[1,2]}(G)$. We discussed the graphs with $\gamma_{c[1,2]}(G) = n$ and the graphs with $\gamma_{c[1,2]}(G) = \gamma_c(G)$. In the end, the CONNECTED [1, 2]-SET Problem has been proved to be NP-complete for bipartite graphs.

Keywords: [1, 2]-set · Connected [1, 2]-set · NP-complete

1 Introduction

Let $G = (V, E)$ be a simple connected graph with vertex set $V(G)$, edge set $E(G)$, and *order* $n = |V(G)|$, *size* $m = |E(G)|$. The *neighborhood*, and *closed neighborhood*, *degree* of a vertex v in G are respectively denoted by $N(v) = \{u \in V(G)|uv \in E(G)\}$, $N[v] = N(v) \cup \{v\}$, and $d(v) = |N(v)|$. Each vertex in $N(v)$ is called a neighbor of v, a vertex v called a *leaf* if $deg(v) = 1$ and its neighbor is called a *support vertex*. The *minimum degree* of G is $\delta(G) = min_{v \in V(G)}\{d(v)\}$ and the *maximum degree* is $\Delta(G) = max_{v \in V(G)}\{d(v)\}$. The *open neighborhood* of a set $S \subseteq V(G)$ is $N(S) = \bigcup_{v \in S} N(v)$, while the *closed neighborhood* of a set S is the set $N[S] = \bigcup_{v \in S} N[v]$. The graph induced by S in G is the subgraph $G[S]$. We consider undirected finite simple graphs only, and refer to [1] for undefined notations and terminology.

A set $S \subseteq V(G)$ is a *dominating set* for G if every vertex of G either belongs to S or is adjacent to a vertex of S. The *domination number* $\gamma(G)$ is the minimum cardinality of a dominating set, and the minimum dominating set also marked as $\gamma(G)$-set. A dominating set for G is a *connected dominating set* if it induces a connected subgraph of G. The minimum cardinality of a connected dominating set for G is called the *connected domination number* of G and is denoted by $\gamma_c(G)$ [3], and the minimum connected dominating set is $\gamma_c(G)$-set.

Supported by Natural science fundation of Zhejiang province (No. LY14F020040), Natural Science Foundation of China (No. 61173002)and Natural Science Foundation of Jiangsu University (No. 16KJB110011).

L. Li et al. (Eds.): NCTCS 2018, CCIS 882, pp. 93–98, 2018.
https://doi.org/10.1007/978-981-13-2712-4_7

A set $S \subseteq V(G)$ in G is called a $[j,k]$-set if for every vertex $v \in V(G) \setminus S$, $j \leq |N(v) \cap S| \leq k$, that is every vertex in $V(G) \setminus S$ is adjacent to at least j vertices, but not more than k vertices in S. So we get the $[j,k]$-set S is a dominating set for $j \geq 1$. The $[j,k]$-sets of graphs mainly studied in references [2,4].

Definition 1. A set $S \subseteq V(G)$ in G is called a *connected $[j,k]$-set* if it satisfies that $G[S]$ is both a connected subgraph of G and a $[j,k]$-set. The *connected $[i,j]$-domination number* is the minimum cardinality of S, denoted by $\gamma_{c[i,j]}(G)$.

In this paper, we mainly study connected [1,2]-sets of graph G. In Sect. 2, we discuss the graphs G with $\gamma_{c[1,2]}(G) = \gamma_c(G)$ and the graphs with $\gamma_{c[1,2]}(G) = n$. In Sect. 3, we prove that Connected [1, 2]-Set Problem in bipartite graphs is NP-complete. In the end, we pose some open problems.

Note that the graph mentions in the following text refers to a connected graph.

2   Bounds

Every connected graph G has a connected [1,2]-set S, for every vertex $v \in V \setminus S$, $1 \leq |N(v) \cap S| \leq 2$. A connected [1,2]-set of graph G is a connected dominating set of graph G. Hence, we have

Theorem 1. *For any connected graph of order n, $\gamma_c(G) \leq \gamma_{c[1,2]}(G) \leq n$.*

Next we consider the sharpness of these bounds.

2.1   For Which Graphs G is $\gamma_c(G) = \gamma_{c[1,2]}(G)$?

Theorem 2. *If G have maximum degree $\Delta(G) \leq 2$, then $\gamma_c(G) = \gamma_{c[1,2]}(G)$.*

Proof. Note that $\gamma_c(G)$-set S is the $\gamma_{c[1,2]}(G)$-set. Since the graphs has maximum degree $\Delta(G) \leq 2$, there is not a vertex in $V \setminus S$ be adjacent to more than 2 vertices in S, so we have $\gamma_c(G) = \gamma_{c[1,2]}(G)$.

Corollary 1. *For paths $G = P_n$ or cycles $G = C_n$, $\gamma_c(G) = \gamma_{c[1,2]}(G)$.*

Proof. This follows from Theorem 2, the path or cycle is with $\Delta(G) \leq 2$.

Proposition 1. *If every vertex v of a graph G of order $n \geq 2$ is either a support vertex or has degree at most 2, then $\gamma_c(G) = \gamma_{c[1,2]}(G)$.*

Proof. Let S to be any $\gamma_c(G)$-set containing all the support vertices of G and some vertices of degree 2 which are adjacent to the support vertices. Then every vertex in $V \setminus S$ has one or two neighbors in S. So, S is a $[1, 2]$-set of G, $\gamma_{c[1,2]}(G) \leq |S| = \gamma_c(G)$.

A tree for which the removal of all its leaves results in a path is called a caterpillar. Every vertex in a caterpillar is either a support vertex or has degree at most 2, by Proposition 1, we have

Corollary 2. *If G is a caterpillar which is a tree for removing of all its leaves results in a path, then $\gamma_c(G) = \gamma_{c[1,2]}(G)$.*

The corona $G \circ K_1$ is the graph obtained from a graph $G = (V, E)$ by attaching a leaf to each vertex $v \in V$, similarly, $G \circ K_2$ is by attaching a complete graph K_2 to each vertex $v \in V$.

Corollary 3. *If G is a corona $H \circ K_1$ or $H \circ K_2$, then $\gamma_c(G) = \gamma_{c[1,2]}(G)$.*

Proof. This follows from Proposition 1, since every vertex in a corona $H \circ K_1$ is either a support vertex or a leaf. In corona $H \circ K_2$, all the vertices in H construct a $\gamma_c(G)$-set S, and S is also a $\gamma_{c[1,2]}(G)$-set of G, so $\gamma_c(G) = \gamma_{c[1,2]}(G)$.

Theorem 3. *If T is a tree, then $\gamma_c(T) = \gamma_{c[1,2]}(T)$.*

Proof. For a graph G with order n, $\gamma_c(G) = n - l(G)$, and $l(G)$ is the maximum number of leaves in a spanning tree of G. A spanning tree of a tree T is itself, so $\gamma_c(T) = n - l(T)$. Let S be a γ_c-set of tree T, then every vertex in $V \backslash S$ is a leaf of tree T and adjacent to one vertex of S. Hence S is also a $\gamma_{c[1,2]}$-set, and $\gamma_c(G) = \gamma_{c[1,2]}(G)$.

Theorem 4. *If $\Delta(G) = n-1$ or there are two vertices u, v such that $uv \in E(G)$ and $N[u] \cup N[v] = V(G)$, then $\gamma_c(G) = \gamma_{c[1,2]}(G)$.*

Proof. If $\Delta(G) = n - 1$, then $\gamma_c(G) = \gamma_{c[1,2]}(G) = 1$. If there are two vertices u, v such that $uv \in E(G)$ and $N[u] \cup N[v] = V(G)$, then $\gamma_c(G) = \gamma_{c[1,2]}(G) = 2$.

Corollary 4. $\gamma_c(K_n) = \gamma_{c[1,2]}(K_n)$, $\gamma_c(K_{n,m}) = \gamma_{c[1,2]}(K_{n,m})$.

Corollary 5. *If G is a connected graph with $\Delta(G) = n - 2$, then $\gamma_c(G) = \gamma_{c[1,2]}(G)$.*

Proof. $\Delta(G) = n - 2$. Let $deg(u) = n - 2$, and $V \backslash N[u] = \{w\}$. Since G is connected, there is a vertex v such that v is adjacent to w. Then $uv \in E(G)$ and $N[u] \cup N[v] = V(G)$. By Theorem 4, $\gamma_c(G) = \gamma_{c[1,2]}(G)$.

In general, $\gamma_c(G) \leq \gamma_{c[1,2]}(G)$, we consider a problem that the upper bound of difference between $\gamma_c(G)$ and $\gamma_{c[1,2]}(G)$. We construct a class of graphs G_k as below (shown in Fig. 1):

Let $V(G_k) = \bigcup_{i=1}^{k} V_i, E(G_k) = (\bigcup_{i=1}^{k} E_i) \bigcup (\bigcup_{i=1}^{k-1} \{u_5^i u_1^{i+1}\})$;
$V_i = \{u_j^i : 0 \leq j \leq 5\}, 1 \leq i \leq k$;
$E_i = \{u_0^i u_2^i, u_0^i u_3^i, u_0^i u_4^i, u_j^i u_{j+1}^i : 1 \leq j \leq 4\}, 1 \leq i \leq k$.
By the definitions of γ_c-set and $\gamma_{c[1,2]}$-set, we have

Proposition 2. $\gamma_c(G_k) = 5k - 2$ and $\gamma_{c[1,2]}(G_k) = 6k - 2$.

So, we have

Theorem 5. *There is a class of graphs G_k such that $\gamma_{c[1,2]}(G_k) - \gamma_c(G_k) = k$, k is an arbitrary integer.*

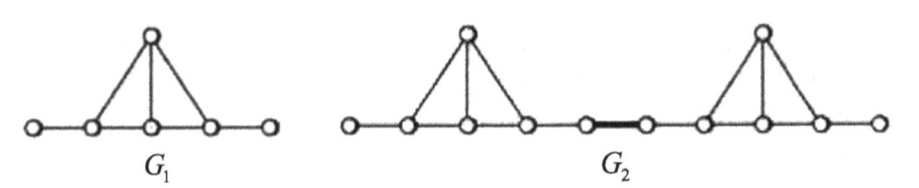

Fig. 1. G_1 and G_2

2.2 For Which Graphs G is $\gamma_{c[1,2]}(G) = n$?

By the definition the [1,2]-domination number and connected [1,2]-domination number, we have

Theorem 6. *For any connected graph of order n, $\gamma_{[1,2]}(G) \leq \gamma_{c[1,2]}(G) \leq n$.*

Theorem 7. *For the graph G with order n, if $\gamma_{[1,2]}(G) = n$, then $\gamma_{c[1,2]}(G) = n$.*

Proof. Let $\gamma_{[1,2]}(G) = n$. By Theorem 6, $n = \gamma_{[1,2]}(G) \leq \gamma_{c[1,2]}(G) \leq n$, then $\gamma_{c[1,2]}(G) = n$.

Let p and k be two integers with $p \geq k+2$. Let $G_{p,k}$ be the graph obtained from a complete graph K_p as follows. For every k-element subset S of the vertices $V(K_p)$, we add a new vertex x_S and the edges $x_S u$ for all $u \in S$. Note that the total number of added vertices is $\binom{p}{k}$, and the number of added edges is $k\binom{p}{k}$. Yang et al. [4] remark that the result of the following theorem for k = 3 is due to Chellali et al. [2].

Theorem 8. *Let p and k be two integers, and $G_{p,k}$ be the graph of order n in the above construction. If $p \geq k+2$ and $k \geq 3$, then $\gamma_{[1,2]}(G_{p,k}) = |V(G_{p,k})| = n$.*

By Theorems 7 and 8, we have

Corollary 6. *Let p and k be two integers, and $G_{p,k}$ be the graph of order n in the above construction. If $p \geq k+2$ and $k \geq 3$, then $\gamma_{c[1,2]}(G_{p,k}) = |V(G_{p,k})| = n$.*

Yang et al. [4] discussed the planar graph, bipartite graphs and triangle-free graphs with $\gamma_{[1,2]}(G) = n$. Obviously, $\gamma_{c[1,2]}(G) = n$ for these graphs G.

Is there a graph such that $\gamma_{[1,2]}(G) < n$ and $\gamma_{c[1,2]}(G) = n$? The answer is positive.

Let G_1 and G_2 be the graph with $\gamma_{c[1,2]}(G_1) = n_1$ and $\gamma_{c[1,2]}(G_2) = n_2$, here, n_1 and n_2 are orders of G_1 and G_2. To connect one vertex of G_1 and one vertex of G_2 by a path P_m, we obtain a class of graph H with order n. By definition of the connected [1,2]-domination number, we have

Theorem 9. $\gamma_{c[1,2]}(H) = |V(H)| = n$.

Proof. Since $\gamma_{c[1,2]}(P_m) = \gamma_c(P_m)$, Obviously $\gamma_{c[1,2]}(H) = n$.

For the path P_m, if $m \geq 3$, then $\gamma_{[1,2]}(H) < n$.

3   Complexity

Chellali et al. [2] discussed the complexity of [1,2]-SET Problem, and we consider CONNECTED [1,2]-SET Problem as below.

Set-Cover: Given a collection C of subsets of a base set X and a positive integer $k \leq |X|$, determine whether C contains a set cover with cardinality at most k, where a set cover is a subcollection C' of C such that every element of X appears in at least one subset in C'.

Set-Cover is a well-known NP-complete problem, by constructing a reduction from it to Min-CDS (Minimum-Connected Dominating Set Problem). We know Min-CDS is a NP-hard problem. Assume the cardinality of arbitrary element of C is 3, then $k = \lceil |X|/3 \rceil$. So we get another problem.

Exact 3-Cover (X3C): A finite set X with $|X| = 3q$ and a collection C of 3-element subsets of X, is there a subcollection C' of C such that every element of X appears in exactly one element of C'?

Exact 3-Cover is a NP-complete problem, and we defined the CONNECTED [1,2]-SET Problem as follows.

CONNECTED [1,2]-SET: For connected graph $G = (V, E)$, positive integer $k \leq |V|$, does G have a connected $[1, 2]$-set of cardinality at most k?

Theorem 10. *CONNECTED [1,2]-SET Problem is NP-complete for bipartite graphs.*

Proof. [1,2]-SET Problem is NP-complete, since it is easy to verify a yes instance of Connected [1,2]-Set in polynomial time. We can construct a reduction from Exact 3-Cover to Connected [1,2]-Set of G.

Let $X = \{x_1, x_2, \ldots, x_{3q}\}$ and $C = \{C_1, C_2, \ldots, C_t\}$ be an arbitrary instance of X3C. For input collection X and C we first construct a bipartite graph G. For each $C_j \in C$, we built a vertex u_j, and add two vertices v, w, and v is adjacent to w and every u_j for $j = 1, 2, \ldots, t$. Add new vertices $x_1, x_2, \ldots, x_{3q}$ and edges $x_i u_j$ if $x_i \in C_j$, $i = 1, 2, \ldots, 3q$. Thus, we get a bipartite graph G with $t + 3q + 2$. Let $k = q + 1$.

Suppose that the instance X, C of X3C has a solution C'. Then the vertices u_j with labels in C', that is every u_j for each $x_i \in C'$, together with v form a Connected [1,2]-Set S in graph G. Since the cardinality of C' is precisely q, and so $|S| = q + 1 = k$.

Conversely, suppose that G has a Connected [1,2]-Set S with $|S| \leq q+1 = k$. Note that S must contains vertex v in order to dominating w. Also, for each x_i, S contains either x_i or some u_r adjacent to x_i. Now, since each u_j dominates only three vertices of $\{x_1, x_2, \ldots, x_{3q}\}$, it follows that we need at least q additional vertices in S to dominate the set X. Hence, $|S| \geq q + 1 = k$, and we have $|S| = q + 1 = k$. Therefore, $C' = \{C_j | u_j \in S\}$ is an exact cover for C.

4 Open Questions

The most problems in the reference [2] can discuss on the connected [1,2]-sets of graphs, we only select some problems as below:

Question 1. Let G be a graph of order n, how to determine bounds on $\gamma_{c[1,2]}(G)$?

Question 2. Is there a polynomial algorithm for deciding if $\gamma_{c[1,2]}(G) < n$?

Question 3. Can you characterize a class of graphs G with $\gamma_{c[1,2]}(G) \leq n-k$, determine the bound of k.

Question 4. Is it true for grid graphs G that $\gamma_c(G) = \gamma_{c[1,2]}(G)$?

References

1. Bondy, J.A., Murty, U.S.R.: Graph Theory with Applications. Macmillan, London (2008)
2. Chellali, M., Haynes, T.W., Hedetniemi, S.T., McRae, A.: [1,2]-sets in graphs. Discret. Appl. Math. **161**, 2885–2893 (2013)
3. Sampathkumar, E., Walikar, H.B.: The Connected domination number of a graph. J. Math. Phys. Sci. **13**, 607–613 (1979)
4. Yang, X., Wu, B.: [1,2]-domination in graphs. Discret. Appl. Math. **175**, 79–86 (2014)

Study of Multilevel Parallel Algorithm of KPCA for Hyperspectral Images

Rulin Xu$^{(\boxtimes)}$, Chang Gao, and Jingfei Jiang

School of Computer, National University of Defense Technology, Changsha, China
xurulin@gmail.com, gaochangjiyi@126.com, jingfeijiang@126.com

Abstract. Hyperspectral remote sensing image data has been widely used in a variety of applications due to its continuous spectrum and high spectral resolution. However, reducing huge dimensions with high data relevance is time-consuming, and parallel processing is required to accelerate this process. In the previous work, the KPCA (Kernel Principal Component Analysis), a nonlinear dimensionality reduction method was studied, and a parallel KPCA algorithm was proposed based on heterogeneous system with a single GPU, and achieved the desired experimental results. However, as data scale grows, the proposed solution would consume all the available memory on a single node and encounter performance bottleneck. Therefore, to tackle the limitation of insufficient memory caused by the reduction of large-scale hyperspectral data dimension, in this paper the intra-node parallelization using multi-core CPUs and many-core GPUs are exploited to improve the parallel hierarchy of distributed-storage KPCA. Finally, we designed and implemented a multilevel hybrid parallel KPCA algorithm that achieves 2.75–9.27 times speedup compared to the traditional coarse-grained parallel KPCA method on MPI.

Keywords: Hyperspectral image · Nonlinear dimensionality reduction
KPCA · GPU · Heterogeneous system · Multilevel parallel

1 Introduction

Hyperspectral remote sensing exploits the imaging spectrometer to obtain many continuous-spectrum features image with nanometer resolution. With the spatial information, radiation information and spectral information integrated, hyperspectral remote sensing is used in a wide array of applications, including geography, biology, agriculture, forestry, marine science, space exploration, anti-terrorism, and military etc [1].

Evolving from traditional two-dimensional images, hyperspectral remote sensing images introduce the spectral dimension to form a three-dimensional hyperspectral data cube. Continuous feature spectrum information can effectively distinguish spectral characteristic of surface material and excavate the hidden information. However, it also has many problems: (1) high resolution

© Springer Nature Singapore Pte Ltd. 2018
L. Li et al. (Eds.): NCTCS 2018, CCIS 882, pp. 99–115, 2018.
https://doi.org/10.1007/978-981-13-2712-4_8

leads to high correlation between continuous bands and weakens the characteristics of different ground target classifications, thus impairing the classification accuracy; (2) tremendous information redundancy brings great challenges to reduce the time and space complexity of execution. In view of above issues, hyperspectral data dimensionality reduction is proposed, which is crucial part of hyperspectral image analysis.

Dimensionality reduction is a large-scale and computation-intensive task. The traditional serial processing method is time-consuming and computationally complex, which makes it difficult to apply to real problems. With the rapid development of parallel processing, it has become a predominant strategy to design efficient parallel algorithms that make the best of hardware resources to solve many scientific computing problems. The combination of the dimensionality reduction method and the advanced parallel technology not only brings tremendous performance benefits, but also helps to expand business scale without causing additional costs.

The common dimension reduction methods fall into two categories: linear dimensionality reduction and nonlinear dimensionality reduction. In comparison, the former's result is composed of finite parameters, making it convenient and intuitive to explain the data composition. However, there could be some nonlinear data clusters in the hyperspectral image, on which applying linear processing will cause original characteristic loss and result in the hyperspectral data ineffectiveness. The results in [2] prove that the nonlinear dimension reduction technique is appropriate for data with nonlinear features such as hyperspectral image. However, due to the high computational complexity, long elapsed time and insufficient running space, it is difficult to apply nonlinear methods to massive hyperspectral data.

The kernel-based dimension reduction algorithm is an important branch of the nonlinear dimension-descending algorithm family. Based on the Gaussian kernel and Principal Component Analysis, the KPCA (Kernel Principal Component Analysis) algorithm was initially proposed in the kernel-based dimensionality reduction field, where it has solid theoretical basis and significant application prospects. Hence, its parallelization is of great importance in hyperspectral processing field.

In our previous work [3], we proposed a parallel KPCA algorithm (KPCA_G) based on CPU/GPU heterogeneous system with a single GPU, which achieved good parallel performance. However with the further study, we find that as data scale grows, the proposed solution would consume all the available memory on a single node and encounter performance bottleneck. Therefore, in this paper we are focused on intra-node parallelization and performance optimization of KPCA algorithm, and the content is organized as follows: The second section discusses the related work. The third section briefly describes the KPCA algorithm and pinpoints the accelerating hotspot. In the fourth section, our previous work on single GPU is introduced briefly. In the fifth section, inspired by the multi-level cooperative parallel technology and optimization strategy based on CPU/GPU heterogeneous system, we realize the distributed-storage

KPCA algorithm (KPCA_M) and multilevel parallel algorithms (KPCA_M_O and KPCA_M_O_G). These methods provide effective solutions especially for large-scale hyperspectral data nonlinear dimensionality reduction. Section 6 explores the performance improvements of different parallel algorithms through extensive experiments. The last section provides a summary and some outlooks.

2 Related Work

In recent years, parallel computing on CPU/GPU heterogeneous systems has emerged in the field of hyperspectral remote sensing image processing. Bernabe [4] designed a parallel automatic target detection algorithm (ATDCA) on the GPU platform to meet the real-time processing demands. In some domain of hyperspectral applications, such as feature target detection and anomaly identification [5], the parallel design of algorithms on GPU has become key technology and is widely applied. Agathos [6] and Torti [7] employed the GPU and realized a parallel hyperspectral unmixing algorithm, which handles the tremendous complex computing tasks. For processing larger scale of data, Sanchez [8] achieved real-time hyperspectral unmixing using a GPU cluster. On the other hand, Keymeulen [9] and Santos [10] accelerated hyperspectral image lossless and lossy compression algorithm on GPU respectively; ElMaghrbay [11] proposed a fast GPU algorithm for extracting hyperspectral image features.

As for linear dimensionality reduction of hyperspectral image, Fang [12] proposed a parallel principal component analysis (PCA) algorithm, which obtained 128 times speedup on two GPUs. In the same year, Fang [13] implemented a three-level hybrid parallel FastICA algorithm for hyperspectral image dimensionality reduction on a CPU/GPU heterogeneous system. This method gained 159 times performance speedup, in which the computation component got accelerated by 169 times. Wu [14] improved the maximum noise fractional transform (MNF) algorithm and implemented a GPU-based G-OMNF algorithm. As for nonlinear method, Gao [3] gave a parallel KPCA algorithm based on single GPU platform, which achieved up to 173x speedup over the original serial KPCA.

In summary, GPUs have been used to facilitate the speed of various hyperspectral algorithms due to their powerful computing ability and memory bandwidth, and they gradually become a research and development trend in hyperspectral remote sensing. Regarding the hyperspectral dimensionality reduction, parallel research of the linear algorithm has become more sophisticated, while the parallelization of the nonlinear dimensionality reduction algorithm is still in the infancy and exploration stage. To fill in the gaps, this paper proposes new parallel algorithms and provides performance optimization on the heterogeneous system with multiple CPUs and GPUs.

3 KPCA Algorithm and the Analysis of Hot Spot

Through implicit space transformation, KPCA algorithm maps the original data onto an infinite-dimensional Hilbert Space. The results will have linear properties and the PCA procedure can be applied to extract features hereafter [15]. For the convenience of presentation, we Define the HSI data set as $\boldsymbol{X} = \{\boldsymbol{X}_1, \boldsymbol{X}_2, \cdots \boldsymbol{X}_I\} = \{\boldsymbol{Y}_1, \boldsymbol{Y}_2, \cdots \boldsymbol{Y}_B\}^{\mathrm{T}}$ (in which $I = W \times H$, W and H are spatial dimensions, and B denotes the spectral dimension). Actually, $\boldsymbol{X}$ can be expressed by a three-dimensional data cube extracted from B images and has a size of $W \times H$. After dimensionality reduction, m (m < B) features are extracted from B original spectral bands. The KPCA approach conceptually involves four steps:

(1) Compute the Gaussian kernel matrix $\boldsymbol{K} = Gauss(\boldsymbol{X})$ and get the centering matrix $\boldsymbol{K}_L = Gaussmodify(\boldsymbol{K})$;
(2) Perform matrix eigenvalue decomposition of $\boldsymbol{K}_L$: $\boldsymbol{V}^{-1}\boldsymbol{K}_L\boldsymbol{V} = \boldsymbol{\Lambda}$, where $\boldsymbol{\Lambda}$ ($diag\{\lambda_1, \lambda_2, \cdots, \lambda_I\}$) is a diagonal matrix, $\boldsymbol{V} = \{v_1, v_2 \cdots, v_I\}$ denotes eigenvalue matrix and v_i represents i^{th} eigenvector that satisfies the condition of $\lambda_i (v_i \cdot v_i) = 1$;
(3) Sort eigenvalues $\{\lambda_1, \lambda_2, \cdots, \lambda_I\}$ in descending order and rearrange eigenvectors in accordance with the eigenvalues' new sequence. Select the first m eigenvectors to form $\boldsymbol{V}_m$;
(4) Execute the KPCA mapping according to the function $\boldsymbol{P} = \boldsymbol{K}_L\boldsymbol{V}_m^T$.

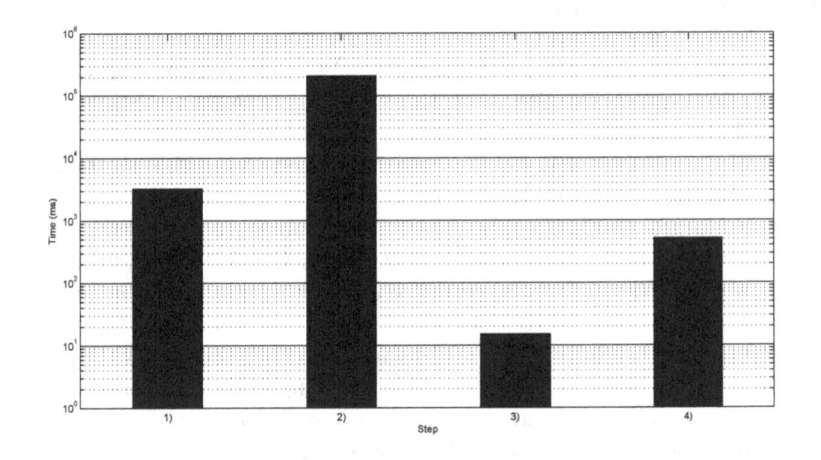

Fig. 1. The elapse time of all steps in serial KPCA.

We have implemented the serial KPCA algorithm according to the above steps, in which the Bilateral Jacobi Iteration is applied to conduct symmetric matrix eigenvalue decomposition. In our implementation, the termination of the Jacobi iteration is when the maximum absolute value is smaller than the setting accuracy (e.g. $ep = 0.001$).

When profiling the algorithm, we cut out a segment with size of 32 * 32 * 224 from the hyperspectral image to excavate its acceleration module. As shown in Fig. 1 (see Fig. 1), Jacobi Iteration, calculating Gaussian kernel matrix and KPCA mapping, which are denoted by step (2), (1) and (4), are the critical bottlenecks.

4   A GPU-Based Parallel KPCA Algorithm

In this section, we briefly present the previous research on parallel design and performance optimization of KPCA algorithm on many-core GPU platform. And here is focused on program design and optimization strategy of Jacobi iteration, which is the main hotspot of KPCA. The details could be found in [3].

4.1   Design and Optimization of Jacobi Iteration on GPU

The Jacobi iteration method reduces the non-diagonal elements of the symmetric matrix KL to zero by plane rotation (Givens transformation). The transformation equation is:

$$(\boldsymbol{Q}_k^T...(\boldsymbol{Q}_1^T \boldsymbol{K}_L \boldsymbol{Q}_1)...\boldsymbol{Q}_k) = \boldsymbol{\Lambda} \tag{1}$$

Matrix $\boldsymbol{Q}_i$ represents the Givens transformation matrix. Givens transformation is an orthogonal similarity transformation. The rotation transformation matrix is shown in Eq. 2, in which p and q indicate the number of lines where the parameters located.

$$\boldsymbol{Q}_i(p,q,\theta) = \begin{pmatrix} 1 & & & & & \\ & \ddots & & & & \\ & & \cos\theta & & \sin\theta & \\ & & & \ddots & & \\ & & -\sin\theta & & \cos\theta & \\ & & & & & \ddots \\ & & & & & 1 \end{pmatrix} \begin{matrix} \\ \\ (p) \\ \\ (q) \\ \\ \end{matrix} \tag{2}$$

Let a_{ij} be the $i-rowj-column$ element of matrix $\boldsymbol{K}_{L(k)}$ ($\boldsymbol{K}_L$ iteration for k times), bij is the $i-rowj-column$ element of matrix $\boldsymbol{K}_{L(k+1)}$. The Givens transformation can be denoted by $\boldsymbol{K}_{L(k+1)} = \boldsymbol{Q}_{k+1}^T \boldsymbol{K}_{L(k)} \boldsymbol{Q}_{k+1}$. Related data updates are shown in Eq. 3–7:

$$b_{ip} = b_{pi} = a_{pi}\cos\theta - a_{qi}\sin\theta, i \neq p, q \tag{3}$$

$$b_{iq} = b_{qi} = a_{pi}\sin\theta + a_{qi}\cos\theta, i \neq p, q \tag{4}$$

$$b_{pp} = a_{pp}\cos^2\theta + a_{qq}\sin^2\theta - a_{pq}\sin 2\theta \qquad (5)$$

$$b_{qq} = a_{pp}\sin^2\theta + a_{qq}\cos^2\theta + a_{pq}\sin 2\theta \qquad (6)$$

$$b_{pq} = b_{qp} = a_{pq}\cos 2\theta + \frac{a_{pp} - a_{qq}}{2}\sin 2\theta \qquad (7)$$

In order to transform element b_{pq} with the coordinate (p, q) to zero, we set Eq. 7 to zero to get the parameter θ. In Eq. 3–7, only elements in row p, q and column p, q of matrix $\boldsymbol{K}_{L(k)}$ are updated, while other elements are unchanged, which shows the localization of data updates in Givens transformation. In summary, if the corresponding parameters (p, q) in $\boldsymbol{Q}_i$ are not intersect, a number of $I/2$ Givens transformations can be executed in parallel, which reduces $I/2$ non-diagonal elements to zero and updates the entire matrix elements. Figure 2 shows the work-flow of the parallel algorithm on the GPU platform (see Fig. 2).

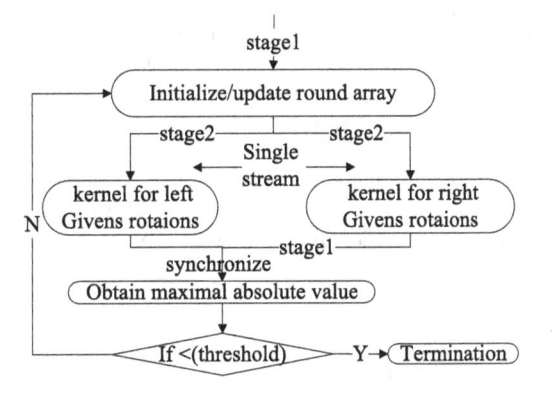

Fig. 2. Bilateral Jacobi iteration parallel algorithm based on GPU.

In the GPU-based parallel framework, step 2 contains the left and right Givens transformation that are executed in a serial manner. In step 3, the element with absolute maximum value is detected after each round of updates, and if it is less than the setting threshold, the Jacobi iteration stops.

4.2   Parallel KPCA on GPU

Finally, we select the optimal optimization of the three bottlenecks to implement GPU-based parallel KPCA algorithm, the model of which is shown here (see Fig. 3).

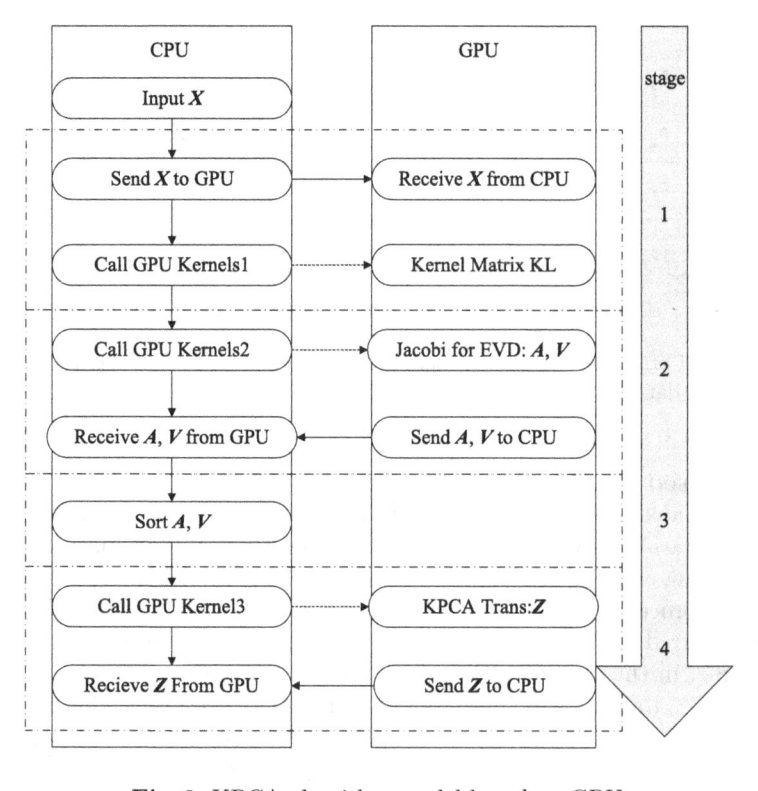

Fig. 3. KPCA algorithm model based on GPU.

5   Parallel Dimensionality Reduction Scheme of Hyperspectral Image Based on Multilevel Parallelism

As data scale grows, the proposed solution would encounter memory bottleneck. In this section, we provide a MPI-based KPCA algorithm based on multi-node systems and exploit parallelization mechanism of intra-node with many-core GPU for better dimensionality reduction performance.

5.1   MPI-Based KPCA Algorithm

(1) MPI-based Gaussian Kernel Matrix calculation

Considering the specialty of hyperspectral data, we divide the data and propose a parallel computing scheme of gauss matrix (see Fig. 4).

In this figure, C is the result matrix. Each processor maintains two buffer (bufA and bufB) to cache the intermediate local data. The computation flow is illustrated in Fig. 4a. P_i reads $block_i$ into bufA and bufB, and then all the processors start calculating the data blocks placed on the diagonal line. After that, the data in bufA remain unchanged but the data in bufB move upwards recursively, which is shown in Fig. 4b.

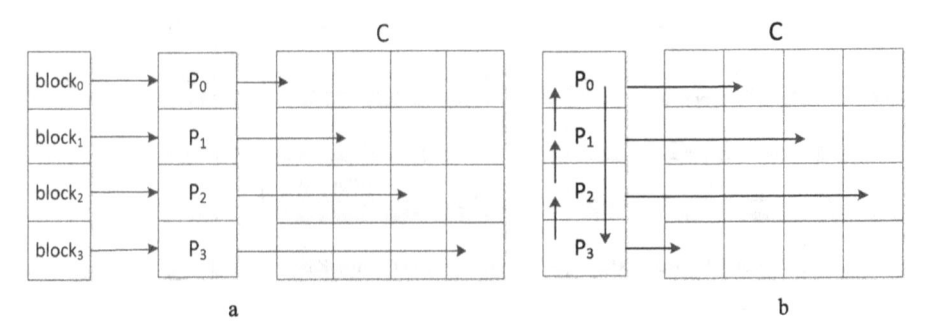

Fig. 4. Parallel program of Gaussian matrix calculation based on the characteristics of hyper-spectral data on GPU.

(2) MPI-based Jacobi iteration

The basic idea of Jacobi iteration is to make any off-diagonal element close to 0 through iterations of Givens transformation, so that the result matrix (denoted as K_L^*) is diagonalized. To analyze parallelism, we partition K_L^* into several blocks. The process of transforming off-main-diagonal elements in a data block into 0 is referred to as a sub-task. In each sub-task, data locality is observed. For example, in the process of left-hand Givens transformation, $block(i,j)$ has two input lines i and j, which are independent from each other. However, there are some issues to be addressed if multiple sub-tasks were executed in parallel.

Issue 1: if sub-tasks belonging to different processes are placed on the same row or column, part of the Givens transformation will be applied on the same data block. This part of data may subject to out-of-order updates imposed by different processes, eventually leading to non-reproducible results and data inconsistency.

Issue 2: the bilateral Jacobi iterations in each sub-task involve left transformations (update row block) and right transformations (update column block). If data matrix is partitioned in row, then the column data block to be updated will not be fully preserved on local storage, vice versa.

To solve issue 1, we partition the tasks and data (see Fig. 5) to make sure that the transformation will not cause inter-process interference. Each sub-task therefore has disjoint indices and the data blocks to be updated are independent from each other.

Figure 6 shows the holistic mapping of sub-tasks and data blocks in the Jacob iteration (see Fig. 6). On the left-hand side lies the partitioning of diagonal sub-tasks (the partition granularity is denoted by L). Local diagonal elements in these sub-tasks are global diagonal elements, so they do not need to be transformed into 0. The right-hand sub-figure illustrates how the non-diagonal sub-tasks are assigned to each process (the granularity $R = L/2$). The arrow to each process (P_i) represents that all the blocks in the row are preserved locally.

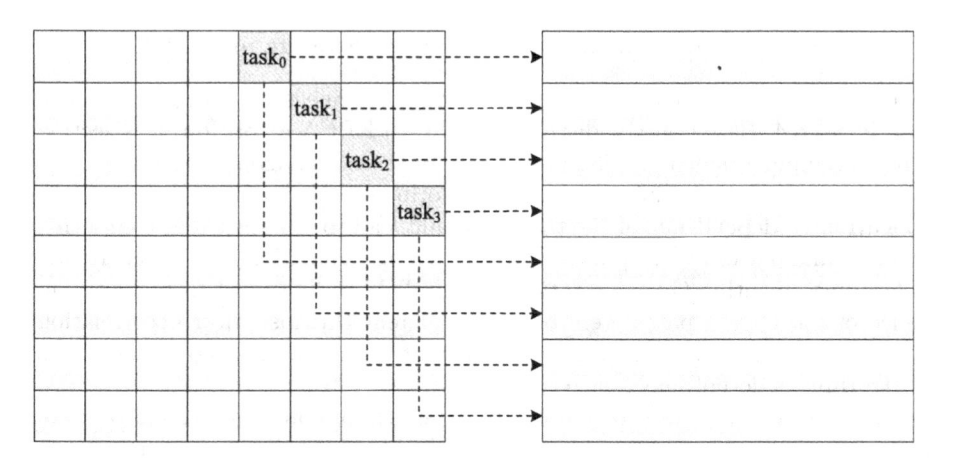

Fig. 5. Task allocation scheme.

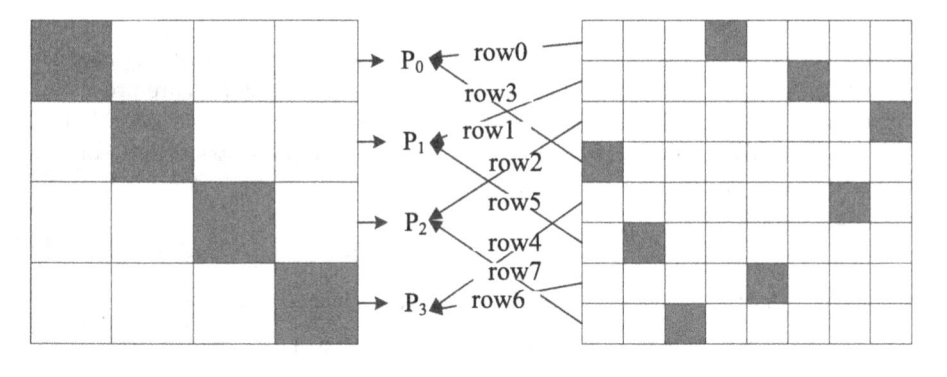

Fig. 6. Global mapping of Jacobi iteration subtasks and related data.

During the right-hand Givens transformation, parts of the data blocks to be updated and parameters of updates are dispersed on different processes. It results in the data dependency among different processes. To tackle the second issue, after updating each row in left-hand Givens rotation, the collection and broadcast of parameters is performed to obtain the global parameter list, so that each process store all the needed data on local storage.

In summary, the parallel KPCA process first partitions data for Gaussian calculation and outputs the Gaussian matrix blocks to the local storage, then it performs the Jacob iteration to integrate principle eigenvectors to form the mapping matrix, and broadcast it to all the processes for them to execute the KPCA mapping independently.

5.2   The KPCA Algorithm on Distributed Storage and GPU

The parallel mechanism of the sub-tasks on diagonal line is similar to the description in Sect. 4. Based on the distributed storage KPCA algorithm, this section studies the fine-grained parallel mechanism of the non-diagonal sub-tasks.

When utilizing multiple threads to perform several Givens transformations concurrently, dependency of the threads would lead to issues such as computing overlaps and out-of-order updates, yielding wrong calculation results. Therefore, before implementing Givens rotations in parallel, we first need to remove relevance of the Givens parameters between different threads. After decorrelation operation, all the p and q are distinctive, so that the operations and data updates of the threads do not affect each other.

Because the line numbers and column numbers of non-diagonal sub-task are different, we can combine each row and column randomly as a return-to-zero element's coordinate, all of the coordinate forming an independent sequence. The max degree of parallelism in non-diagonal sub-task is *blocksize*. For covering all the elements in non-diagonal block, Fig. 7 illustrates how the independent sequence of non-diagonal sub-task is scheduled (see Fig. 7). By enabling parallel computation within the nodes, the independent Givens transforms are processed at the same time. In Fig. 8, we implement the programming model of "MPI + CUDA". The MPI process is responsible for data communication and coarse-grained parallel calculation, while the GPU is focused on high-density floating point operations.

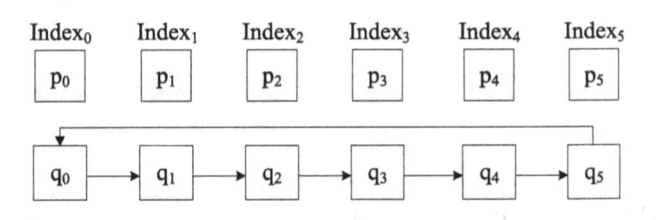

Fig. 7. Scheduling policy of independent sequence.

The execution of the sub-tasks has both independence and correlation, that is, the row-related data blocks are stored locally, and the column-related blocks are scattered at each node. Then independent left-hand Givens transformations launch so that row blocks are updated in parallel, which is referred as a round of circulation (see Fig. 8). Since the Givens-right-transformed data for column update is scattered on different nodes, parameter gather and broadcast are required between the two modules, after which column blocks update begin. The inner loop contains scheduling the independent sequence and repeating the above procedure in a node.

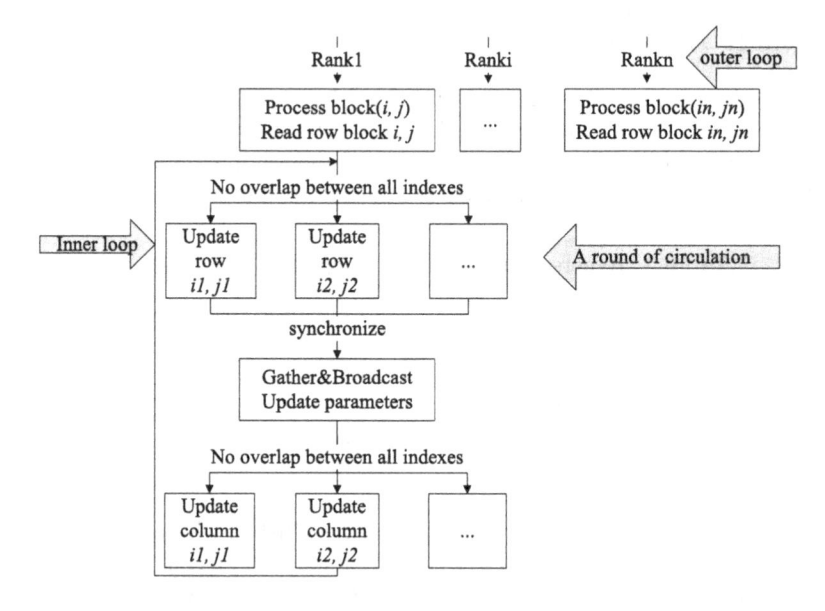

Fig. 8. Jacobi algorithm based on MPI+CUDA.

5.3 KPCA Algorithm Based on Distributed/Shared Storage and GPU

As discussed in Sect. 5.1, the data and tasks are partitioned and dispatched on distributed storage. Section 5.2 has expatiated on how the large-scale computing tasks in Givens transform are handled by GPU. In this section, other suitable parallel tasks, such as Gaussian kernel calculation and Givens parameter calculation, are processed using multi-thread OpenMP, achieving the three-level parallel KPCA algorithm based on MPI + OpenMP + CUDA. The multilevel hybrid parallel KPCA makes full use of different platform resources and is suitable for large-scale data processing with good scalability and portability.

In the MPI implementation of the KPCA algorithm, each process reads its own data and calculates the Gaussian kernel function. The calculation procedure include three circulations, the first two represent data coordinates, while the inner loop carries out the specific Gaussian operations. The operations in outer layer are independent to each other, and therefore can be allocated to different threads to perform parallel execution. In the Givens parameter calculation, the independent sequence is updated, in which the parameters are calculated corresponding to the reducing point in coordinate of (p, q). Without data correlation, the parameter calculation processes are independent and can be executed by multi-threads.

6   Result Analysis

We use the hyperspectral image data provided by AVIRIS in the United States to run the experiments. Table 1 lists the three sets of hyperspectral image data used in the experiment. They are extracted from the original hyperspectral image and the number of pixels is 1024,4096 and 16,384, respectively.

Table 1. Hyperspectral remote sensing image information

ID	Width	Height	Bands
1	32	32	224
2	64	64	224
3	128	128	224

The experimental platform is a heterogeneous cluster, where the CPU/GPU heterogeneous nodes are equipped with two 8-core Intel (R) Xeon (R) CPU E5-2670 and two Kepler architecture NVIDIA Tesla K20c GPUs. The system environment includes Red Hat Enterprise Linux Server release 6.2 (Santiago), GCC-4.4.6 compiler, CUDA release 5.5 toolkit and the MPICH library compiler. The spectral information is transformed into pixel information, the original 16-bit integer data is converted into un-signed char type (unsigned char).

6.1   GPU-Based KPCA Algorithm

The KPCA algorithm is executed on a single node using different processor configurations, including single-core (CPU), multi-core (CPU) and many-core (GPU). Table 2 reports the execution time and the speedup of the three KPCA implementations. These include KPCA_S (the serial KPCA), KPCA_O (a multi-thread parallel implementation on OpenMP using 16 processors) and KPCA_G which is based on the many-core GPU architecture. The experimental result is listed in Table 2. The more details could be found in [3].

Table 2. Time (ms) and speedup of KPCA

	Data1		Data2	
	Time	Speedup	Time	Speedup
KPCA_S	82,017.55	-	15,710,746.06	-
KPCA_O	18,519.99	4.43	6,300,228.22	2.49
KPCA_G	1,817.25	45.13	90,778.75	173.07

The results show that KPCA_O and KPCA_G achieve 2.49–4.43 and 45.13–173.07 times performance improvement compared to KPCA_S, and the acceleration ratio of the GPU-based implementation increases along with the volume of the test data, which proves that it is more scalable than the multi-thread implementation.

The experimental platform used in Sect. 6.1 is a single CPU/GPU heterogeneous node. Due to the limited running space, only the first two sets of data can be calculated. The subsequent multi-node parallel experiment will test the large-scale data and provide further discussion.

6.2   Analysis of the MPI-Based KPCA

In the Jacobian iteration that is based on distributed storage, obtaining the global maximum absolute value requires frequent data exchange between nodes, which results in huge performance loss in production-scale data processing and gives uncontrollable results. In this paper, we simplify the end-point discrimination process and set the terminating condition of the Jacobi iteration as the fixed number of cycles, i.e., all non-diagonal elements are reduced to zero once. Table 3 shows the execution time of the algorithm.

Table 3. Time (s) of serial KPCA and main modules

Data	1	2	3
KPCA	16.30	1,781.53	170,553.54

Our experiments also evaluate the KPCA algorithm on MPI, where n in KPCA_M (n) is the number of launched processes. We use three sets of data to test the experiment, and record the execution time of the slowest process. Table 4 records the execution time of overall KPCA_M procedure. We also compare KPCA and KPCA_M algorithms and show the acceleration effect of KPCA_M (see Fig. 9). The results show that, the speed ratio increases along with the growing number of processes. However, when the volume of data increases, the performance of KPCA rises and then falls. Among all the test cases, the KPCA_M using 8 processes has the best result, obtaining 7.78–18.24 times performance improvement.

Table 4. Time (s) of KPCA_M and main modules

Data	KPCA_M(2)	KPCA_M(4)	KPCA_M(8)
1	4.77	2.30	1.14
2	438.71	188.15	97.65
3	40,228.89	28,506.95	21,918.38

As the process number grows, the partition granularity of KPCA_M decreases, so the performance gains. When the data scale is large, the overall performance has witnessed a significant degradation, and the performance of these three types of KPCA_M is not comparable to the previous test cases using smaller size of data sets. Our analysis shows that the main factor is the MPI group communication adopts the "many times, smaller amount" style of transmission, so with the increase of the data scale, the transmission time also increases, and results in poor performance. Therefore, when the data size is large, it may be appropriate to increase the number of nodes to reduce the amount of communication data and avoid performance degradation.

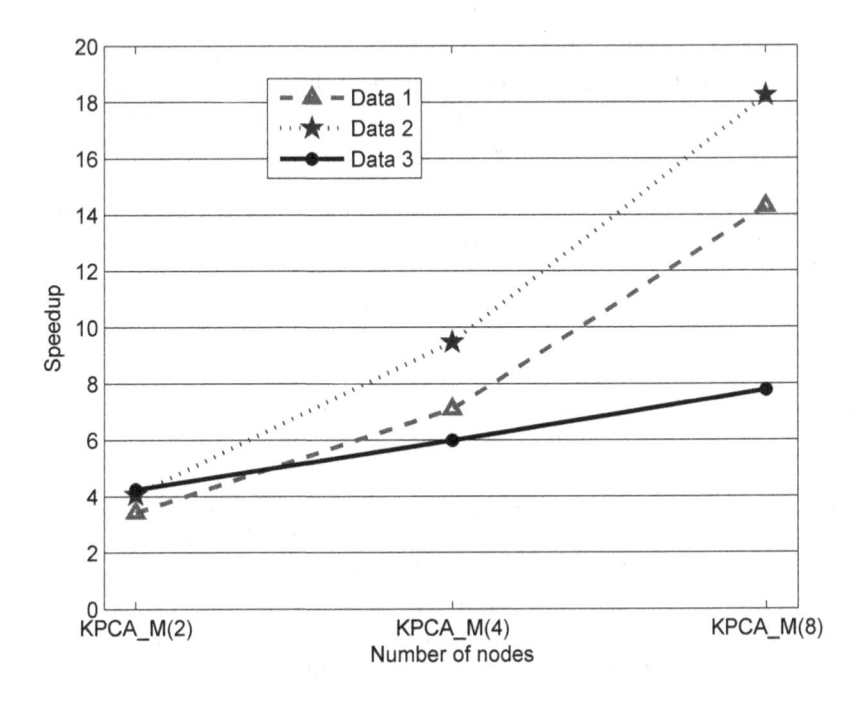

Fig. 9. Speedup of KPCA_M algorithm.

6.3   Analysis of KPCA Algorithm Based on MPI + CUDA

In the experiment of parallel KPCA algorithm based on MPI + CUDA, two processes are launched, each of which is equipped with a GPU.

By recording the execution time of the KPCA_M_G and KPCA_M algorithm, we calculates the performance improvement comparing the KPCA_M_G (default 2 processes) with KPCA_M algorithm (see Fig. 10): the introduction of GPU parallelization in the nodes has enabled the KPCA_M_G to be faster 2.56–9.03 times than the original KPCA_M(2), and KPCA_M_G is faster than the extended 4-process KPCA_M by 1.24–6.4 times. In addition, when using the smallest data set, performance of KPCA_M_G is poorer than the 8-process extended KPCA_M. When the last two sets of data are used, its performance improves by 1.25 and 4.92 times than 8-process extended KPCA_M. The experimental results show that with the increase of the data volume, the proportion of the calculation in the node increases, so that the advantage of utilizing GPU gradually appears to make it suitable for the fine granularity parallelism in the node.

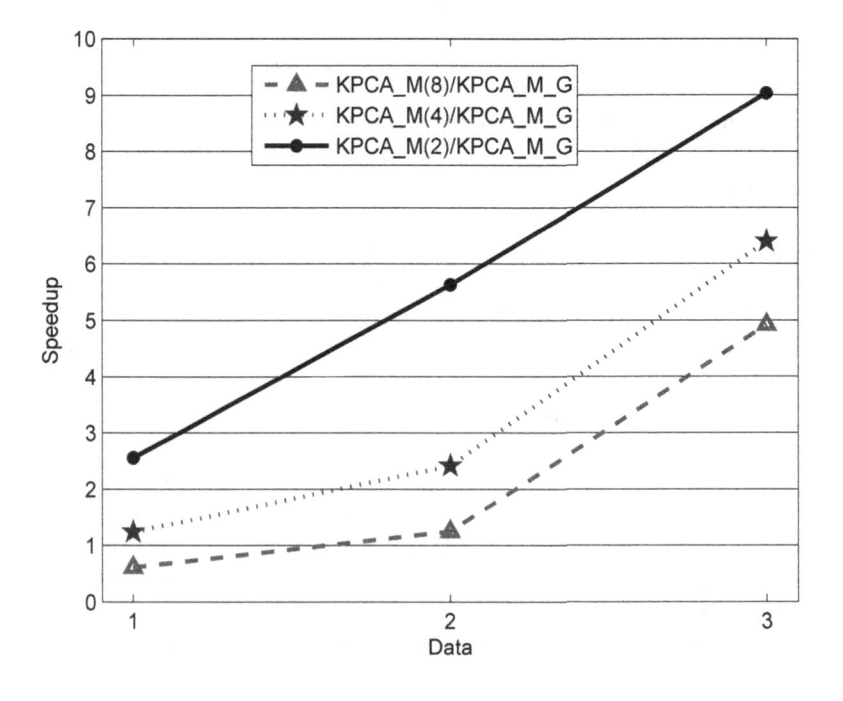

Fig. 10. Performance comparison between KPCA_M and KPCA_M_G.

6.4 Analysis of KPCA Algorithm Based on MPI + OpenMP + CUDA

This section implements the three-level parallel KPCA algorithm based on MPI + OpenMP + CUDA. Table 5 records the execution time of various parallel KPCA algorithms. KPCA_M_O_G uses two CPU + GPU heterogeneous nodes and obtains the acceleration ratio of 2.75–9.27 compared with 2-process KPCA_M, as well as the acceleration ratio of 1.33–6.57 and 1.39–5.05 compared with 4-process and 8-process KPCA_M algorithm. By comparing with the KPCA_M algorithm extending the number of nodes, we can effectively reduce the number of nodes and reduce the cluster size under the same performance requirements by KPCA_M_O_G.

When the minimum data set (Data 1) is used for the KPCA_M_O_G experiment, compared with KPCA_M(8), the performance does not rise but fall, mainly because the use of GPU optimization algorithm will introduce some additional over-head, including GPU warming up, kernel boot, data transmission between host and device. Based on the experimental results, we can draw the following conclusions:

Table 5. Time (s) of KPCA in different ways

Data	KPCA_M_O_G	KPCA_M_G	KPCA_M(2)
1	1.73	1.86	4.77
2	70.22	77.90	438.71
3	4,340.47	4,457.39	40,228.89

(1) When the size of the original hyperspectral data is suitable for a single machine, the KPCA_G algorithm can greatly improve the efficiency of data reduction;

(2) When the data size increases, and the memory requirement for processing is beyond the limit of a single-node, the distributed and parallel heterogeneous cluster platform is an inevitable choice. This paper presents the MPI + OpenMP + CUDA, a multilevel hybrid parallel algorithm and provides a good application demo.

7   Summary and Outlook

Taking KPCA algorithm for example, this paper reviews KPCA_G algorithm on CUDA, and designs KPCA_M_G algorithm on MPI + CUDA and KPCA_G_O_G algorithm on MPI + OpenMP + CUDA. The experiments prove that all these algorithms achieve remarkable performance improvements on the CPU/GPU heterogeneous system.

The research of GPU-based parallel algorithms for nonlinear dimension reduction of hyperspectral images is still on preliminary stage, there are lots of open research questions left to be answered, we put forward the following ideas for the future work: (1) it's necessary to develop a specialized parallel function library for hyperspectral dimensionality reduction, which can unify standard, simplify procedure, and promote application of hyperspectral dimensionality reduction algorithm. (2) With the rapid development of high performance computing technology, optimization of algorithm on different high performance computing system will be a long-lasting topic.

References

1. Zhang, Z., Zhang, L.: Hyperspectral Remote Sensing. Wuhan University Press, Wuhan (2005). (in Chinese)
2. Ainsworth, T.L., Bachmann, C.M., Fusina, R.A.: Local intrinsic dimensionality of hyper-spectral imagery from non-linear manifold coordinate. In: IEEE International on Geoscience and Remote Sensing Symposium, pp. 1541–1542 (2007)
3. Gao, C., Zhou, H., Fang, M.: Parallel Algorithm and Performance Optimization of Kernel Principal Component Analysis on GPUs for Dimensionality Reduction of HIS, HPC China, pp. 611–614 (2016)
4. Bernabe, S., Lopez, S., Plaza, A., Sarmiento, R.: GPU implementation of an automatic target detection and classification algorithm for hyperspectral image analysis. IEEE Geosci. Remote Sens. Lett. **10**(2), 221–225 (2013)

5. Lokman, G., Yilmaz, G.: Anomaly detection and target recognition with hyperspectral images. In: 2014 22nd Signal Processing and Communications Applications Conference (SIU), pp. 1019–1022, 23–25 2014
6. Agathos, A., Li, J., Petcu, D., Plaza, A.: Multi-GPU implementation of the minimum volume simplex analysis algorithm for hyperspectral unmixing. IEEE J. Sel. Topics Appl. Earth Obs. Remote Sens. **7**(6), 2281–2296 (2014)
7. Torti, E., Danese, G., Leporati, F., Plaza, A.: A hybrid CPU-GPU real-time hyperspectral unmixing chain. IEEE J. Sel. Topics Appl. Earth Obs. Remote Sens. **9**(2), 945–951 (2016)
8. Sanchez, S., Ramalho, R., Sousa, L., Plaza, A.: Real-time implementation of remotely sensed hyperspectral image unmixing on GPUs. J. Real-Time Image Process. **10**, 469–483 (2012)
9. Keymeulen, D., Aranki, N., Hopson, B., Kiely, A., Klimesh, M., Benkrid, K.: GPU lossless hyperspectral data compression for space applications. In: 2012 IEEE Aerospace Conference, pp. 1–9, 3–10 March 2012
10. Santos, L., Magli, E., Vitulli, R., Lopez, J.F., Sarmiento, R.: Highly-parallel GPU architecture for lossy hyperspectral image compression. IEEE Sel. Topics Appl. Earth Obs. Remote Sens. **6**(2), 670–681 (2013)
11. ElMaghrbay, M., Ammar, R., Rajasekaran, S.: Fast GPU algorithms for endmember extraction from hyperspectral images. In: 2012 IEEE Symposium Computers and Communications (ISCC), pp. 000631–000636, 1–4 July 2012
12. Fang, M., Zhou, H., Shen, X.: Multilevel parallel algorithm of PCA dimensionality reduction for hyperspectral image on GPU. Dongbei Daxue Xuebao/J. Northeastern Univ. **35**(S1), 238–243 (2014). (in Chinese)
13. Fang, M., Zhou, H., Zhang, W., Shen, X.: A parallel algorithm of FastICA dimensionality reduction for hyperspectral image on GPU. Dongbei Daxue Xuebao/J. Northeastern Univ. **37**(4), 65–70 (2015). (in Chinese)
14. Wu, Y., Gao, L., Zhang, B., Zhao, H., Li, J.: Real-time implementation of optimized maximum noise fraction transform for feature extraction of hyperspectral images. J. Appl. Remote Sens. **8**(1), 084797 (2014)
15. Scholkopf, B., Smola, A.J., Muller, K.: Nonlinear component analysis as a kernel eigenvalue problem. Neutral Comput. **1**, 1299–1319 (1998)

A New Approximation Algorithm
for Flow Shop with Transporter
Coordinate

Xin Han[1] and Yinling Wang[2(✉)]

[1] Software School, Dalian University of Technology,
Dalian 116024, Liaoning, People's Republic of China
hanxin@dlut.edu.cn
[2] School of Mathematical Sciences, Dalian University of Technology,
Dalian 116024, Liaoning, People's Republic of China
yinling_wang@foxmail.com

Abstract. In this paper, we study a problem of the two-machine flow shop scheduling problem with intermediate transportation. This problem has been studied in [2,4,17]. The best approximation algorithm was presented in [17] with a two approximation ratio to our best knowledge. We propose a $(\frac{5}{3} + \varepsilon)$-approximation algorithm for this problem, where $\varepsilon > 0$. Moreover, our algorithm can reach the lower bound $\frac{5}{3}$ asymptotically given by [2] when ε is close to 0.

Keywords: Flow shop · Bin-packing · Approximation algorithms

1 Introduction

The machine scheduling problems with transporter coordination are obtaining more and more attention because of the need from the manufacturing and distribution systems. These problems combine the job scheduling and transporting together, while the traditional scheduling problems only consider job scheduling. These combinatorial problems are more practical and applicable in the supply chain compared to the traditional scheduling problem.

In this paper, we study the following problem. There are two flow shop machines denoted by A and B respectively and a transporter called V with limited capacity. A set of n jobs $J_1, J_2, \ldots, J_n$ are first processed on machine A then transported to machine B by a transporter V for further processing. Each job has their size and processing time on machines A and B. We assume that machine A can store unlimited number of the half-finished jobs. Transporter V initially locates on machine A, then it takes t_1 units of time for delivering jobs from machine A to machine B and t_2 for the return, it stays at the location of machine B after all the jobs arrive at the machine B. In this paper we assume that $t_1 \geq t_2$. In each time. the total size of jobs delivered by the transporter V cannot exceed its capacity. The objective is to minimize the makespan, i.e., the completion time of the last job.

© Springer Nature Singapore Pte Ltd. 2018
L. Li et al. (Eds.): NCTCS 2018, CCIS 882, pp. 116–140, 2018.
https://doi.org/10.1007/978-981-13-2712-4_9

This problem can be denoted as $TF2|s_j|C_{max}$ according to the three-field notation introduced by Graham et al. [5]. The T means there is one transporter, $F2$ implies two flow machines, s_j corresponds to the size of job J_j, the goal is to minimize the makespan.

When each job has the same size, then the problem can be denoted by $TF2|c|C_{max}$ where c corresponds to the maximal number of jobs that the transporter V can carry in each batch. As we can see, the problem $TF2|s_j|C_{max}$ is a generalization of $TF2|c|C_{max}$. It was first investigated by Lee and Chen [11], the complexity of this problem is proved to be NP-hard [8, 10, 11], thus $TF2|s_j|C_{max}$ is also NP-hard.

Hence in this paper, we focus on approximation algorithm. Unlike the optimal algorithm, the approximation algorithm will give an approximate feasible solution in polynomial time. The approximation ratio measures the approximation algorithm. Given an instance I with a minimization problem, $A(I)$ is the objective value obtained by approximation algorithm A while $OPT(I)$ represents the optimal value of I. The approximation ratio ρ is:

$$\rho = \max_{\forall I} \left\{ \frac{A(I)}{OPT(I)} \right\},$$

We also can call algorithm A the ρ-approximation algorithm.

Related Works. There are two main sets of job transportation problems studied in the literature. One set is that jobs are delivered for further processing, i.e. job intermediate transportation, another is to delivery the finished jobs to the customer [11].

For the problems that delivering the completed jobs to the customers, Cheng et al. considered the single machine case with jobs due-date assignment, the objective is to simultaneously minimize the total cost of earliness and tardiness, they proposed a dynamic optimal algorithm [1]. Lee and Chen considered the objective of minimize the makespan, they studied the case that each job has same size [11]. Chang and Lee considered a more general case that each job has arbitrary size [16].

The problems of job intermediate transportation between machines are mostly studied with the flowshop system. They are generated from the requirement of industry and manufacturing, such as the half-finished jobs are required to be delivered to another factory for further processing. [11] and [13] studied the problems that several transporters are delivering the jobs between two flow machines. Lee and Chen proved the NP-hardness of some model [11].

For our problem, Gong and Tang [4] firstly studied this problem. They gave a $\frac{7}{3}$-approximation algorithm. In the algorithm, all the jobs are packed according to FFD (First Fit Decreasing) [14] algorithm in advance. According to the packing result, they applied the Johnson rule [12] to each batch. Then they proved that the approximation ratio of the algorithm cannot overcome 2 no matter which kind of bin-packing algorithm is used to wrap the items in advance. Then, Dong et al. [2] improved the approximation ratio to $\frac{11}{5}$. At the same time, Zhong and

Chen [17] gave a 2-approximation algorithm. According to the lower bound 2 in [4], the result in [17] matches the lower bound.

Since the bin-packing problem is a particular case of $TF2|s_j|C_{max}$, deciding whether 2 or 3 bins are enough to pack all the items is NP-complete [3]. Then the worst case is that the optimal schedule only needs $(2t_2 + t_1)$ units of time to delivery all jobs, the length of the schedule we can get within polynomial time in worst case is at least $(3t_1 + 2t_2)$ unless $P = NP$. When $t_1 = t_2$, a lower bound of $\frac{5}{3}$ is immediately obtained on the approximation ratio, mentioned by Dong et al. [2]. Therefore there is still the gap for this problem.

In problem $F3||C_{max}$, there are three flow machines M_1, M_2 and M_3, each job needs to be processed on machine M_1 first, then M_2, M_3 last, the goal is to minimize the makespan. This problem is similar to our problem since only the middle processor is different. For problem $F3||C_{max}$, Hall [6] gave $(1 + \varepsilon)$-approximation algorithm where $\varepsilon > 0$.

Contributions. It is impossible to get a better approximation ratio than two whenever we pack the jobs in advance. We then consider the jobs size, the processing time in order to get the better algorithm. In this paper, we propose a $(\frac{5}{3} + \varepsilon)$-approximation algorithm for arbitrary $\varepsilon > 0$, when ε is close to 0, it asymptotically matches the immediate lower bound of $\frac{5}{3}$. When the round-trip time t is short enough, our algorithm even can get the approximation ratio $(\frac{3}{2} + \varepsilon)$.

Structure of the Paper. The paper is organized as follows. In Sect. 2, we introduce the bin-packing problem and propose some useful properties, then we give the main idea of our algorithm. In Sect. 3, we propose a $(\frac{5}{3} + \varepsilon)$-approximation algorithm and give the analysis. In the last section, we give the conclusion.

2   Preliminary

2.1   Definition of the Problem

In this paper, we study a flow shop scheduling problem with two flow shop machines denoted by A and B respectively and a transporter called V between the two machines. A set of n jobs $J_1, J_2, \ldots, J_n$ need to be processed on machine A then transported to machine B by transporter V for further processing. The processing time of J_i on machines A, B is donated by a_i and b_i respectively. Each job J_i has their size s_i where $0 \le s_i \le 1$. We assume that the buffer of A is infinite such that each job can be stored for a while after the processing step on machine A. The transporter V initially locates on A, and it will stay at the location of machine B after all the jobs arrive at machine B. We say each transporting operation as a batch. The capacity of transporter V is limited to 1, i.e., the total size of jobs in each batch cannot exceed 1. It takes t_1 units of time for transporter V delivering jobs from machine A to B and t_2 units of time for the return. Since transporter V is loaded with some jobs from machine A to machine B and empty for the return, we assume $t_1 \ge t_2$ without loss of generality. We use $t = t_1 + t_2$ to denote the round-trip time. The objective is to minimize the makespan, i.e., the completion time of the last job.

2.2   Bin-Packing

Definition 1 (Bin-packing). *In the classical one-dimensional bin packing problem, there are n items $x_1, x_2, \cdots, x_n$, each item x_i has size s_i in $[0, 1]$. There are unlimited bins with capacity one. The goal is to pack all the items into a minimum number of bins. This problem is proved to be NP-complete [3].*

FFD (First Fit Decreasing) Algorithm: FFD algorithm is a well-known algorithm for the bin-packing problem proposed by Johnson et al. [9]. FFD algorithm first sorts the items in **non-increasing order** of the size, then assign items to the bins according to the sorted order one by one. The detail is: assign the first item in the first bin, every time we place a new item to the **lowest indexed** bin which can accommodate the items. FFD is proved to be a $\frac{3}{2}$-approximation algorithm [14]. FFD will be used in this paper to pack the jobs into batches.

We propose the following two lemmas on FFD algorithm These two lemmas give the base idea of the assignment of the jobs on transporter V.

Lemma 1. *Consider any input I of the bin-packing problem, then we can construct a new input $I^{'}$ with the following two conditions such that $FFD(I^{'}) \leq \frac{3}{2}OPT(I)$*

Condition 1: $I^{'}$ has the same items as the I of size $\geq \varepsilon$, where $\varepsilon \leq \frac{1}{3}$.
Condition 2: the total size of all items in $I^{'}$ is at most the total of all items in I.

Proof. There are two cases obtained by the FFD algorithm to the $I^{'}$:

Case 1: The last bin has at least one item with size $\geq \varepsilon$. In this case, we can see that the items with size $\geq \varepsilon$ decide the number of batches. Since $I^{'}$ has the identical items of size $\geq \varepsilon$ as L, thus $FFD(I^{'}) \leq \frac{3}{2}OPT(I)$.

Case 2: The last bin only contains the items with size $< \varepsilon$. It means all the other bins must have size at least $(1 - \varepsilon)$. If FFD uses at least $(\frac{3}{2}OPT(I) + 1)$ bins, then FFD actually packs jobs with total size $> (\frac{3}{2}OPT(I) + 1)(1 - \varepsilon)$. Since $\varepsilon \leq \frac{1}{3}$, then we have a contradiction: the total size of $I^{'}$ is larger than $OPT(I)$. Thus in this case we have $FFD(I^{'}) \leq \frac{3}{2}OPT(I)$. $\qquad\square$

Lemma 2. *Consider any input I with x items with size in $(\frac{1}{2}, 1]$, y items with size in $(\frac{1}{3}, \frac{1}{2}]$ of the bin-packing problem, then we can construct a new input $I^{'}$ with the following two conditions such that $FFD(I') \leq \frac{3}{2}OPT(I) + 1$*

Condition 1: the total size of $I^{'}$ is at most the total size of I.
Condition 2: $I^{'}$ has at most x, y number of items with size in $(\frac{1}{2}, 1], (\frac{1}{3}, \frac{1}{2}]$ respectively.

Proof. There are two cases after running the FFD algorithm to the $I^{'}$:
Case 1: The last bin has at least one item with size $> \frac{1}{3}$.

In this case, the worst case of packing results of $I^{'}$ is that the each job with size in $(\frac{1}{2}, 1]$ takes one bin, every two jobs of size in $(\frac{1}{3}, \frac{1}{2}]$ take one bin. Then we have $FFD(I^{'}) \leq \lceil \frac{y}{2} \rceil + \lceil \frac{x}{2} \rceil$. We also have

$$OPT(I) \geq \begin{cases} x & x \geq y \\ x + \lceil \frac{y-x}{2} \rceil & x < y \end{cases}$$

Then we get $FFD(I^{'}) \leq \frac{3}{2} OPT(I) + 1$.

Case 2: the last bin only contains the items with size $\leq \frac{1}{3}$. The prove is similar to the case 2 of the prove in Lemma 1. See more detail in appendix.   □

2.3   The Main Idea of the Algorithm

The algorithms presented in [2,4,17] all pack the jobs to batches in advance. Gong and Tang [4] showed that the approximation ratio of the algorithms could not be smaller than 2 as long as they pack the jobs into batches in advance. They only consider the size of the jobs when they pack the jobs into batches. In our algorithm, we take into account the size, processing time of each job, and the transporting time of transporter V.

The works in [6,7] inspire our result, we extend their works to let their technique can not only handle the jobs with processing time but also with the size. Our algorithm is divided into three parts. We first separate the jobs set into disjoint subsets. Then on machines A B, we adopt the similar method from [6]. On transporter V, unlike the classical scheduling problem, the jobs has its size, each batch requires the delivery time and has the capacity constraints. Therefore we propose these properties 1 and 2 to handle the operations on transporter V (i.e. assign jobs to batches). The two properties can give some interesting structural guide to get a better approximation algorithm for the scheduling problem with transporter coordination.

Thus there are three main steps in our algorithm: 1. Divide the jobs into large jobs and small jobs. 2. Guess the main structures. 3. Find the assignment of small Jobs. 4. Restrict the number of demanded batches. 5. Transfer the main structures to the schedules.

1. *Divide the jobs into large jobs and small jobs:* We first divide the jobs set into two subsets: The large jobs set and small jobs set. The jobs with long processing time or large size can be bounded by a constant. These jobs will be grouped into the large jobs set, and the left jobs belong to the small jobs set.

2. *Guess the main structures:* If we want to guess out the exact optimal schedule, it requires exponential time to n. To decrease the time complexity to polynomial time, we will not guess the exact optimal schedule but rough information of the optimal schedule. First, we divide the time into the constant number of time intervals. Then for the large jobs, we guess each large job starts to be processed or delivered in which time interval since the number of large

jobs and time intervals is bounded by constant. For the small jobs, we can not guess the same information since the number of small jobs might not be constant. Thus on machines A, B we only guess the approximate length of the time for processing the small jobs in each time interval. On transporter V, we guess the number of needed batches, the number of jobs with big size started to be delivered in each time interval.

3. *Find the assignment of small jobs:* We can build the linear programming to find an assignment: the small jobs start to be processed or delivered at which time intervals according to the information of the main structure.

4. *Bound the number of needed batches in each time interval:* We will adapt the FFD [14] algorithm to pack the jobs assigned in each time interval into batches respectively. According to the properties 1 and 2, the number of batches assigned in each time interval will not be too far from the optimal schedule.

5. *Transfer the known information to a schedule:* We see the operations assigned in each time interval as a block on machines A, B. On transporter V, we see the total packed batches assigned in each time interval as a single block also. Then we process the block one by one on each processor according to some rules. Then we will get the schedule which is feasible on each processor: there might exist some overlap between different processor. Then we use delay operation to remove the overlap inside the schedule.

Remark: From above, we can see that if we guess the correct main structure of the optimal schedule, then we can transfer that main structure to a feasible schedule. In real, we will not know if we get the main structure of the optimal schedule. Thus our algorithm will exhaust all the possible main structures. Hence the optimal solution must be included. Then we transfer each main structure to a schedule by the main steps 3, 4 and 5. Finally, we choose the shortest feasible schedule as the output. The length of the output must be no longer than the length of the feasible schedule obtained from the main structure of the optimal schedule.

2.4   Definition of Some Values

Assume ε is an arbitrary small rational number in the interval $(0, 1]$ while $\frac{1}{\varepsilon}$ is an integer. Since there is already the 2-approximation algorithm for this problem, we only consider the case that $\varepsilon < 1$. Suppose the value of ε is fixed which is not a part of the input, thus we can see $\frac{1}{\varepsilon}$ as a constant. After we run the 2-approximation algorithm, then we will get a feasible schedule with length T. When $T = 0$, it is easy to see that we get the optimal solution, thus we will focus on the case that $T > 0$. When $T > 0$, let $T' = \frac{7}{6}T$, we will have $OPT < T' \leq \frac{7}{3}OPT$. We can see that T' is a strict upper bound of the optimal solution.

Before we give the definition of the large and small job, we partition the time interval $[0, T')$ into $\chi = \frac{27}{\varepsilon}$ pieces of length $\delta = \frac{\varepsilon T'}{27}$. We call the interval $[(k-1)\delta, k\delta)$ as the δ-interval k, where $1 \leq k \leq \chi$. We let $\varepsilon' = \frac{\varepsilon}{81}$, $\gamma = \frac{\varepsilon^2 T'}{1485}$, and $\frac{\delta}{\gamma} = \frac{55}{\varepsilon}$.

If $t \in [\frac{\delta}{2}, \delta)$, then we let $\chi = \frac{54}{\varepsilon}, \varepsilon' = \frac{\varepsilon}{162}, \delta = \frac{\varepsilon T'}{54}$ and $\gamma = \frac{\varepsilon^2 T'}{2970}$. By this way, we can always let either $t \geq \delta$ or $t < \frac{\delta}{2}$ happen. In the following analysis of the algorithm, we will adapt the original value of the χ, δ, γ since the following lemmas and theorems still hold when we contract $\delta, \gamma, \varepsilon'$ to half and expand χ to 2χ.

3   The $(\frac{5}{3} + \varepsilon)$-Approximation Algorithm

In this section, we give the $(\frac{5}{3} + \varepsilon)$-approximation algorithm. The algorithm first divides the jobs set into large jobs and small jobs, and then we exhaust all the possible main structures. For each main structure, the algorithm runs the procedure H to generate the schedule. In the end, the algorithm chooses the shortest feasible schedule as the output. We first define the large and small jobs, then define the main structure, then propose the procedure H. Finally, we give the analysis of the algorithm.

When all the jobs can be packed into a single batch and $\sum_{i=1}^{n}(a_i + b_i) \leq t$, then the length of the optimal solution is $\sum_{i=1}^{n}(a_i + b_i) + t_1 \leq t + t_1$, otherwise the length of the optimal solution must $\geq (t + t_1)$. Thus in the following, we only consider the case that the length of the optimal solution is $\geq (t + t_1)$.

Now we give the detailed algorithm.

3.1   The Algorithm

Definition of Large and Small Jobs
When $t \geq \gamma$

- Large jobs: The processing time of a job on machine A or B is $\geq \gamma$, or the size is $\geq \varepsilon'$.
- Small jobs: All the jobs except the large jobs.

When $t < \gamma$:

- Large jobs: The processing time of the job on machine A or B is $\geq \gamma$.
- Small jobs: All the jobs except large jobs.

From the above definition, we can obtain the following observations:

- When $t < \gamma$, the quantity of the large jobs is bounded by $\frac{2T'}{\gamma} = \frac{2970}{\varepsilon^2}$, a constant number.
- When $t \geq \gamma$: 1. For the jobs with processing time on A or B $\geq \gamma$, the number is bounded by $\frac{2T'}{\gamma} = \frac{2970}{\varepsilon^2}$. 2. For the jobs with size $\geq \varepsilon'$, since $t \geq r$, thus there are at most $\frac{1485}{\varepsilon^2}$ number of batches assigned in the whole schedule (i.e. the total size of all jobs is bounded by $\frac{1485}{\varepsilon^2}$). Hence there are at most $\frac{1485 \times 81}{\varepsilon^3}$ number of jobs with size $\geq \varepsilon'$. Thus there are at most $\frac{2970}{\varepsilon} + \frac{1485 \times 81}{\varepsilon^3}$ number of large jobs when $t \geq \gamma$, a constant as well.

– The quantity of the small jobs cannot be bounded by a constant number, but their processing time and transporting time is concise, which can be assigned in the left space of each time interval.

The Main Structure

After we divide the jobs into large jobs and small jobs, we list all the possible main structures of the optimal schedule. The two schedules will be grouped if they have the same main structure. In the algorithm, The information of the main structure is different when $t \geq \gamma$ and $t < \gamma$.

When $t \geq \gamma$, the information contained inside the main structure is as blow:

1. The δ-interval where each operation of each *large job* begins.
2. For each δ-interval of the transporter, the times that the transporter V begins delivering the jobs to machine B in that δ-interval (i.e., the number of batches assigned in that δ-interval).
3. For each δ-interval of machines A and B, the approximate length of the total processing time of the operation of the small jobs that start to be processed in that δ-interval. Here the length is approximated by rounding up to the nearest multiple of the length of γ.

When $t < \gamma$, the information contained inside the main structure is as blow:

1. The δ-interval where each operation of each *large job* begins.
2. For each δ-interval of the transporter, the number of batches assigned in that δ-interval.
3. For each δ-interval of the transporter, the number of jobs with size in $(\frac{1}{2}, 1]$ and size in $(\frac{1}{3}, \frac{1}{2}]$ that assigned in that δ-interval.
4. For each δ-interval of machines A and B, the approximate length of the total processing time of the operation of small jobs that start to be processed in that δ-interval. Here the length is approximated by rounding up to the nearest multiple of the length of γ.

Remark: The length of the optimal schedule is strictly shorter than T', and the main structure of optimal schedule will not have the operation that start to be processed after time T'. Thus we only consider the δ-interval 1 to χ, another main structures are not among the main structures of the optimal solutions.

If the schedule meets all the requires of the main structure, then we can say the schedule is associated with the main structure (i.e., belongs to that main structure). As we can see, each main structure contains many schedules, and each schedule is associated with a single main structure. All the possible main structures are the partition of all feasible schedules. Now we first prove this partition contains at most the polynomial number of main structures. It shows that the algorithm can list all the possible main structure in polynomial time.

Lemma 3. *The partition contains at most the polynomial number of the main structures.*

Proof. We only prove of the case that $t < \gamma$, for the case $t \geq \gamma$, see the appendix.

If the feasible schedules are grouped into the same main structure, then it means these schedules share the same aforementioned characteristics.

When $t < \gamma$: the first character will generate at most $\chi^{\frac{2970}{\varepsilon}}$ number of main structures. The second character will produce at most n^{χ} number of main structures since each interval can be assigned with at most n batches. Similar to the second character, the third character will generate at most $n^{2\chi}$ number of main structures. In the last characteristic, at most $\left(\frac{55}{\varepsilon}\right)^{\chi}$ number of main structures will be obtained.

The number of the partition beforementioned can be bounded by the product of the above number of the main structures generated by the given characteristics respectively. Since $\chi, \frac{1}{\varepsilon}$ are constant, the number of the main structures of the partition is bounded by $O(n^{3\chi})$.   □

We can get all the main structure of the problem by the exhaustive method. Then we will generate the schedule according to each main structure, then to choose the shortest feasible schedule as the output. The Algorithm 1 gives the structure of the approximation algorithm. For each main structure, we run the procedure H (lines 5–7) to transfer the main structure to the schedule. In the end, the algorithm will output the shortest feasible schedule.

Algorithm 1. Approximation algorithm for $TF2|s_j|C_{max}$

Require: n jobs, ε,
1: //Find all the possible main structures.
2: Initialize a set $\mathcal{S} = \emptyset$.
3: **for** each main structure **do**
4:     //Run procedure H:
5:     Step 1. Use Linear programming (see LP1 and LP2) to assign the small jobs.
6:     Step 2. Assign the jobs to prefixed interval on each processor respectively.
7:     Step 3. Remove the overlaps on different processors:
8:     **if** the generated schedule S is feasible **then**
9:         $\mathcal{S} \leftarrow \mathcal{S} \cup S$
10:    **end if**
11: **end for**
12: **return** The shortest feasible schedule $\sigma = \arg\min\{C_{\max}(S) \mid S \in \mathcal{S}\}$ where $C_{\max}(S)$ denotes the length of the schedule S.

Now we describe how the procedure H generate a schedule according to the main structure of the input.

The Procedure H

Step 1: we first build the linear programming to find the assignment for the small jobs, here the assignment means the operations of each job start to be processed in which δ-interval. We will give two different linear programmings for cases that $t \geq \gamma$ (see LP1) and $t < \gamma$ (see LP2).

Assume $J_1, J_2, \cdots, J_{n'}$ are the small jobs, then we will have the following linear programming. The decision variables are denoted as $x_{j,(o,p,q)}$, where $1 \leq j \leq n', 0 \leq o \leq p, p + \lfloor \frac{\delta}{t} \rfloor \leq q \leq \chi$. $x_{j,(o,p,q)} = 1$ means that the small job J_j begins processing(delivering) in the δ-interval o on machine A, δ-interval p on transporter V, δ-interval q on machine B. In the linear programmings, we use the α_i, β_i to denote the length of the time for processing the short jobs from the main structure(the multiple of the amount of γ) of the δ-interval i, L_i to denote the number of the batches assigned in the δ-interval i, S_i' and S_i'' to denote the number of jobs with size in $(\frac{1}{2}, 1]$ and $(\frac{1}{3}, \frac{1}{2}]$ respectively. To represent the number of small jobs assigned in the δ-interval i with size in $(\frac{1}{2}, 1]$ and $(\frac{1}{3}, \frac{1}{2}]$, we let $s_j' = 1$ if $s_j \in (\frac{1}{2}, 1]$, $s_j' = 0$ otherwise, $s_j'' = 1$ if $s_j \in (\frac{1}{3}, \frac{1}{2}]$, $s_j'' = 0$ otherwise. On transporter V, we assume that the total size of the large jobs assigned in the δ-interval i is l_i where $1 \leq i \leq \chi$.

The goal of the linear programmings LP1 and LP2 are to find a basic feasible solution. When $t \geq \gamma$, the procedure H will run the linear programming LP1, when $t < \gamma$, the procedure H will run the linear programming LP2.

The LP1:

$$\sum_{o,p,q} x_{j,(o,p,q)} = 1, \qquad j = 1, 2, \cdots, n' \qquad (1)$$

$$\sum_{j,p,q} a_j x_{j,(o,p,q)} \leq \alpha_o, \qquad o = 1, 2, \cdots, \chi \qquad (2)$$

$$\sum_{j,o,q} s_j x_{j,(o,p,q)} + l_p \leq L_p, \qquad p = 1, 2, \cdots, \chi \qquad (3)$$

$$\sum_{j,o,p} b_j x_{j,(o,p,q)} \leq \beta_q, \qquad q = 1, 2, \cdots, \chi \qquad (4)$$

$$x_{j,(o,p,q)} \geq 0 \qquad j = 1, 2, \cdots, n' \qquad (5)$$

The LP2:

$$\sum_{o,p,q} x_{j,(o,p,q)} = 1, \qquad j = 1, 2, \cdots, n' \qquad (6)$$

$$\sum_{j,p,q} a_j x_{j,(o,p,q)} \leq \alpha_o, \qquad o = 1, 2, \cdots, \chi \qquad (7)$$

$$\sum_{j,o,q} s_j x_{j,(o,p,q)} + l_p \leq L_p, \qquad p = 1, 2, \cdots, \chi \qquad (8)$$

$$\sum_{j,o,q} s_j' x_{j,(o,p,q)} \leq S_p', \qquad p = 1, 2, \cdots, \chi \qquad (9)$$

$$\sum_{j,o,q} s_j'' x_{j,(o,p,q)} \leq S_p'', \qquad p = 1, 2, \cdots, \chi \qquad (10)$$

$$\sum_{j,o,p} b_j x_{j,(o,p,q)} \leq \beta_q, \qquad\qquad q = 1, 2, \cdots, \chi \qquad (11)$$

$$x_{j,(o,p,q)} \geq 0 \qquad\qquad j = 1, 2, \cdots, n' \qquad (12)$$

The constraints (6) and (1) guarantee that each small job is scheduled exactly once. The constraints (7), (11), (3) and (4) ensure that the total length of the operation of small jobs assigned in δ-interval i on machines A and B is bounded by the α_i, β_i. The constraints (8), (3) (resp. (9) and (10)) ensure that the number of batches (resp. number of jobs with size in $(\frac{1}{2}, 1], (\frac{1}{3}, \frac{1}{2}])$ assigned in δ-interval i on transporter V is bounded by the L_i (resp. S', S'').

When $t \geq \gamma$, in the basic feasible solution of the linear programming LP1, there are at most $(n' + 3\chi)$ rows in the matrix of constraints, thus we have at most $(n' + 3\chi)$ decision variables that will receive positive value. Moreover, each small job associated with at least one fractional positive assignment. Thus there are at most 3χ small jobs that will get the fractional assignment while the other small jobs will get an integral assignment. The number of small jobs with the fractional assignment is bounded by 3χ. Moreover, we know the small jobs have the size $\leq \varepsilon'$, i.e., the fractional small jobs can be packed into one batch. Here the procedure H will schedule the small jobs with the fractional assignment in the last single batch. By this way, the fractional jobs will be scheduled in $(t_1 + 6\chi\gamma)$ amount of time, assume the V stays at the machine A, as we can see it is a small expense.

When $t < \gamma$, in the basic feasible solution of the linear programming LP2, at most 5χ small jobs will receive the fractional assignment. Since the round-trip time is short, the procedure H here will schedule the fractional small jobs in the last and each fractional jobs is delivered by a whole batch one by one. By this way, the fractional jobs will be scheduled in $(5\chi + 2)\gamma$ amount of time, also a small expense.

In the next step, we will only process the remaining jobs including the large jobs and the small jobs with the integral assignment.

Step 2: In this step, we only process the jobs that we know they are assigned to which δ-interval. We will give the schedule which is feasible on processors A, V, and B respectively. On the machines A, B, the operations assigned in the same δ-interval are processed without the idle time, and the longest operation assigned in each δ-interval is processed in the end. On the transporter T, we use the FFD algorithm to pack the jobs assigned in the same δ-interval into batches respectively. All the batches obtained in the same δ-interval are also requested to be transported without idle time. The operations assigned in each δ-interval can be saw as a block. Assume O denotes the machine or the transporter and v_i^O denotes the length of the block (assume here the length of each batch is t) assigned in the δ-interval i. Let δ-interval ϖ^O be the last interval with the operation assigned on processor O. Now we decide the starting time and the end time of each block assigned in each δ-interval. We use ζ_i^O (resp. ι_i^O) to denote the starting time (resp. end time) of the block assigned in the δ-interval i on processor O where $1 \leq i \leq \varpi^O$. The values of ζ_i^O and ι_i^O can be calculated as follows:

When $t \geq \delta$, we extend the length of each δ-interval to $(\delta + \gamma)$, and we have:

$$\zeta_i^O = \begin{cases} 0 & i = 1 \\ \max\{(i-1)(\delta + \gamma), \iota_{i-1}^O\} & 2 \leq i \leq \varpi^O \end{cases}$$

$$\iota_i^O = \zeta_i^O + v_i^O \qquad 1 \leq i \leq \varpi^O.$$

When $t < \frac{\delta}{2}$, we extend the length of each δ-interval to $(\frac{3}{2}\delta + \frac{9}{4}\gamma)$, and we have:

$$\zeta_i^O = \begin{cases} 0 & i = 1 \\ \max\{(i-1)(\frac{3}{2}\delta + \frac{9}{4}\gamma), \iota_{i-1}^O\} & 2 \leq i \leq \varpi^O \end{cases}$$

$$\iota_i^O = \zeta_i^O + v_i^O \qquad 1 \leq i \leq \varpi^O.$$

In step 2, we only concentrate on letting schedule to be feasible on each processor. When we integrate the schedules on A, V, and B to a whole schedule, this schedule is unlikely to be feasible since there will be some overlap between some jobs, such as the jobs are processed on the different processor at the same time or in the wrong order. Thus in step 3, we will remove the overlap inside this schedule.

Step 3: In step 2, we avoid overlaps within machines or transporter respectively, but the overlap may occur between the machines and transporter. The third step will remove the overlaps between the machines and transporter by delaying operation. Delaying operation means that we delay the starting time of some specific operations.

When $t \geq \delta$, we first delay all the batches on the transporter T by $2(\delta + \gamma)$ units of time, and all the operations on the machine B by $4(\delta + \gamma)$ units of time.

When $t < \frac{\delta}{2}$, we first delay all the batches on the transporter T by $2(\frac{3}{2}\delta + \frac{9}{4}\gamma)$ units of time, and all the operations on the machine B by $4(\frac{3}{2}\delta + \frac{9}{4}\gamma)$ units of time.

3.2   The Analysis of the Algorithm

In the algorithm, we list all the possible of the main structures. Thus there must be the main structure which is associated with the optimal schedule. In this section, we will prove the procedure H can generate a feasible schedule with length at most $(\frac{5}{3} + \varepsilon)OPT$ according to the main structure of the optimal schedule.

Assume that the main structure associated with the optimal schedule is Π^*. In the optimal schedule, we use e_i^O and c_i^O to denote the starting time and completion time of the operation assigned in the δ-interval i on the processor O, the total length of the operation assigned in δ-interval i on processor O is denoted by u_i^O where $u_i^O \leq c_i^O - e_i^O$. The schedule obtained from Π^* in the second step is denoted by S_1^*, the schedule obtained from Π^* finally is denoted by S_2^*. In the schedule S_1^*, we use U_i^O denotes the length of each block assigned in the δ-interval i on processor O, E_i^O (resp. C_i^O) to denote the starting time (resp. end time) of the block assigned in the δ-interval i on processor O where $1 \leq i \leq \omega^O$, here the δ-interval ω^O denotes the last interval with the operation assigned on processor O. The processor O can be A, B and V.

We now give the following lemmas for analyzing the approximation ratio of the Algorithm 1.

The Lemma 4 shows that the linear programming LP1 and LP2 must get the basic feasible solutions such that the procedure H can go to the second step successfully.

Lemma 4. *For the main structure Π^*, in the first step of procedure H, we can get the basic feasible solutions from the linear programmings LP1 and LP2.*

Proof. The main structure Π^* is associated with some feasible schedules (at least the optimal schedule). On the machines A, B, the main structure Π^* overestimates the time for processing the small jobs. For the transporter V, the main structure Π^* has the exact number of batches assigned in each δ-interval. it also has the exact number of the jobs of size in $(\frac{1}{2}, 1]$ and $(\frac{1}{3}, \frac{1}{2}]$ in each δ-interval. According to the above analysis, we can see that a feasible solution corresponding to the main structure Π^* (in particular the optimal schedule) can also be feasible in the proposed linear programmings. $\square$

The following Lemmas 5, 6, 7 and 8 show that the length of the schedule S_1^* is not far from the length of the optimal schedule.

Lemma 5. *For the δ-interval i of the optimal schedule and the associated interval of S_1^*, on machines O ($O = A$ or B) we have:*

– $t \geq \delta$: $U_i^O \leq u_i^O + \gamma$ when $1 \leq i \leq \omega^O$.
– $t < \frac{\delta}{2}$: $U_i^O \leq \frac{3}{2}u_i^O + \frac{9}{4}\gamma$ when $1 \leq i \leq \omega^O$.

Proof. On the machines A and B, in each main structure, we overestimate the total processing time of small jobs by at most γ units of time in each δ-interval and $\gamma \leq \frac{\delta}{2}$, so the lemma holds on the machines A and B. $\square$

Lemma 6. *For the δ-interval i of the optimal schedule and the associated time interval of S_1^*, on transporter V we have:*

– $t \geq \delta$: $U_i^V \leq u_i^V + \gamma$ when $1 \leq i \leq \omega^V - 1$, and $U_{\omega^V}^V \leq u_{\omega^V}^V + \gamma + t_2$
– $t < \frac{\delta}{2}$: $U_i^V \leq \frac{3}{2}u_i^V + \frac{9}{4}\gamma$ when $1 \leq i \leq \omega^V - 1$, and $U_{\omega^V}^V \leq \frac{3}{2}(u_{\omega^V}^V + t_2) + \frac{9}{4}\gamma$.

Proof. Here we consider three cases:

1. When $t \geq \delta$, we first consider the time interval i where $1 \leq i \leq \omega^V - 1$, in this case, each time interval only can assign at most 1 batch, we can see that if the optimal schedule only have one batch in the δ-interval i, then the jobs assigned in associated time interval of schedule S_1^* will also be packed to a single batch. Thus $U_i^V \leq u_i^V + \gamma$ holds. Then we consider the time interval ω^V. In the schedule S_1^*, there is only one batch assigned in the associated time interval ω^V, we have $U_{\omega^V}^O \leq t$. In the optimal schedule, the transporter V might not need to go back to machine A, thus we can obtain $u_{\omega^V}^V \geq t_1$. Hence we have $U_{\omega^V}^O \leq u_{\omega^V}^V + \gamma + t_2$.

2. When $\gamma \leq t < \frac{\delta}{2}$, the prove is similar to the case that $t \geq \delta$. The appendix shows the detailed prove.
3. When $t < \gamma$, it can be proved by the Lemma 2 and the idea of case $t \geq \delta$. See the appendix for more details.   □

Lemma 7. *On machine O (i.e., $O = A$, B), for the δ-interval i $(1 \leq i \leq \omega^O)$ of the optimal schedule and the associated time interval of S_1^*, we have:*

1. *When $t \geq \delta$, then $E_i^O \leq e_i^O + (i-1)\gamma$ and $C_i^O \leq c_i^O + i\gamma$.*
2. *When $t < \frac{\delta}{2}$, then $E_i^O \leq \frac{3}{2}e_i^O + \frac{9}{4}(i-1)\gamma$ and $C_i^O \leq \frac{3}{2}c_i^O + \frac{9}{4}i\gamma$.*

Proof. We will prove two different cases respectively:

1. When $t \geq \delta$: In the time interval 1, we have:

$$E_1^O = 0 \leq e_1^O \text{ and } C_1^O = 0 + U_0^O \leq 0 + u_0^O + \gamma \leq c_1^O + \gamma$$

When $i = k(1 \leq k \leq \omega^O - 1)$, assume the equations $E_k^O \leq e_k^O + (k-1)\gamma$ hold. Then when $i = k + 1$, we have:

$$E_{k+1}^O = \max\{k(\delta + \gamma), E_k^O + U_k^O\} \qquad C_{k+1}^O \leq E_{k+1}^O + U_{k+1}^O$$
$$\leq \max\{k(\delta + \gamma), E_k^O + u_k^O + \gamma\} \qquad \leq e_{k+1}^O + k\gamma + u_{k+1}^O + \gamma$$
$$\leq \max\{k(\delta + \gamma), e_k^O + (k-1)\gamma + u_k^O + \gamma\} \qquad \leq (e_{k+1}^O + u_{k+1}^O) + (k+1)\gamma$$
$$\leq e_{k+1}^O + k\gamma \qquad \leq c_{k+1}^O + (k+1)\gamma$$

Thus when $i = k + 1$, the lemma holds.
2. When $t < \frac{\delta}{2}$: we first have: $E_1^O = 0 \leq e_1^O$ and $C_1^O = 0 + U_0^O \leq 0 + \frac{3}{2}u_0^O + \frac{9}{4}\gamma \leq \frac{3}{2}c_1^O + \frac{9}{4}\gamma$ When $i = k(1 \leq k \leq \omega^O - 1)$, assume the equations $E_k^O \leq \frac{3}{2}e_k^O + \frac{9}{4}(k-1)\gamma$ hold.
Then when $i = k + 1$, we have:

$$E_{k+1}^O = \max\{\frac{3}{2}k\delta + \frac{9}{4}(k-1)\gamma, E_k^O + U_k^O\}$$
$$\leq \max\{\frac{3}{2}k\delta + \frac{9}{4}(k-1)\gamma, \frac{3}{2}e_k^O + \frac{9}{4}(k-1)\gamma + \frac{3}{2}u_k^O + \frac{9}{4}\gamma\}$$
$$\leq \frac{3}{2}\max\{k\delta, e_k^O + u_k^O\} + \frac{9}{4}k\gamma$$
$$\leq \frac{3}{2}e_{k+1}^O + \frac{9}{4}k\gamma$$
$$C_{k+1}^O = E_{k+1}^O + U_{k+1}^O$$
$$\leq \frac{3}{2}e_{k+1}^O + \frac{9}{4}k\gamma + \frac{3}{2}u_{k+1}^O + \frac{9}{4}\gamma$$
$$\leq \frac{3}{2}(e_{k+1}^O + u_{k+1}^O) + \frac{9}{4}(k+1)\gamma$$
$$\leq \frac{3}{2}c_{k+1}^O + \frac{9}{4}(k+1)\gamma$$

Thus when $i = k + 1$, the lemma holds.   □

Lemma 8. *On transporter V, for the δ-interval i of the optimal schedule and the associated time interval of S_1^*, we have:*

1. *When $t \geq \delta$: $E_i^V \leq e_i^V + (i-1)\gamma$, $C_i^V \leq c_i^V + i\gamma$ where $1 \leq i \leq \omega^V - 1$, and $E_{\omega^V}^V \leq e_{\omega^V}^V + (\omega^V - 1)\gamma$, $C_\omega^V \leq c_{\omega^V}^V + \omega^V \gamma + t_2$.*
2. *When $t < \frac{\delta}{2}$: $E_i^V \leq \frac{3}{2}e_i^V + \frac{9}{4}(i-1)\gamma$, $C_i^V \leq \frac{3}{2}c_i^V + \frac{9}{4}i\gamma$ where $1 \leq i \leq \omega^V - 1$, and $E_{\omega^V}^V \leq \frac{3}{2}e_{\omega^V}^V + \frac{9}{4}(\omega^V - 1)\gamma$, $C_{\omega^V}^V \leq \frac{3}{2}(c_{\omega^V}^V + t_2) + \frac{9}{4}\omega^V \gamma$.*

Proof. We can apply the similar method as in Lemma 7 and the conclusion from Lemma 6 to prove this lemma. $\qquad\square$

From Lemmas 7 and 8, we can get the following corollary:

Corollary 1. *Assume OPT is the length of the optimal schedule, the length of the schedule S_1^* is bounded by:*

1. *$\frac{3}{2}OPT + \frac{3}{2}t_2 + \frac{9}{4}\chi\gamma$ when $t < \frac{\delta}{2}$.*
2. *$OPT + \chi\gamma + t_2$ when $t \geq \delta$.*

Lemma 9. *In schedule S_1^*, each operation with length $\geq \gamma$ assigned in the δ-interval $i \in [1, \chi]$ of the main structure Π^* starts processing in time interval:*

1. *$[(i-1)(\delta+\gamma), i(\delta+\gamma))$ when $t \geq \delta$;*
2. *$[(i-1)(\frac{3}{2}\delta + \frac{9}{4}\gamma), i(\frac{3}{2}\delta + \frac{9}{4}\gamma) + \frac{\delta}{4})$ when $t < \frac{\delta}{2}$.*

On the other side, in schedule S_1^*, each operation with length $< \gamma$ assigned in δ-interval $i \in [1, \chi]$ of the main structure Π^* starts and completes processing in time interval:

1. *$[(i-1)(\delta+\gamma), i(\delta+\gamma) + \gamma)$ when $t \geq \delta$;*
2. *$[(i-1)(\frac{3}{2}\delta + \frac{9}{4}\gamma), i(\frac{3}{2}\delta + \frac{9}{4}\gamma) + \frac{3}{2}\gamma)$ when $t < \frac{\delta}{2}$.*

Proof. Remark: In the main structure Π^*, since there is no operation assigned in the δ-interval $(\omega^O + 1)$ to χ on processor O(O can be A, B or V), we will only focus on the δ-interval 1 to ω^O on processor O.

Clearly the operations assigned in δ-interval i starts to process after $(i-1)(\delta+\gamma)$ in the associated time interval i of the schedule S_1^* when $t \geq \delta$, when $t < \frac{\delta}{2}$, the operation assigned in associated time interval i in schedule S_1^* starts to process after $(i-1)(\frac{3}{2}\delta + \frac{9}{4}\gamma)$. Thus all we need to show is that the last operation does not start too late:

First we consider the transporter V. In the optimal schedule, we have $c_i^V - t < i\delta$ when $1 \leq i \leq \omega^V - 1$. In the δ-interval ω^V, since the optimal schedule only need t_1 amount of time to delivery the jobs and does not need to go back to machine A, thus we have $c_{\omega^V}^V - t_1 < \omega^V \delta$. According to the Lemma 8, we have:

1. When $t \geq \delta$ we have:

$$\text{When } 1 \leq i \leq \omega^V - 1: \qquad\qquad \text{When } i = \omega^V:$$
$$C_i^V - t \leq c_i^V + i\gamma - t \qquad\qquad C_i^V - t \leq c_i^V + i\gamma + t_2 - t$$
$$= (c_i^V - t) + i\gamma \qquad\qquad\qquad = (c_i^V - t_1) + i\gamma$$
$$\leq i(\delta + \gamma) \qquad\qquad\qquad\qquad \leq i(\delta + \gamma)$$

2. When $\gamma \le t < \frac{\delta}{2}$ we have:

When $1 \le i \le \omega^V - 1$:

$$C_i^V - t \le \frac{3}{2}c_i^V + \frac{9}{4}i\gamma - t$$
$$= \frac{3}{2}(c_i^V - t) + \frac{t}{2} + \frac{9}{4}i\gamma$$
$$\le i(\frac{3}{2}\delta + \frac{9}{4}\gamma) + \frac{\delta}{4}$$

When $i = \omega^V$:

$$C_i^V - t \le \frac{3}{2}(c_i^V + t_2) + \frac{9}{4}i\gamma - t$$
$$= \frac{3}{2}(c_i^V - t_1) + \frac{9}{4}i\gamma + \frac{t}{2}$$
$$\le i(\frac{3}{2}\delta + \frac{9}{4}\gamma) + \frac{\delta}{4}$$

3. When $t < \gamma$ we have:

When $1 \le i \le \omega^V - 1$:

$$C_i^V \le \frac{3}{2}c_i^V + \frac{9}{4}i\gamma$$
$$= \frac{3}{2}(c_i^V - t) + \frac{3}{2}t + \frac{9}{4}i\gamma$$
$$\le i(\frac{3}{2}\delta + \frac{9}{4}\gamma) + \frac{3}{2}\gamma$$

When $i = \omega^V$:

$$C_i^V \le \frac{3}{2}(c_i^V + t_2) + \frac{9}{4}i\gamma$$
$$= \frac{3}{2}(c_i^V - t_1) + \frac{9}{4}i\gamma + \frac{3}{2}t$$
$$\le i(\frac{3}{2}\delta + \frac{9}{4}\gamma) + \frac{3}{2}\gamma$$

Next we consider the machine O (O can be A or B). We consider two cases, here $1 \le i \le \omega^O$:

Case 1: There is at least one operation with length $\ge \gamma$ assigned in the δ-interval i of the main structure Π^*, these operations all belong to the large jobs and are scheduled in the associated time interval i of the schedule S_1^*. Assume that the operation with longest length (The length is denoted as x and $x \ge \gamma$) is schedule in the last in the associated time interval i of the schedule S_1^*. In the optimal schedule, suppose the length of the last processed operation is y and $c_i^O - y \le i\delta$. We also have $x \ge y$. According to the Lemma 7 and Corollary 1, we can obtain:

When $t \ge \delta$:

$$C_i^O - x \le c_i^O + i\gamma - x$$
$$\le (c_i^O - y) + i\gamma$$
$$\le i(\delta + \gamma)$$

When $t < \frac{\delta}{2}$:

$$C_i^O - x \le E_i^O + U_i^O - y$$
$$\le \frac{3}{2}s_i^O + \frac{9}{4}(i-1)\gamma + u_i^O + \gamma - y$$
$$\le \frac{3}{2}(s_i^O + u_i^O - y) - \frac{1}{2}(u_i^O - y) + \frac{9}{4}i\gamma$$
$$\le \frac{3}{2}(c_i^O - y) + \frac{9}{4}i\gamma$$
$$\le i(\frac{3}{2}\delta + \frac{9}{4}\gamma)$$

Case 2: in the δ-interval i of the main structure Π^*, all the assigned operations are with length $< \gamma$. In this case, all the assigned operations must have length $< \gamma$ in the optimal schedule, thus we have $c_i^O < i\delta + \gamma$. Then we obtain:

$$C_i^O \le \begin{cases} c_i^O + i\gamma \le i\delta + \gamma + i\gamma = i(\delta + \gamma) + \gamma & t \ge \delta \\ \frac{3}{2}c_i^O + \frac{9}{4}i\gamma \le \frac{3}{2}(i\delta + \gamma) + \frac{9}{4}i\gamma \le i(\frac{3}{2}\delta + \frac{9}{4}\gamma) + \frac{3}{2}\gamma & t < \frac{\delta}{2} \end{cases}$$

$\square$

In the following Lemma 10, we prove that the step 3 of procedure H will modify the schedule S_1^* to a feasible schedule.

Lemma 10. *The resulting schedule S_2^* is feasible.*

Proof. To prove the feasibility, we focus on an arbitrary job and prove each job is scheduled correctly without overlap. We will consider the large jobs and short jobs respectively.

Given a large job J_j, we first analyse its operations on the machine A and transporter V. In the optimal schedule, assume they are assigned in the δ-interval k and l separately, then the time difference of the starting time of the job J_j on machine A and transporter V is guaranteed to be at most

$$l\delta - (k-1)\delta = (l-k+1)\delta$$

In the schedule S_1^*, the time difference of the starting time of the job J_j on machine A and transporter V is at least

$$(l-1)(\delta+\gamma) - k(\delta+\gamma) \geq (l-k+1)\delta - 2(\delta+\gamma) \text{ when } t \geq \delta$$

$$(l-1)(\tfrac{3}{2}\delta + \tfrac{9}{4}\gamma) - k(\tfrac{3}{2}\delta + \tfrac{9}{4}\gamma) \geq (l-k+1)\delta - 2(\tfrac{3}{2}\delta + \tfrac{9}{4}\gamma) \text{ when } t < \frac{\delta}{2}$$

After the step 3, we delay the schedule by $2(\delta+\gamma)$ when $t \geq \gamma$ (resp. $2(\tfrac{3}{2}\delta+\tfrac{9}{4}\gamma)$ when $t < \frac{\delta}{2}$) units of time on the transporter V, then the starting time of two operations can be separated by at least $(l-k+1)\delta$ units of time, $\geq$ the time difference of the optimal schedule. Thus the large jobs are schedule feasibly on machine A and transporter V. This proof also holds for the operations on V and B of large jobs. Thus we can see the delay operations can remove the overlap for the large jobs.

For the small jobs, the assignments of operations might not follow the optimal schedule, which is not identical to the large jobs.

First consider a small job J_j with operations on machine A and transporter V. In schedule S_1^*, assume these two operations are assigned in δ-interval k and l separately with $k \leq l$. We discuss two cases: $t \geq \delta$ and $t < \frac{\delta}{2}$:

Case 1: $t \geq \delta$. From Lemma 9, we can know the operations on machine be finished before $k(\delta+\gamma)+\gamma$ and transporter V starts to delivery the job J_j at or after time $(l-1)(\delta+\gamma)$. After delaying $2(\delta+\gamma)$ units of time, the transporter V starts to delivery the job J_j at or after time $(l-1)(\delta+\gamma)+2(\delta+\gamma) > k(\delta+\gamma)+\gamma$. Thus the small jobs are scheduled feasibly on machine A and transporter V when $t \geq \delta$.

Case 2: $t < \frac{\delta}{2}$. From Lemma 9, we can know the job J_j must be finished on machine A before $k(\tfrac{3}{2}\delta + \tfrac{9}{4}\gamma) + \tfrac{3}{2}\gamma$ and transporter V starts to delivery the job J_j at or after time $(l-1)(\tfrac{3}{2}\delta + \tfrac{9}{4}\gamma)$. After delaying $2(\tfrac{3}{2}\delta + \tfrac{9}{4}\gamma)$ units of time, the transporter V starts to delivery the job J_j at or after time $(l-1)(\tfrac{3}{2}\delta + \tfrac{9}{4}\gamma) + 2(\tfrac{3}{2}\delta + \tfrac{9}{4}\gamma) > k(\tfrac{3}{2}\delta + \tfrac{9}{4}\gamma) + \tfrac{3}{2}\gamma$. Thus the small jobs are scheduled feasibly on machine A and transporter V when $t < \frac{\delta}{2}$.

Then consider the small job J_j with operations on transporter V and machine B. In the main structure Π^*, the two operations are assigned in δ-interval p and q respectively where $p + \lfloor \frac{t}{\delta} \rfloor \leq q$. We discuss two cases: $t \geq \delta$ and $t < \frac{\delta}{2}$:

Case 1: $t \geq \delta$. In the schedule S_1^*, the job J_j must arrive to machine B before $p(\delta + \gamma) + t_1$ and starts on the machine B at or after $(q - 1)(\delta + \gamma)$. After step 3 of procedure H, The operation on machine B starts at or after time $(q - 1)(\delta + \gamma) + 2(\delta + \gamma) \geq (p + \lfloor \frac{t}{\delta} \rfloor)(\delta + \gamma) + \delta + \gamma \geq p(\delta + \gamma) + t_1$. Thus the small jobs are scheduled feasibly on transporter V and machine B when $t \geq \delta$.

Case 2: $t < \frac{\delta}{2}$. In the schedule S_1^*, the job J_j must arrive to machine B before $p(\frac{3}{2}\delta + \frac{9}{4}\gamma) + \frac{\delta}{4}$ and starts on the machine B at or after $(q - 1)(\frac{3}{2}\delta + \frac{9}{4}\gamma)$. After delaying $2(\frac{3}{2}\delta + \frac{9}{4}\gamma)$ units of time, the operation on machine B starts at or after time $(q-1)(\frac{3}{2}\delta + \frac{9}{4}\gamma) + 2(\frac{3}{2}\delta + \frac{9}{4}\gamma) \geq (p + \lfloor \frac{t}{\delta} \rfloor)(\frac{3}{2}\delta + \frac{9}{4}\gamma) + \frac{3}{2}\delta + \frac{9}{4}\gamma > p(\frac{3}{2}\delta + \frac{9}{4}\gamma) + \frac{\delta}{4}$. Thus the small jobs are scheduled feasibly on transporter V and machine B when $t < \frac{\delta}{2}$.

According to the above analysis, there is no overlap for the small jobs in the schedule S_2^*. $\square$

Theorem 1. *The Algorithm 1 can generate a feasible schedule within the length $(\frac{5}{3} + \varepsilon)OPT$ in polynomial time. When $t < \frac{\delta}{2}$, the algorithm will obtain the approximation ratio $(\frac{3}{2} + \varepsilon)$.*

Proof. First, we prove the length of the schedule (See Appendix for more details): From the above lemma, assume the length of the S_2^* is T^* and we have $T' \leq \frac{7}{3}OPT$.

When $t \geq \delta$, since $t \leq \frac{2}{3}OPT$. Then we can obtain:

$$T^* \leq OPT + t_2 + \chi\gamma + 4(\delta + \gamma) + t_1 + 6\chi\gamma \leq \left(\frac{5}{3} + \varepsilon\right)OPT$$

When $\gamma \leq t < \frac{\delta}{2}$, we obtain:

$$T^* \leq \frac{3}{2}OPT + \frac{9}{4}\chi\gamma + \frac{3}{2}t_2 + \chi\gamma + 4\left(\frac{3}{2}\delta + \frac{9}{4}\gamma\right) + t_1 + 6\chi\gamma \leq \left(\frac{3}{2} + \varepsilon\right)OPT$$

When $t < \gamma$, we can obtain:

$$T^* \leq \frac{3}{2}OPT + \frac{3}{2}t_2 + 4\left(\frac{3}{2}\delta + \frac{9}{4}\gamma\right) + (5\chi + 2)\gamma < \left(\frac{3}{2} + \varepsilon\right)OPT$$

Second we show that the time complexity of the algorithm. We already showed that the algorithm would generate all main structures with time complexity $O(n^{\frac{81}{\varepsilon}})$. For each main structure, we run procedure H to generate the schedule. The step 2 and 3 of procedure H runs in linear time, the bottle neck of the procedure H is step 1 that finding a feasible solution of the linear programming (a polynomial-time procedure). Each linear program has at most $O(n\frac{27^3}{\varepsilon^3})$ variables and $O(n + \frac{135}{\varepsilon})$ constraints. Assume the input size is N which is polynomial with, then the algorithm of [15] can solve the linear program in time

$O\left((n\frac{27^3}{\varepsilon^3} + n + 5\frac{27}{\varepsilon})^{1.5}n\frac{27^3}{\varepsilon^3}N\right)$, since $\frac{1}{\varepsilon}$ is the constant, thus the complexity of solving the linear programme is $O(n^{2.5}N)$. Hence total running time of the Algorithm 1 would be $O(n^{2.5+\frac{81}{\varepsilon}}N)$. Since N is polynomial to n, the Algorithm 1 runs in polynomial time.   □

4   Conclusion

In this paper, we study the problem $TF2|s_i|C_{max}$. Unlike the previous algorithm that only focuses on the size of each job, we consider the size, processing time of each job and the transporting time together. By this way, we improve the approximation ratio and get a $(\frac{5}{3} + \varepsilon)$-approximation algorithm for this problem. When the transporting time is short enough, the algorithm even can reach approximation ratio of $(\frac{3}{2} + \varepsilon)$.

Even this algorithm has a better approximation ratio theoretically, but the algorithm is slower than the known algorithm [2,4,17]. It will be interesting to find a faster algorithm that can remove the ε from the approximation ratio.

Appendix

Lemma 2. *Consider any input L with x items with size in $(\frac{1}{2}, 1]$, y items with size in $(\frac{1}{3}, \frac{1}{2}]$ of the bin-packing problem. Then we can construct a new input L' with the following two conditions such that $FFD(L') \leq \frac{3}{2}OPT(L) + 1$.*

Condition 1: the total size of L' is at most the total size of all items in L.
Condition 2: L' has at most x, y number of items with size in $(\frac{1}{2}, 1], (\frac{1}{3}, \frac{1}{2}]$ respectively.

Proof. There are two cases after running the FFD algorithm to the L':
    Case 1: The last bin has at least one item with size $>\frac{1}{3}$.
    In this case, the worst case of packing results of L' is that the each job with size in $(\frac{1}{2}, 1]$ takes one bin, every two jobs of size in $(\frac{1}{3}, \frac{1}{2}]$ take one bin. Then we have $FFD(L') \leq \lceil\frac{y}{2}\rceil + \lceil\frac{x}{2}\rceil$. We also have

$$OPT(L) \geq \begin{cases} x & x \geq y \\ x + \lceil\frac{y-x}{2}\rceil & x < y \end{cases}$$

    Then we get $FFD(L') \leq \frac{3}{2}OPT(L) + 1$.
    Case 2: the last bin only contains the items with size $\leq\frac{1}{3}$. As we can see, all the other bins contain at least $\frac{2}{3}$ size of items. If FFD uses at least $\frac{3}{2}OPT(L)+2$ bins, then FFD packs at least $(\frac{3}{2}OPT(L) + 1) \times \frac{2}{3} = OPT(L) + \frac{2}{3}$ size of items, so we get a contradiction: the total size of the items of L' is larger than $OPT(L)$ while $OPT(L)$ is larger than the total size of the items in L. Thus we have $FFD(L') \leq \frac{3}{2}OPT(L) + 1$.   □

Lemma 3. *The partition contains at most the polynomial number of the main structures.*

Proof. If the feasible schedules are grouped into the same main structure, then it means these schedules share the same characteristics which are aforementioned.
When $t \geq \gamma$: the first characteristic will generate at most $\chi^{\frac{2970}{\varepsilon} + \frac{1485 \times 81}{\varepsilon^3}}$ number of main structures. The second characteristic will produce at most $\left(\frac{55}{\varepsilon}\right)^\chi$ number of main structures since each δ-interval can assign at most $\frac{\delta}{\gamma} = \frac{55}{\varepsilon}$ batches. In the last characteristic, we will also obtain at most $\left(\frac{55}{\varepsilon}\right)^\chi$ number of main structures.

When $t < \gamma$: the first character will generate at most $\chi^{\frac{2970}{\varepsilon}}$ number of main structures. The second character will produce at most n^χ number of main structures since each interval can be assigned at most n batches. Similar to the second character, the third character will generate at most $n^{2\chi}$ number of main structures. In the last characteristic, at most $\left(\frac{55}{\varepsilon}\right)^\chi$ number of main structures will be obtained.

The number of the partition beforementioned can be bounded by the product of the above number of the main structures generated by the given characteristics respectively. Since χ is an constant, the number of the main structures of the partition is bounded by $O(n^{3\chi})$. $\qquad\square$

Lemma 6. *For the δ-interval i of the optimal schedule and the associated time interval of S_1^*, on transporter V we have:*

- *$t \geq \delta$: $U_i^V \leq u_i^V + \gamma$ when $1 \leq i \leq \omega^V - 1$, and $U_{\omega V}^V \leq u_{\omega V}^V + \gamma + t_2$*
- *$t < \frac{\delta}{2}$: $U_i^V \leq \frac{3}{2}u_i^V + \frac{9}{4}\gamma$ when $1 \leq i \leq \omega^V - 1$, and $U_{\omega V}^V \leq \frac{3}{2}(u_{\omega V}^V + t_2) + \frac{9}{4}\gamma$*

Proof. Here we consider three cases:

1. When $t \geq \delta$, we first consider the time interval i where $1 \leq i \leq \omega^V - 1$, in this case, each time interval only can assign at most 1 batch, we can see that if the optimal schedule only have one batch in the δ-interval i, then the jobs assigned in associated time interval of schedule S_1^* will also be packed to a single batch. Thus $U_i^V \leq u_i^V + \gamma$ holds. Then we consider the time interval ω^V. In the schedule S_1^*, there is only one batch assigned in the associated time interval ω^V, we have $U_{\omega V}^O \leq t$. In the optimal schedule, the transporter V might not need to go back to machine A, thus we can obtain $u_{\omega V}^V \geq t_1$. Hence we have $U_{\omega V}^O \leq u_{\omega V}^V + \gamma + t_2$.

2. When $\gamma \leq t < \frac{\delta}{2}$, we first consider the time interval i where $1 \leq i \leq \omega^V - 1$. From the Lemma 1, we can see that if the optimal schedule only need the L_i^* batches in the δ-interval i, then the jobs assigned in the associated time interval in the schedule S_1^* needs $\frac{3}{2}L_i^*$ batches. Thus $U_i^V \leq \frac{3}{2}u_i^V + \frac{9}{4}\gamma$ holds. Then we consider the time interval ω^V, in this time interval, the transporter V in schedule S_1^* needs to go back to machine A for delivering the left fractional jobs while the optimal solution does not need. Here we have $u_{\omega V}^V \geq (L^* - 1)t + t_1$, $U_{\omega V}^V \leq \frac{3}{2}L^*t$, since $t_1 + t_2 = t$, then we have $U_{\omega V}^V \leq \frac{3}{2}\left(u_{\omega V}^V + t_2\right) \leq \frac{3}{2}\left(u_{\omega V}^V + t_2\right) + \frac{9}{4}\gamma$.

3. When $t < \gamma$, from the Lemma 2, we can see that if the optimal schedule only need the L_i^* batches in the δ interval i, then the jobs assigned in the associated time interval in schedule S_1^* can be packed into $\frac{3}{2}L_i^* + 1$ batches. When $1 \leq i \leq \omega^V - 1$, since the transporter V in optimal solution and the schedule S_1^* both need to go to machine A, and $t \leq \gamma$, thus the lemma holds. When $i = \omega^V$, the optimal solution does not need to go back to machine A in the last batch. Hence we have $u_{\omega^V}^V \geq (L^* - 1)t + t_1$, $U_{\omega^V}^V \leq \frac{3}{2}(L^* + 1)t$, since $t < \gamma$ and $t_2 < \frac{\gamma}{2}$, then we can obtain $U_i^O \leq \frac{3}{2}u_i^O + \frac{9}{4}\gamma \leq \frac{3}{2}\left(u_{\omega^V}^V + t_2\right) + \frac{9}{4}\gamma$.

$\square$

Lemma 8. *On transporter V, for the δ-interval i of the optimal schedule and the associated time interval of S_1^*, we have:*

1. *When $t \geq \delta$: $E_i^V \leq e_i^V + (i - 1)\gamma$, $C_i^V \leq c_i^V + i\gamma$ where $1 \leq i \leq \omega^V - 1$, and $E_{\omega^V}^V \leq e_{\omega^V}^V + (\omega^V - 1)\gamma$, $C_{\omega^V}^V \leq c_{\omega^V}^V + \omega^V\gamma + t_2$.*
2. *When $t < \frac{\delta}{2}$: $E_i^V \leq \frac{3}{2}e_i^V + \frac{9}{4}(i - 1)\gamma$, $C_i^V \leq \frac{3}{2}c_i^V + \frac{9}{4}i\gamma$ where $1 \leq i \leq \omega^V - 1$, and $E_{\omega^V}^V \leq \frac{3}{2}e_{\omega^V}^V + \frac{9}{4}(\omega^V - 1)\gamma$, $C_{\omega^V}^V \leq \frac{3}{2}(c_{\omega^V}^V + t_2) + \frac{9}{4}\omega^V\gamma$.*

Proof. We will prove two different cases respectively:

1. When $t \geq \delta$: In the time interval 1, we have:
   $E_1^V = 0 \leq e_1^V$ and $C_1^V = 0 + U_0^V \leq 0 + u_0^V + \gamma \leq c_1^V + \gamma$
   When $i = k(1 \leq k \leq \omega^V - 2)$, assume the equations $E_k^V \leq e_k^V + (k - 1)\gamma$ hold. Then when $i = k + 1$, we have:

$$
\begin{aligned}
E_{k+1}^V &= \max\{k(\delta + \gamma), E_k^V + U_k^V\} \\
&\leq \max\{k(\delta + \gamma), E_k^V + u_k^V + \gamma\} \\
&\leq \max\{k(\delta + \gamma), e_k^V + (k - 1)\gamma + u_k^V + \gamma\} \\
&\leq e_{k+1}^V + k\gamma
\end{aligned}
\qquad
\begin{aligned}
C_{k+1}^V &\leq E_{k+1}^V + U_{k+1}^V \\
&\leq e_{k+1}^V + k\gamma + u_{k+1}^V + \gamma \\
&\leq (e_{k+1}^V + u_{k+1}^V) + (k + 1)\gamma \\
&\leq c_{k+1}^V + (k + 1)\gamma
\end{aligned}
$$

When $i = \omega^V$, we have:

$$
\begin{aligned}
E_{\omega^V}^V &= \max\{(\omega^V - 1)(\delta + \gamma), E_{\omega^V - 1}^V + U_{\omega^V - 1}^V\} \\
&\leq \max\{(\omega^V - 1)(\delta + t_2 + \gamma), E_{\omega^V - 1}^V + u_{\omega^V - 1}^V + \gamma\} \\
&\leq \max\{(\omega^V - 1)(\delta + \gamma), e_{\omega^V - 1}^V + (\omega^V - 2)\gamma + u_{\omega^V - 1}^V + \gamma\} \\
&\leq e_{\omega^V}^V + (\omega^V - 1)\gamma \\
C_{\omega^V}^V &\leq E_{\omega^V}^V + U_{\omega^V}^V \\
&\leq e_{\omega^V}^V + (\omega^V - 1)\gamma + u_{\omega^V}^V + \gamma + t_2 \\
&\leq (e_{\omega^V}^V + u_{\omega^V}^V) + \omega^V\gamma + t_2 \\
&\leq c_{\omega^V}^V + \omega^V\gamma + t_2
\end{aligned}
$$

2. When $t < \frac{\delta}{2}$: we first have: $E_1^V = 0 \leq e_1^V$ and $C_1^V = 0 + U_0^V \leq 0 + \frac{3}{2}u_0^V + \frac{9}{4}\gamma \leq \frac{3}{2}c_1^V + \frac{9}{4}\gamma$.

When $i = k(1 \leq k \leq \omega^V - 2)$, assume the equations $E_k^V \leq \frac{3}{2}e_k^V + \frac{9}{4}(k-1)\gamma$ hold.

Then when $i = k + 1$, we have:

$$E_{k+1}^V = \max\{\frac{3}{2}k\delta + \frac{9}{4}(k-1)\gamma, E_k^V + U_k^V\}$$

$$\leq \max\{\frac{3}{2}k\delta + \frac{9}{4}(k-1)\gamma, \frac{3}{2}e_k^V + \frac{9}{4}(k-1)\gamma + \frac{3}{2}u_k^V + \frac{9}{4}\gamma\}$$

$$\leq \frac{3}{2}\max\{k\delta, e_k^V + u_k^V\} + \frac{9}{4}k\gamma$$

$$\leq \frac{3}{2}e_{k+1}^V + \frac{9}{4}k\gamma$$

$$C_{k+1}^V = E_{k+1}^V + U_{k+1}^V$$

$$\leq \frac{3}{2}e_{k+1}^V + \frac{9}{4}k\gamma + \frac{3}{2}u_{k+1}^V + \frac{9}{4}\gamma$$

$$\leq \frac{3}{2}(e_{k+1}^V + u_{k+1}^V) + \frac{9}{4}(k+1)\gamma$$

$$\leq \frac{3}{2}c_{k+1}^V + \frac{9}{4}(k+1)\gamma$$

When $i = \omega^V$, we have:

$$E_{\omega^V}^V = \max\{\frac{3}{2}(\omega^V - 1)\delta + \frac{9}{4}(\omega^V - 2)\gamma, E_{\omega^V - 1}^V + U_{\omega^V - 1}^V\}$$

$$\leq \max\{\frac{3}{2}(\omega^V - 1)\delta + \frac{9}{4}(\omega^V - 2)\gamma, \frac{3}{2}e_{\omega^V}^V + \frac{9}{4}(\omega^V - 2)\gamma + \frac{3}{2}u_{\omega^V - 1}^V + \frac{9}{4}\gamma\}$$

$$\leq \frac{3}{2}\max\{(\omega^V - 1)\delta, e_{\omega^V - 1}^V + u_{\omega^V - 1}^V\} + \frac{9}{4}(\omega^V - 1)\gamma$$

$$\leq \frac{3}{2}e_{\omega^V}^V + \frac{9}{4}(\omega^V - 1)\gamma$$

$$C_{\omega^V}^V = E_{\omega^V}^V + U_{\omega^V}^V$$

$$\leq \frac{3}{2}e_{\omega^V}^V + \frac{9}{4}(\omega^V - 1)\gamma + \frac{3}{2}u_{\omega^V}^V + \frac{9}{4}\gamma + \frac{3}{2}t_2$$

$$\leq \frac{3}{2}(e_{\omega^V}^V + u_{\omega^V}^V) + \frac{9}{4}\omega^V\gamma + \frac{3}{2}t_2$$

$$\leq \frac{3}{2}c_{\omega^V}^V + \frac{9}{4}\omega^V\gamma + \frac{3}{2}t_2$$

Thus the lemma holds.

$\square$

Theorem 1. *The Algorithm 1 can generate a feasible schedule within the length $(\frac{5}{3} + \varepsilon)OPT$ in polynomial time. When $t < \frac{\delta}{2}$, the algorithm will obtain the approximation ratio $(\frac{3}{2} + \varepsilon)$.*

Proof. In the Lemma 10, we already prove that the algorithm will produce the feasible schedule.

First, we prove the length of the schedule: From the above lemma, assume the length of the S_2^* is T^* and we have $T' \leq \frac{7}{3}OPT$.

When $t \geq \delta$, since $OPT \geq t + t_1$, $t_1 \geq t_2$, then we have $t \leq \frac{2}{3}OPT$. Then we can obtain:

$$
\begin{aligned}
T^* &\leq OPT + t_2 + \chi\gamma + 4(\delta + \gamma) + t_1 + 6\chi\gamma \\
&\leq OPT + t + (7\chi + 4)\gamma + 4\delta \\
&\leq \frac{5}{3}OPT + (7\chi + 4)\gamma + 4\delta \\
&\leq \frac{5}{3}OPT + \left(\frac{4}{27} + \frac{7 \times 27 + 4}{1485}\right)\varepsilon T' \\
&\leq \frac{5}{3}OPT + \frac{8}{27}\varepsilon T' \\
&\leq \left(\frac{5}{3} + \varepsilon\right)OPT
\end{aligned}
$$

When $\gamma \leq t < \frac{\delta}{2}$, we obtain:

$$
\begin{aligned}
T^* &\leq \frac{3}{2}OPT + \frac{9}{4}\chi\gamma + \frac{3}{2}t_2 + \chi\gamma + 4\left(\frac{3}{2}\delta + \frac{9}{4}\gamma\right) + t_1 + 6\chi\gamma \\
&< \frac{3}{2}OPT + \left(\left(\frac{9}{4} + 6\right)\chi + 9\right)\gamma + 6\delta + t + \frac{t_2}{2} \\
&\leq \frac{3}{2}OPT + \left(\left(\frac{9}{4} + 6\right)\chi + 9\right)\gamma + 6\delta + \frac{\delta}{2} + \frac{\delta}{8} \\
&\leq \frac{3}{2}OPT + \left(\frac{27 \times 33}{4\varepsilon} + 9\right)\frac{\varepsilon^2 T'}{1485} + \frac{53\varepsilon T'}{216} \\
&< \frac{3}{2}OPT + \varepsilon OPT \\
&\leq \left(\frac{3}{2} + \varepsilon\right)OPT
\end{aligned}
$$

When $t < \gamma$, we can obtain:

$$
\begin{aligned}
T^* &\leq \frac{3}{2}OPT + \frac{3}{2}t_2 + 4\left(\frac{3}{2}\delta + \frac{9}{4}\gamma\right) + (5\chi + 2)\gamma \\
&< \frac{3}{2}OPT + \left(\left(\frac{9}{4} + 5\right)\chi + 11\right)\gamma + 6\delta \\
&< \frac{3}{2}OPT + \left(\frac{29 \times 27}{4\varepsilon} + 11\right)\frac{\varepsilon^2 T'}{1485} + \frac{6\varepsilon T'}{27} \\
&\leq \frac{3}{2}OPT + \varepsilon OPT \\
&< \left(\frac{3}{2} + \varepsilon\right)OPT
\end{aligned}
$$

Second we show that the time complexity of the algorithm. We already showed that the algorithm would generate all main structures with time complexity $O(n^{\frac{81}{\varepsilon}})$. For each main structure, we run procedure H to generate the schedule. The step 2 and 3 of procedure H runs in linear time, the bottle neck of the procedure H is step 1 that finding a feasible solution of the linear programming (a polynomial-time procedure). Each linear program has at most $O(n^{\frac{27^3}{\varepsilon^3}})$ variables and $O(n + \frac{135}{\varepsilon})$ constraints. Assume the input size is N which is polynomial with, then the algorithm of [15] can solve the linear program in time $O\left((n^{\frac{27^3}{\varepsilon^3}} + n + 5\frac{27}{\varepsilon})^{1.5} n^{\frac{27^3}{\varepsilon^3}} N\right)$, since $\frac{1}{\varepsilon}$ is the constant, thus the complexity of solving the linear programme is $O(n^{2.5}N)$. Hence total running time of the Algorithm 1 would be $O(n^{2.5+\frac{81}{\varepsilon}} N)$. Since N is polynomial to n, the Algorithm 1 runs in polynomial time. $\qquad\square$

References

1. Cheng, T.C.E., Gordon, V.S.: Batch delivery scheduling on a single machine. J. Oper. Res. Soc. **45**(10), 1211–1216 (1994)
2. Dong, J., Wang, X., Hu, J., Lin, G.: An improved two-machine flowshop scheduling with intermediate transportation. J. Comb. Optim. **31**(3), 1316–1334 (2016)
3. Garey, M.R., Johnson, D.S.: Computers and Intractability: A Guide to the Theory of NP-Completeness. W. H. Freeman & Co., New York (1979)
4. Gong, H., Tang, L.: Two-machine flowshop scheduling with intermediate transportation under job physical space consideration. Comput. Oper. Res. **38**(9), 1267–1274 (2011)
5. Graham, R.L., Lawler, E.L., Lenstra, J.K., Rinnooy Kan, A.H.G.: Optimization and approximation in deterministic sequencing and scheduling: a survey. Ann. Discret. Math. **5**(1), 287–326 (1979)
6. Hall, L.A.: Approximability of flow shop scheduling. Math. Program. **82**(1), 175–190 (1998)
7. Hall, L.A., Shmoys, D.B.: Approximation schemes for constrained scheduling problems. In: 1989 30th Annual Symposium on Foundations of Computer Science, pp. 134–139. IEEE (1989)
8. Hurink, J., Knust, S.: Makespan minimization for flow-shop problems with transportation times and a single robot. Discret. Appl. Math. **112**(1), 199–216 (2001)
9. Johnson, D.S., Demers, A., Ullman, J.D., Garey, M.R., Graham, R.L.: Worst-case performance bounds for simple one-dimensional packing algorithms. SIAM J. Comput. **3**(4), 299–325 (1974)
10. Lan, Y., Han, X., Wu, Z., Guo, H., Chen, X.: Complexity of problem $TF2|v = 1, c = 2|C_{max}$. Inf. Process. Lett. **116**(1), 65–69 (2016)
11. Lee, C.Y., Chen, Z.L.: Machine scheduling with transportation considerations. J. Sched. **4**(1), 3–24 (2001)
12. Johnson, S.M.: Optimal two- and three-stage production schedules with setup times included. Nav. Res. Logist. Q. **1**(1), 61–68 (1954)
13. Maggu, P.L., Das, G.: On $2 \times n$ sequencing problem with transportation times of jobs. Am. J. Ind. Med. **12**(6), 574–83 (1980)
14. Simchi-Levi, D.: New worst-case results for the bin-packing problem. Nav. Res. Logist. **41**(4), 579 (1994)

15. Vaidya, P.M.: Speeding-up linear programming using fast matrix multiplication. In: Proceedings of the 30th Annual Symposium on Foundations of Computer Science, pp. 332–337 (1989)
16. Chang, Y.-C., Lee, C.Y.: Machine scheduling with job delivery coordination. Eur. J. Oper. Res. **158**(2), 470–487 (2004)
17. Zhong, W., Chen, Z.L.: Flowshop scheduling with interstage job transportation. J. Sched. **18**(4), 411–422 (2015)

A Kernel Method with Manifold Regularization for Interactive Segmentation

Haohao Chen[1], En Zhu[1(✉)], Xinwang Liu[1], Junnan Zhang[1], and Jianping Yin[2]

[1] College of Computer, National University of Defense Technology,
Changsha 410073, Hunan, China
HaohaoChen666@163.com, {enzhu,xinwangliu,zhangjunnan12}@nudt.edu.cn
[2] Dongguan University of Technology, Dongguan 523000, Guangzhou, China
jpyin@dgut.edu.cn

Abstract. Interactive segmentation has been successfully applied to various applications such as image editing, computer vision, image identification. Most of existing methods require interaction for each single image segmentation, which costs too much labor interactions. To address this issue, we propose a kernel based semi-supervised learning framework with manifold regularization for interactive image segmentation in this paper. Specifically, by manifold regularization, our algorithm makes similar superpixel pair bearing the same label. Moreover, the learned classifier on one single image is directly used to similar images for segmentation. Extensive experimental results demonstrate the effectiveness of the proposed approach.

Keywords: Interactive image segmentation
Semi-supervised learning · Manifold regularization

1 Introduction

Image segmentation, aiming to separate foreground from a given image, is one of the most important and basic tasks in computer vision. Fully automatic segmentation is arguably an intrinsically ill-posed problem because the region of interest to users is uncertain and manual segmentation is time-consuming. Interactive image segmentation has demonstrated great practical importance and popularity [1]. In an interactive segmentation method, it is fed with an image and the corresponding interactions and outputs the segmentation result.

So far, many algorithms for interactive image segmentation have been proposed. The existing methods can be divided into four categories according to the interaction mode: seed/scribble based [2–4,11], contours based [5], bounding boxes based [6–8] and query based [9,10]. There are two categories for the existing methods considering the algorithm's principle. One is based on probability estimation, which segments the image by estimating the probability of each pixel or super pixel as foreground given the seed. The another is based

L. Li et al. (Eds.): NCTCS 2018, CCIS 882, pp. 141–149, 2018.
https://doi.org/10.1007/978-981-13-2712-4_10

on graph, where there are two subcategories: MRF model based [1,6] and Random walker based [3,16]. The Markov random field (MRF) theory provides an effective and consistent way of modeling contextual information such as image pixels and features. In this model, the mutual influences among pixels can be formulated into conditional MRF distributions. The solution of random walker probabilities has been found the same as minimizing a combinatorial Dirichlet problem [11]. The existing interactive image segmentation algorithms have been able to meet most tasks of image segmentation. However, when a user encounters a group of similar images, for example, medical images in a specific medical diagnosis problem often have the same color space distribution, interacting with each image is a tedious task. Existing methods interacting with each image does not take advantage of the prior knowledge when dealing with a set of similar images. The proposed method can segment a set of similar images by interacting with only a single image within the set.

This paper proposes an interactive segmentation algorithm that can deal with batches of similar image segmentation tasks. Unlike the previous method, this paper uses a semi-supervised learning method to train a kernel classifier, taking labeled foreground and background pixel as positive and negative samples for training, and other pixels as unlabeled training samples. By adding manifold regularization term [12], the geometric distributions of the classification hyperplane and the superpixel feature space fit more closely. Under the trained classifier, all the superpixels will be divided into two classes, foreground and background. Therefore, the classifier trained for similar image features can still be used for the image data set with similar feature distribution, and the segmentation process on the new data set is automatic.

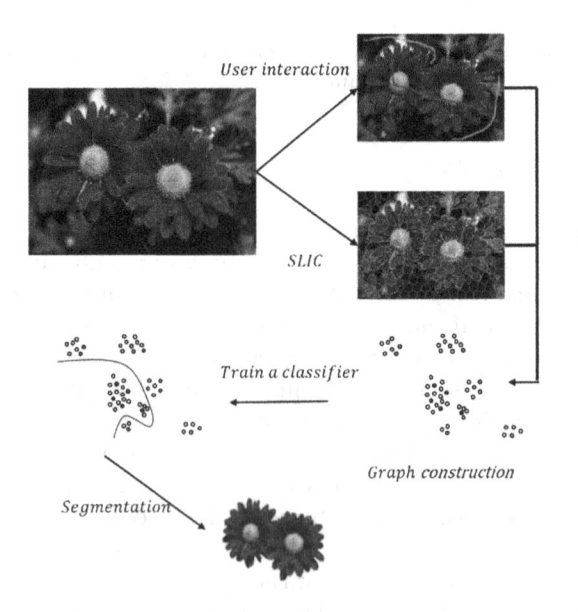

Fig. 1. The steps of the interactive segmentation method using manifold regularization (Color figure online)

2   Related Works

2.1   Graph-Based Interactive Segmentation

Interactive segmentation based on graph has been the mainstream method. The state-of-art methods Graphcut, Grabcut and random walking all are graph-based methods. They use pixels or superpixels as nodes and define a weight for each edge, and the segmentation of the graph is realized by using the spectral information or the graph cut theory. Graphcut takes full advantage of the map region information and border information. Grabcut is intrinsically a Graphcut algorithm using the distribution of color information. Random walking takes advantage of the color features of pixels and the adjacency between pixels.

2.2   Semi-supervised Learning Framework Using Manifold Regularization

The semi-supervised learning framework using manifold regularization was proposed by Belkin et al. in 2006. It is a graph-based semi-supervised learning framework. This framework exploits the geometry of the probability distribution that generates the data and incorporates it as an additional regularization term [12]. It can use the information of a small number of labeled samples and the sample distribution information represented by most unlabeled samples to fit the classification hyperplane with all samples. It optimizes the model by adding a manifold regular term to the standard regularized learning framework:

$$min\ Loss + \gamma_1 \|f\|_k + \gamma_2 \|f\|_M, \qquad (1)$$

The first term is the loss between $f(x)$ and y. The term $\|f\|_M$ in formula (1) is the manifold regularization which is an appropriate penalty term that should reflect the intrinsic structure of P_x. $\|f\|_k$ is standard regularization controlling the complexity of f. Intuitively, $\|f\|_M$ is a smoothness penalty corresponding to the probability distribution. For example, if the probability distribution is supported on a low dimensional manifold, $\|f\|_M$ may penalize f along that manifold. γ_1 controls the complexity of the function in the ambient space while γ_2 controls the complexity of the function in the intrinsic geometry of [12].

3   Approach

3.1   Graph Construction

We construct a graph $G(V, E, W)$ for an input image I, where $V = [v_i]_{i=1}^N$ is a set of superpixels, and E represents the edge of the pairwise superpixels, and the W represents the weight of the edges. We use SLIC [13] superpixels as samples in our approach to reduce the dimension of matrix calculation in the models mentioned in Sect. ss. The weight on an edge represents the similarity of a pair of superpixels. We define the similarity W_{ij} between superpixel pair (v_i, v_j) as:

$$W_{ij} = \begin{cases} exp(-\beta \, \|x_i - x_j\|_2) \; if(v_i, v_j) \in \aleph \\ \\ 0 \qquad\qquad\qquad otherwise \end{cases} \tag{2}$$

where the x_i and x_j denote the feature at the superpixel v_i and v_j, respectively. $\aleph$ is the set of all adjacent superpixels, and the constant β controls the strength of the similarity. We define the similarity between non-adjacent superpixels as 0, to reduce the computational complexity of the method.

3.2 Learning Model

Laplacian-SVM [12] is a model of the learning framework mentioned at Sect. 2.2, which is to add manifold regularization term to classical SVM. We assume $x_1, x_2, \cdots, x_l, \cdots, x_{l+u}$ represent the feature vectors of superpixels $v_1, v_2, \cdots, v_l$, $\cdots, v_{l+u}$, where $x_1, x_2, \cdots, x_l$ represent the feature vector of labeled superpixels, and $y_1, y_2, \cdots, y_l$ represent the corresponding label, $y_i \in \{1, -1\}$. When $y_i = 1$, the corresponding superpixel v_1 is marked as foreground, and $y_i = -1$ for background. By leveraging a kernel function $\kappa : R^d \times R^d \rightarrow R$ that induces the Re-producing Kernel Hilbert Space, the Representer theorem states that the target classification function is:

$$f(x) = \sum_{i=1}^{N} \kappa(x, x_i)\alpha_i \tag{3}$$

where α_i is the expansion coefficient contributing to the functional base $\kappa(\cdot, x_i)$. Then we establish the Laplacian as minimizing the following objective:

$$\min_{f \in H_k} \frac{1}{l} \sum_{i=1}^{l} (1 - y_i f(x_i)) + \gamma_1 \|f\|_k + \gamma_2 f^T L f \tag{4}$$

where $f = [f(x_1), f(x_2), \cdots, f(x_N)]^T$, L is Laplacian matrix defined with $L = D - W$, and D is a diagonal matrix made up of $D_{ii} = \sum_{j=1}^{N} W_{ij}$, the ith row and jth column element. The first term in the Eq. (4) is hinge loss function $\max[0, 1 - y_i f(x_i)]$. The second term is standard regularization which controls the complexity of the classification function $f(x)$ and the third term is manifold regularization. The function f is to classify the superpixels into foreground and background. We learn the f through the above model, then we can use f to predict the remaining unlabeled superpixels as a result $f^* = K\alpha^*$, where $K = [\kappa(x_i, x_j)]_{1 < i,j < N} \in R^{n \times n}$, and α^* is calculated by optimizing the formula (4).

3.3 User Interaction and Post-processing

The labeled samples are obtained by the way that user mark the pixels by green and red as shown in the Fig. 1, where the superpixels marked green is positive samples and red one negative. We choose the way like draw lines, mark the point as the user interaction.

Using this method will meet a problem that there is much noise in the resulting background, as shown in Fig. 2. We calculate the Maximum Connected Component of the mask of an image may solve this problem, and error rate reduce greatly.

0.2851

0.0295

Fig. 2. Comparison of accuracy and performance before and after post-processing, the left column is error rate, the right column is result of segmentation.

3.4   Similar Images Segmentation

When we are faced with the task of segmenting a group of similar images, the previous method of interactive image segmentation seems less intelligent and needs to provide interactive information for each image, since it ignores the prior knowledge that this group of images are similar. Interacting with one or some of the representative images, obtaining a classifier, also reaches good performance for other similar images. Similar images are of similar color features. Therefore, a classifier trained for one image among a set of similar image can be used for predicting the foreground of the rest images.

We can formally describe the problem. For a segmentation task T, there are S images $I_1, I_2, \cdots, I_S$, we can obtain a feature matrix $X_{N_i \times d}$ for each image I_i, where N_i is the number of superpixel of image I_i and d represents feature's dimension of superpixel. Choosing one tipical image I_t, users mask the foreground and background superpixels, input the interactions into the learning model in Sect. 3.2, and then obtain a classification function $f_t = \alpha^T k_t(x)$, where $k_t(x) = [\kappa(x_1, x), \cdots, \kappa(x_{N_t}, x)]$. We can use this function to predict the other similar images. For image I_i of this task T:

$$Y = K_{1i}\alpha \tag{5}$$

where Y represents the predict label, and $K_{1i} = [\kappa(x_{k_t}, x_{j_i})]_{1 \leq k_t \leq N_t, 1 \leq j_i \leq N_i} \in R^{N_t \times N_i}$.

4 Experiment

In this section, we evaluate the proposed approach on Grabcut dataset and Berkeley Segmentation Dataset 300 and compare it with the state-of-the-art methods. Another experiment on video frames is also conducted and shows the validity of the proposed approach.

4.1 Segmentation of a Single Image

We conduct experiments on Microsoft GrabCut dataset, which includes 50 images with ground truth segmentations. For this dataset, we use the public seeds information [14] as the label information for pixels. For both datasets, we use the SLIC superpixels to produce nearly 250 superpixels per picture, where each superpixel is of about 250 pixels large for a typical 321 * 481 image. We use the average color of pixels in both RGB and Lab color space as features for every superpixel, and thus the number of feature dimensions is 6 (3 for Lab Space, 3 for RGB space). We may treat this superpixel segmentation process as a pre-processing phase, and the entire framework will start after this step. We set the parameters as follows: $\sigma = 0.5, \lambda_1 = 0.1, \lambda_2 = 30$ in this part of experiment, In the we will discuss the relation-ship between the change of parameters and the segmentation result.

Table 1. Mean and variance of error rates of different methods on the Grabcut dataset.

Methods	Error rate (%)
	Mean ($\pm$) Std
GrabCut [6]	5.46 $\pm$ 4.2
Random walker [3]	6.45 $\pm$ 4.8
Sub-Markov random walk [16]	4.61 $\pm$ 3.2(listed [10])
Laplacian coordinates [15]	5.04 $\pm$ 3.8(listed [10])
Nonparametric higher-order model [17]	4.25 $\pm$ 3.7(listed [10])
Pairwise likelihood learning [10]	3.49 $\pm$ 2.6(listed [10])
Ours	2.47 $\pm$ 2.1

To evaluate our method,we compare our results with the six other state-of-the-art methods. We compare the performance of the different methods by comparing the error rate $\varepsilon = \frac{N_{error}}{N_{unlabel}}$, where N_{error} represents the number of wrongly classified pixel, and $N_{unlabel}$ represents the number of all unlabeled pixel. As shown in Table 1, our method based on manifold regularization is effective for interactive image segmentation (Fig. 3).

Fig. 3. The first column is the user's interaction with the images of Grabcut dataset, the second column is the segmentation result of foreground, the third column is the mask of the segmentation result, and the last column is the ground truth.

4.2 Segmentation of a Set of Similar Images

We also use this method to solve the video cutout problem. The frames of a video are a batch of images with similar color distribution. We use one image to train the classifier and then predict the other images. We use the algorithm for several video data in [18] to observe the performance of the method on similar images. The quantitative result is shown in Table 2, and the qualitative results are shown in Fig. 4. Existing interactive methods cannot implement video cutout with little interaction. Therefore, the existing methods and the method in this paper are not comparable in this experiment.

Table 2. Performance on Jumpcut dataset.

Methods	Error rate (%)
	Mean ($\pm$) Std
Bear	2.53 ± 3.83
Cheetah	1.66 ± 0.52
Kung Fu	1.83 ± 1.00
Pig	3.36 ± 1.59

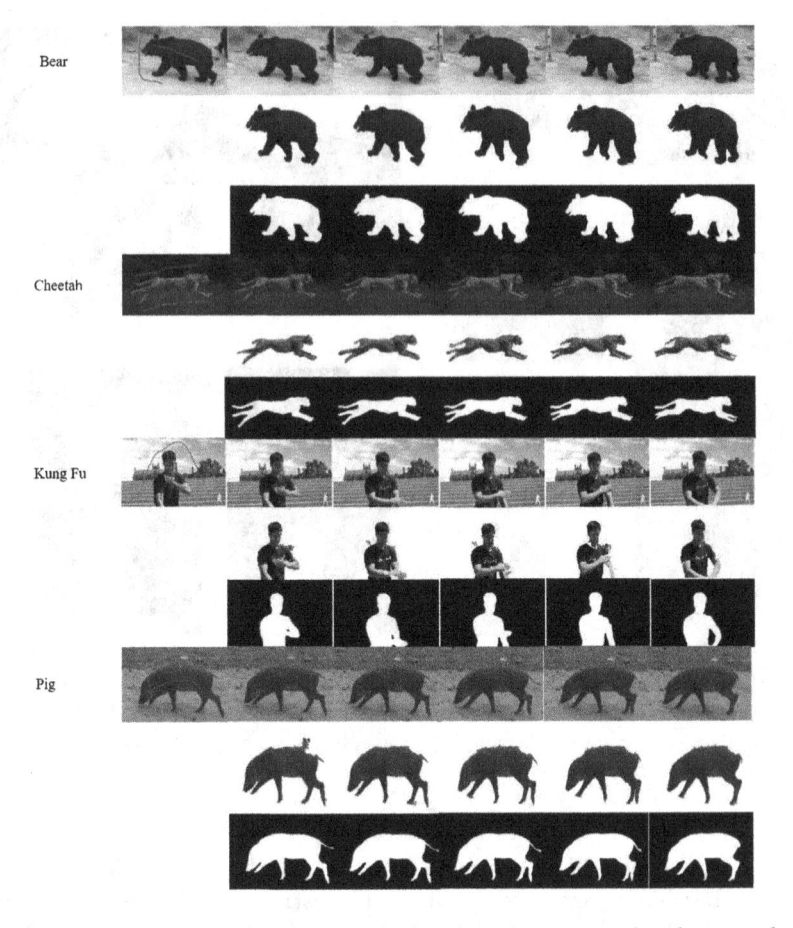

Fig. 4. Examples of cases where the method uses in Jumpcut video dataset, the first row is the interaction and the frames of video, the second is the segmentation results by our method, the last row is the ground truth.

5 Conclusion

In this paper we presented an interactive image segmentation method by a semi-supervised learning framework by incorporating manifold regularization term. To improve the segmentation accuracy and expand the application scenario, we train a classifier for each image as a segmentation discriminator for each superpixel. Good segmentation results obtained for single image and groups of similar images.

Acknowledgement. This work was supported by the National Key R&D program of China 2018YFB1003203 and the National Natural Science Foundation of China (Grant No. 61672528, 61773392).

References

1. Boykov, Y.: Interactive graph cuts for optimal boundary and region segmentation of objects in N-D images. ICCV **1**, 105–112 (2001)
2. Wu, J., Zhao, Y., Zhu, J.Y., et al.: MILCut: a sweeping line multiple instance learning paradigm for interactive image segmentation. In: IEEE Conference on Computer Vision and Pattern Recognition, pp. 256–263. IEEE Computer Society (2014)
3. Grady, L.: Random walks for image segmentation. IEEE Computer Society (2006)
4. Gulshan, V., Rother, C., Criminisi, A., et al.: Geodesic star convexity for interactive image segmentation. In: Computer Vision and Pattern Recognition, pp. 3129–3136. IEEE (2010)
5. Kass, M., Witkin, A., Terzopoulos, D.: Snakes: active contour models. Int. J. Comput. Vis. **1**(4), 321–331 (1988)
6. Rother, C., Kolmogorov, V., Blake, A.: "GrabCut": interactive foreground extraction using iterated graph cuts. ACM Trans. Graph. **23**(3), 309–314 (2004)
7. Dai, J., He, K., Sun, J.: BoxSup: exploiting bounding boxes to supervise convolutional networks for semantic segmentation 1635–1643 (2015)
8. Rupprecht, C., Peter, L., Navab, N.: Image segmentation in twenty questions. In: IEEE Conference on Computer Vision and Pattern Recognition, pp. 3314–3322. IEEE Computer Society (2015)
9. Liang, L., Grauman, K.: Beyond comparing image pairs: setwise active learning for relative attributes. In: IEEE Conference on Computer Vision and Pattern Recognition, pp. 208–215. IEEE Computer Society (2014)
10. Wang, T., Sun, Q., Ge, Q., et al.: Interactive image segmentation via pairwise likelihood learning. In: Twenty-Sixth International Joint Conference on Artificial Intelligence, pp. 2957–2963 (2017)
11. Peng, B., Zhang, L., Zhang, D.: A survey of graph theoretical approaches to image segmentation. Pattern Recogn. **46**(3), 1020–1038 (2013)
12. Belkin, M., Niyogi, P., Sindhwani, V.: Manifold regularization: a geometric framework for learning from labeled and unlabeled examples. JMLR.org (2006)
13. Achanta, R., Shaji, A., Smith, K.: SLIC superpixels compared to state-of-the-art superpixel methods. IEEE Trans. Pattern Anal. Mach. Intell. **34**(11), 2274 (2012)
14. Andrade, F., Carrera, E.V.: Supervised evaluation of seed-based interactive image segmentation algorithms. In: Signal Processing, Images and Computer Vision, pp. 1–7. IEEE (2015)
15. Casaca, W., Nonato, L.G., Taubin, G.: Laplacian coordinates for seeded image segmentation. In: IEEE Conference on Computer Vision and Pattern Recognition, pp. 384–391. IEEE Computer Society (2014)
16. Dong, X., Shen, J., Shao, L., Van Gool, L.: Sub-Markov random walk for image segmentation. IEEE Trans. Image Process. **25**(2), 516–527 (2016)
17. Kim, T.H., Lee, K.M., Lee, S.U.: Nonparametric higher-order learning for interactive segmentation. In: Proceedings of IEEE Conference on Computer Vision and Pattern Recognition, pp. 3201–3208 (2010)
18. Fan, Q., Zhong, F., Lischinski, D.: JumpCut: non-successive mask transfer and interpolation for video cutout. ACM Trans. Graph. **34**(6), 195 (2015)

Chronic Wounds Image Generator Based on Deep Convolutional Generative Adversarial Networks

Junnan Zhang[1], En Zhu[1(✉)], Xifeng Guo[1], Haohao Chen[1], and Jianping Yin[2]

[1] College of Computer, National University of Defense Technology, Changsha 410073, Hunan, China
{zhangjunnan12, enzhu}@nudt.edu.cn,
guoxifeng1990@163.com, HaohaoChen666@163.com
[2] Dongguan University of Technology, Dongguan 523000, China
jpyin@dgut.edu.cn

Abstract. Chronic wounds have a long recovery time, occur extensively, and are difficult to treat. They cause not only great suffering to many patients but also bring enormous work burden to hospitals and doctors. Therefore, an automated chronic wound detection method can efficiently assist doctors in diagnosis, or help patients with initial diagnosis, reduce the workload of doctors and the treatment costs of patients. In recent years, due to the rise of big data, machine learning methods have been applied to Image Identification, and the accuracy of the result has surpassed that of traditional methods. With the fully convolutional neural network proposed, image segmentation and target detection have also achieved excellent results. However, due to the protection of patient privacy, medical images are often difficult to obtain and insufficient training data leads to poor segmentation and recognition. To solve the above problem, we propose the chronic wounds image generator based on DCGANs. First, we select high-quality images of chronic wounds and process them to form a data set containing 520 images. Then we build a generator and discriminator network model to generate new images. Finally, we use the existing methods of chronic wound segmentation and recognition to test. The results show that the generated images can be used to expand the training set and further improve the segmentation and recognition accuracy.

Keywords: Chronic wounds segmentation
Deep convolutional neural networks · Generative adversarial networks

1 Introduction

In recent years, with the rise of big data, the field of artificial intelligence has been aroused a broad concern. AlexNet [1], the champion of ImageNet competition in 2012, uses convolutional neural networks for image classification and recognition. Its accuracy exceeds the traditional method significantly, which makes people pay attention to the application of convolutional neural networks in the field of image classification

© Springer Nature Singapore Pte Ltd. 2018
L. Li et al. (Eds.): NCTCS 2018, CCIS 882, pp. 150–158, 2018.
https://doi.org/10.1007/978-981-13-2712-4_11

again. Afterward, people continued to innovate (VGG [2], GoogleNet [3], Residual Net [4], DenseNet [5], CapsuleNet [6] and other deep neural networks), and further improve the accuracy of image classification. However, in the field of medical image classification and segmentation, there are small image data sets due to the protection of the patient's privacy. Therefore, the application of convolutional neural networks in this area is not effective.

Chronic wound including Diabetic foot ulcers, venous leg ulcers, and acne, has long recovery time and need different methods of treatment at various period. The current treatment of chronic wounds usually takes up a significant amount of medical resources and is not easy to treat [7–9]. Long-term hospitalization is a burden for both hospitals and patients. On the one hand, the resources of the hospital are occupied for an extended period, and it is impossible to provide medical services to other patients in urgent need. On the other hand, the long-term hospitalization costs are too high for most of the patients to afford. It is also very common in some remote areas, patients are far away and inconvenient to see a doctor. These conditions have brought great suffering to the patients.

Hence, it is of great importance to generate more chronic wounds images from the limited number of images that we have. This method helps improve the accuracy of segmentation and classification and the results obtained can assist doctors in diagnosis.

In this paper, we make the following contributions:

We propose chronic wounds image generator based on DCGANs [10] to solve the problem of insufficient dataset.

We design a new generator and discriminator architecture based on the features of the chronic wounds images.

We used the segmentation and identification method of the article [16] to conduct comparative experiments and the results verified that the method could efficiently improve the segmentation and identification performance.

2 Related Work

A major feature of neural networks is that the larger the data set is, the more comprehensive the data is, the less likely it is to produce overfit results, and more likely to obtain the higher accuracy results. When the data set is insufficient, data augmentation methods are needed to augment the original data for obtaining more training and test images. At present, the commonly used data augmentation method is the deformation of data. By enhancing the geometry and color of the image, the operation of rotating, shifting, flipping, and changing the color of the picture is mainly performed. This idea can be traced back to augmentation of the MNIST dataset. These transformation operations can be unified into the following formula:

$$y = wx + b \tag{1}$$

The above ideas are well utilized in the article [11]. The new training data generated by using data augmentation achieve an error rate of 0.35%. Moreover, in addition to the classic affine transformation, digital data can also be elastically transformed.

In addition to traditional data enhancement methods, generating antagonism networks (GANs) has long been considered a powerful technique for automatically generating new training images, and has demonstrated effectiveness in many data generation tasks, such as the generation of novel passages [12]. Antagonistic generation networks (GANs), using neural networks as models, the whole antagonism process can be summarized as follows:

Assume that the generation model is g(z), where z is random noise and g converts this random noise to the data type x. In the area of image augmentation, the output of g is an image. D is a discriminative model. For any input x, the output of D(x) is a real number in the range of 0–1 to determine the probability that the image is a real image. Let Pr and Pg respectively represent the distribution of the real image and the distribution of the generated image. The objective functions of our discriminant model are as follows:

$$\max_D E_{x \sim p_r}[\log D(x)] + E_{x \sim p_g}[\log(1 - D(x)] \tag{2}$$

Similarly, the goal of the generative model is to make the discriminant model indistinguishable from the real image and the generated image. Then the entire optimization objective function is as follows:

$$\min_g \max_D E_{x \sim p_r}[\log D(x)] + E_{x \sim p_g}[\log(1 - D(x))] \tag{3}$$

The optimization method of this maximum minimization objective function is to interactively iterate D and g, fix g, and optimize D. After a period, fix D and optimize g until the process converges.

GANs can also be used to transfer images from one style to another [13] (style transfer). For example, when only photos taken on a sunny day are collected, it is possible to use the generated night or rain picture to train the vehicle for automatic driving at night or on a rainy day. By using transfer learning techniques, GANs have also proven to be effective of relatively small dataset [14]. In addition, GANs also have good applications in medical image segmentation and recognition. For example, the article [15] first uses traditional methods to enhance data, and then use GANs to generate data to increase dataset and diversity further. Compared with methods that only use traditional data augmentation, the method of adding GANs increase accuracy of results significantly. Moreover, the article [10] combine deep convolutional networks with GANs to produce more complicated images. We were inspired by this article and improve the model for the features of chronic wounds images.

3   Method

The model of the article [10] cannot grab the features of the chronic wounds images well (see Fig. 5, row 3). Therefor we made improvements to the model as follows.

3.1   Generator Architecture

The generator is composed of one fully connected layer and five convolutional layers. The fully connected layer takes a 100-dimension noise as input and connects it to 4 * 4 * 1024 neurons. After reshaping them to form 1024-channel feature maps with size 4 by 4, five transposed_convolution layers are followed. Each layer is followed by a batchnorm layer to accelerate the convergence. The kernel size and stride of each convolutional layer are 3 by 3 and 2. They are activated by ReLU except for the last layer which uses Tanh activation (Fig. 1).

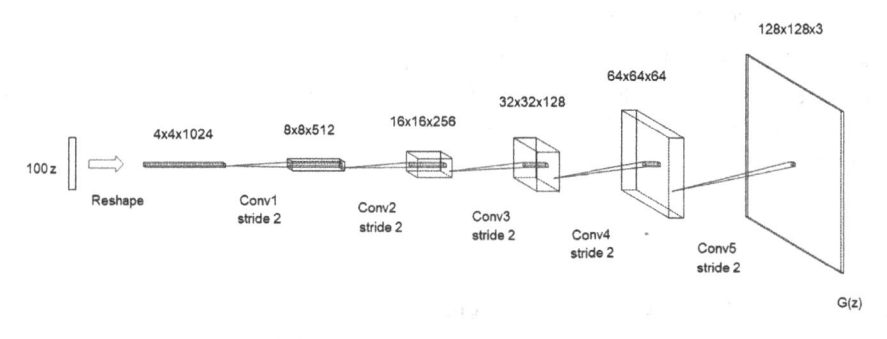

Fig. 1.   The generator architecture.

As the figure shown above, a 100-dimensional uniform distribution Z is reshaped to 4 × 4 × 1024. Five transposed_convolution with stride 2 then converts Z into a 128 × 128 pixel image.

3.2   Discriminator Architecture

The discriminator is composed of ten convolutional layers. The input is a 128 * 128 pixel image, and ten convolutional layers are followed. We then get the 4 * 4 * 1024 output and connect it to one number. (0 or 1, indicating false or true) Each layer is followed by a batchnorm layer to accelerate the convergence. The kernel size and stride of each convolutional layer are 3 by 3 and 1 or 2 (The convolution layer with stride 2 serves as pooling layer, but is better than pooling layer). They are activated by SeLU (Fig. 2).

As the figure shown above, a 128 × 128 pixel image is the input. Five convolution

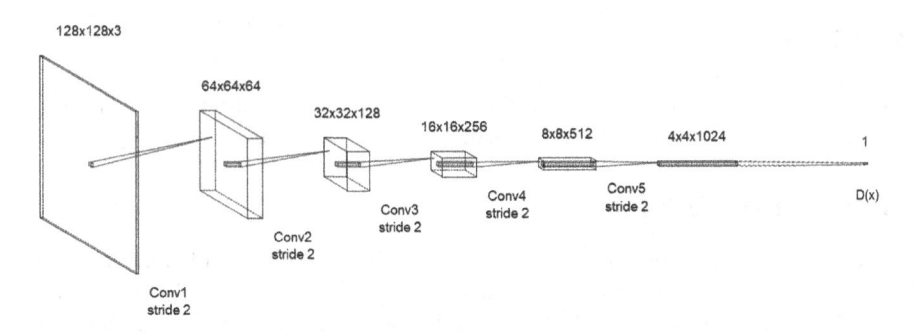

Fig. 2. The discriminator architecture.

layers with stride 1 and five convolution layers with stride 2 convert the input into $4 \times 4 \times 1024$ and finally get a number ranging from 0 to 1.

3.3   Details of Adversarial Training

The model was trained with mini-batch stochastic gradient descent (SGD) with a mini-batch size of 36. All weights were initialized from a zero-centered Normal distribution with standard deviation 0.02. The learning rate of the Adam optimizer was 0.001, and the momentum term was 0.5.

4   Experiment

4.1   Chronic Wounds Images Generating

Experiment Environment. We use an NVIDIA Geforce 1080Ti GPU to speed up parameter learning and evaluate the learned model on a computer with Intel Core i7-8700 K CPU @ 3.70 GHz and 32 GB RAM. The program runs on a 64-bit windows10 home operating system with CUDA 9.0 and Tensorflow 1.7.0-GPU [17] installed.

Data Set. We use the data set that is built by the article [16]. The dataset is collected partly from cooperated medical institutions and partly from Medetec Wound Database [18]. It is made up of chronic wound images. However, some of the images are of low quality, so we carefully pick 450 out of 950 images and then resized in a uniform resolution (128 by 128 pixels).

4.2   Existing Methods for Comparing Experiment

We use the method of the article [16] to evaluate the generated chronic wounds images. First, we use the dataset that we built to train the network and get the segmentation results. Then we add the 284 newly generated chronic wounds images to the dataset to train and get the segmentation results. Finally, we run the results on the same test set and compare the accuracy. The evaluation standard is as follows:

TP: the ground-truth is positive and the prediction is positive.
FN: the ground-truth is positive but the prediction is negative.
FP: the ground-truth is negative but the prediction is positive.
TN: the ground-truth is negative and the prediction is negative.

We use accuracy, mean intersection-over-union (mIoU), and dice similarity coefficient (DSC) to compare the result. They are computed as follows:

$$Acurracy = \frac{TP + TN}{TP + FP + TN + FN} \tag{4}$$

$$mIoU = \frac{TP}{TP + FP + FN} \tag{5}$$

$$DSC = \frac{2 * TP}{2 * TP + TF + FN} \tag{6}$$

5   Results

5.1   Chronic Wounds Images Generating

Figures 3 and 4 show the discriminator loss and generator loss situation. As we can see form the figures, both curves are smooth and more training steps to ensure convergence. Figure 5 shows the results that we got:

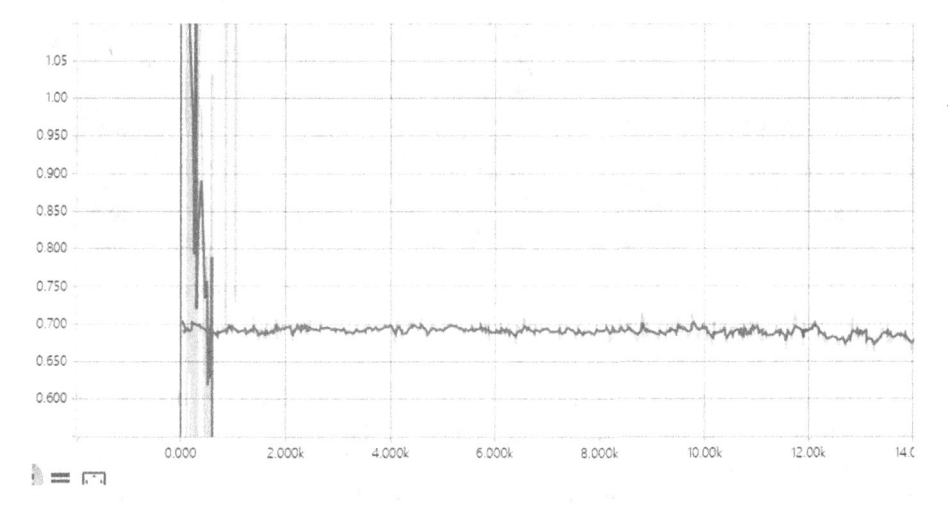

Fig. 3. Discriminator loss

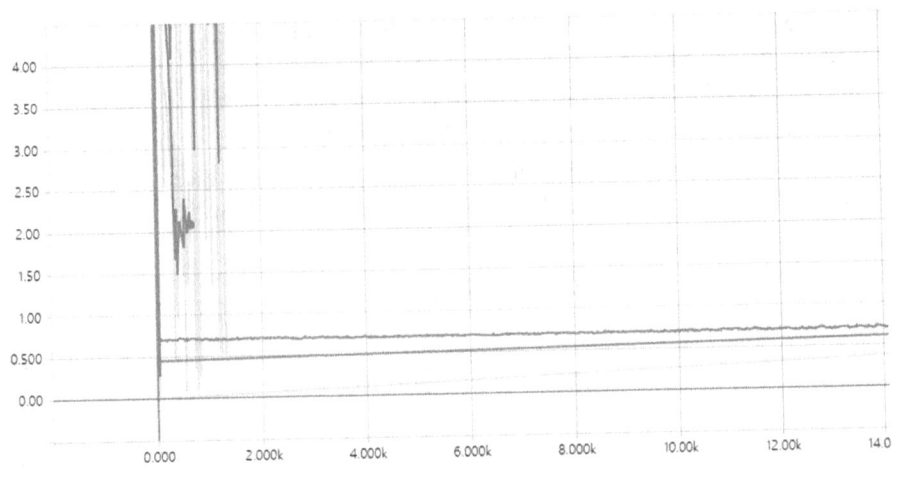

Fig. 4. Generator loss

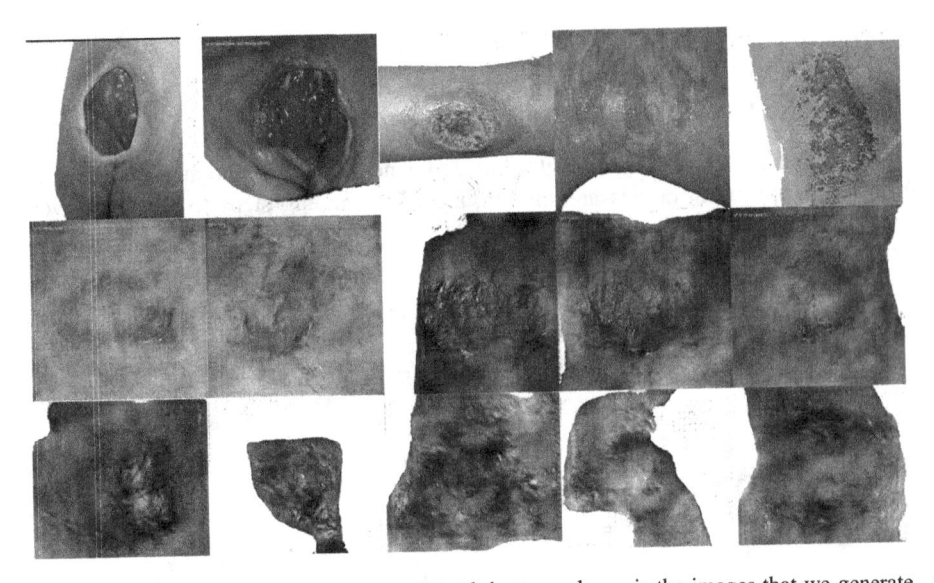

Fig. 5. The first row is the training images and the second row is the images that we generate, the third row is generated by the article [10]

The generated images of our method have mainly all the characters that the chronic wounds images have: the skin, the wound area. People could tell the images immediately and the images are good enough for training. That means the chronic wounds generator works fine. In contrast, the third row shows the model of the article [10] does not fit for chronic wounds images.

5.2   Existing Methods for Comparing Experiment

The following table shows the results of comparing experiment (Table 1):

Table 1. Comparing experiment

Train method	Model	Accuracy (%)	mIoU (%)	DSC (%)
Original dataset	MobileNet × 0.75-fcn16	97.82	82.86	90.92
With traditional method	MobileNet × 0.75-fcn16	97.26	83.29	91.44
With our method	MobileNet × 0.75-fcn16	**98.57**	**85.28**	92.05
With our method and traditional method	MobileNet × 0.75-fcn16	98.53	85.25	**92.76**
Original dataset	VGG16 × 0.75-fcn16	97.96	82.35	90.32
With traditional method	VGG16 × 0.75-fcn16	97.64	83.70	91.70
With our method	VGG16 × 0.75-fcn16	97.91	84.39	92.94
With our method and traditional method	VGG16 × 0.75-fcn16	**98.56**	**84.63**	**92.97**
Original dataset	VGG19 × 0.75-fcn16	97.59	82.44	90.54
With traditional method	VGG19 × 0.75-fcn16	97.76	83.32	91.30
With our method	VGG19 × 0.75-fcn16	98.22	84.22	92.43
With our method and traditional method	VGG19 × 0.75-fcn16	**98.53**	**85.36**	**92.82**

We use the traditional method (flip, crop, rotate) to get another 450 images. We also generate and carefully pick 450 images by comparing with original images using our method. We choose 13/18 of the total images as train set, 1/6 as test set, 1/9 as validation set.

As we can see from the table above, the traditional methods have a certain degree of improvement in terms of accuracy, mIoU and DSC. However, our method has a greater degree of improvement of the three items. Moreover, the testing results of combined our method with traditional methods almost reach the highest accuracy, mIoU and DSC. This is because the new generated images not only increase the number of dataset, but also expand the diversity of the dataset. Therefore, the networks of the article [16] could learn more features and better segment the chronic wounds images.

6   Conclusion

We propose the chronic wounds image generator to generate new chronic wound images based on DCGANs. We then do an experiment comparing the accuracy whether adding the generated chronic wound images for training or not. The results show that the addition of newly generated chronic wound images to the training set lead higher segmentation accuracy. This approach can be considered to generate new medical images when there is an insufficient dataset. Therefore, it can further improve the segmentation and identification accuracy. Moreover, according to the experiment result, it will achieve better results when combined with traditional methods. Further work will focus on transforming the discriminator into a separate network to segment and identify chronic wound images.

Acknowledgements. This work was supported by the National Key R&D Program of China 2018YFB1003203 and the National Natural Science Foundation of China (Grant No. 61672528).

References

1. Krizhevsky, A., Sutskever, I., Hinton, G.E.: ImageNet classification with deep convolutional neural networks. In: NIPS (2012)
2. Simonyan, K., Zisserman, A.: Very deep convolutional networks for large-scale image recognition. arXiv preprint arXiv:1409.1556 (2014)
3. Szegedy, C., et al.: Going deeper with convolutions. In: Proceedings of the IEEE Conference on Computer Vision and Pattern Recognition (2015)
4. He, K., et al.: Deep residual learning for image recognition. In: Proceedings of the IEEE Conference on Computer Vision and Pattern Recognition (2016)
5. Huang, G., et al.: Densely connected convolutional networks. arXiv preprint arXiv:1608.06993 (2016)
6. Sabour, S., Frosst, N., Hinton, G.E.: Dynamic routing between capsules. In: Advances in Neural Information Processing Systems (2017)
7. Shukla, V., Ansari, M.A., Gupta, S.: Wound healing research: a perspective from India. Int. J. Low. Extrem. Wounds 4(1), 7–9 (2005)
8. Sen, C.K., et al.: Human skin wounds: a major and snowballing threat to public health and the economy. Wound Repair Regen. **17**(6), 763–771 (2009)
9. Posnett, J., Franks, P.: The burden of chronic wounds in the UK. Diabet. Med. **14**(5), S7–S85 (2008)
10. Radford, A., Metz, L., Chintala, S.: Unsupervised representation learning with deep convolutional generative adversarial networks. arXiv preprint arXiv:1511.06434
11. Ciresan, D.C., Meier, U., Gambardella, L.M., Schmidhuber, J.: Deep big simple neural nets excel on handwritten digit recognition. CoRR, abs/1003.0358 (2010)
12. Goodfellow, I., et al.: Generative adversarial nets. In: NIPS (2014)
13. Zhu, J., Park, T., Isola, P., Efros, A.A.: Unpaired image to image translation using cycle-consistent adversarial networks. CoRR, abs/1703.10593 (2017)
14. Gurumurthy, S., Sarvadevabhatla, R.K., Radhakrishnan, V.B.: DeLiGAN: generative adversarial networks for diverse and limited data. arXiv e-prints, June 2017
15. Frid-Adar, M., et al.: Synthetic data augmentation using GAN for improved liver lesion classification. In: Proceedings of the IEEE Conference on Computer Vision and Pattern Recognition (2018)
16. Liu, X., et al.: A framework of wound segmentation based on deep convolutional networks. In: Image and Signal Processing, BioMedical Engineering and Informatics (CISP-BMEI) (2017)
17. Abadi, M., et al.: TensorFlow: large-scale machine learning on heterogeneous distributed systems. arXiv preprint arXiv:1603.04467 (2016)
18. Medetec Wound Database.http://www.medetec.co.uk/files/medetec-image-databases.html

Author Index

Printed in the United States
By Bookmasters